THE HUSTLERS
From the Jungle of Africa to the Jungle of Rome

THE HUSTLERS

From the Jungle of Africa to the Jungle of Rome

W.K.C. Onyeka

Spectrum Books Limited
Ibadan
Abuja • Benin City • Lagos • Owerri

Spectrum titles can be purchased on line at
www.spectrumbooksonline.com

Published by
Spectrum Books Limited
Spectrum House
Ring Road
PMB 5612
Ibadan, Nigeria
*e-mail: admin*1*@spectrumbooksonline.com*

in association with
Safari Books (Export) Limited
1st Floor
17 Bond Street
St Helier
Jersey JE2 3NP
Channel Islands
United Kingdom.

Europe and USA Distributor
African Books Collective Ltd
The Jam Factory
27 Park End Street
Oxford OX1, 1HU, UK

First published by Lokenny International Services, Ravenna,
Italy, 2001
This edition published by Spectrum Books Ltd., 2003

ISBN: 978-029-384-1

Printed by Polygraphics Venture Limited Ibadan

Dedication

To my wife, Lois, and daughter, Kennedina

To the memory of

Paul Ajayi, Marcel Igboanugo, Daniel Osuji, Frank Ike, Bright Omokharo, Raph Oguejiofor, Bolanle Omolara-Owambe, Charles Ekenobi Ugochukwu Ugorji (alias Cento) and others whose lives were nipped in the bud.

And to

Mr Boschello Alfonso, the Italian whose love and concern for the welfare of immigrants and the downtrodden remained formidable till his demise.

Contents

Contents

Acknowledgements

Thanks to Hubert Ngadiuba, Ben Nwokenkwo, Gilbert Osueke and Andrea Morini for their immense concern for my welfare.

There are many persons who inspired or read this manuscript, amongst them are: Chika Ibe, Vivian Meremikwu, Nwadimma Nduka, Rose Otote and Tony Iwuoma. Unable to express my appreciation in person, I wish to use this medium to convey my profound gratitude and wishes of God's blessings to all of them.

Chapter 1

From the Eagle's Nest

To Ogemdi who could neither read nor write, the possession of a wristwatch was wasteful and ridiculous. But to Sam, his ten-year-old son, it was a luxury. With his elder sisters gone from home, Sam depended on the early morning sun that penetrated their thatched roof to know when it was time to wake up.

That day was different. No signs of daylight had invaded his room when a hand shook him gently. He opened his eyes to the kerosene lantern which hung on the mud wall and illuminated the room like a lone star on a cloudy night. He scratched his cheeks, rubbed his eyes, spluttered some inaudible curses at whoever it was, and recoiled to sleep.

'Wake up, Samuel,' his father ordered. 'Wake up. You are a man and can go without sleep.'

More out of anxiety than obedience, Sam scrambled to his feet, wondering if anybody had complained of wrong doing against him. His mother went to his side, sat on the wooden bed and beckoned on him to join her. With two hands folded across her chest as if to prop her unbrassiered breasts, she gazed at her husband.

Sam's father drew a chair for himself, brought out his

snuff box from the side pocket of his khaki shorts and tapped on the steel lid twice before he opened it. With his right thumb, he scooped snuff into his nostrils. 'Omumu makes the only genuine tobacco snuff in this town,' he commented and returned the box to his pocket. He cleared his throat and began to speak. 'Your mother and I want to know what you aspire to be.'

As if to drive the question home, his mother added, 'Tell us, Nnadim (my husband's reincarnated father), what do you want to become?'

'Tailor,' Sam replied. 'I want to make money like Dominic who sews my Christmas dresses. I like the wads of naira notes he receives from you and many other customers. I want to have a lot of young men and women around me always. I want children to thank me for making their yearnings for new dresses a reality, and parents…'

'We've heard you!' snapped his father.

'Dominic does a very good job in this hamlet and maybe, he is the richest and most popular person here. He is the only person whose house is roofed with the white man's roofing sheets. Don't the villagers gather there when it rains, with clay pots on their heads to tap water collected from the roof of his house? Was it not in his house that I first stepped my bare feet on a cemented floor? Who else has a motor cycle or a radio in this village?…'

'However,' his father continued, 'beyond here, there are doctors, lawyers, industrialists, engineers and politicians. They run the lives of everybody, including your role model, Dominic, to their advantage. Chief Nso, my age mate, is an example. We were initiated into manhood in our respective villages the same year. As a child, my mother told me that the knife of the local midwife who assisted in his delivery was still dripping with blood when she helped my mother to

2

discharge a stubborn umbilical cord which nearly suffocated me.'

'During our childhood, Nso was not my match in anything. Though he was fat like his late father, I had no problem wrestling him to the ground. He was beaten by almost everybody except those who were scared of his fleshy stature. He was awkward in hunting and weak in farming. It was not out of love but spite that his mother acceded to the catechist's request for a servant to the parish priest. Who in his right senses would offer an industrious son for such an odd role? It was only lazy sons who could be offered as sacrifice. Not me! Not the hard-working and energetic son of Obinedi.'

'Nobody missed Chief Nso when he disappeared with the priest two years later and was forgotten completely. By a twist of fate, he returned after many decades, armed with western education, and wearing dresses associated with Europeans.'

'Why do you think that opportunist is a good model for our son?' Sam's mother protested. 'Nnadim is not weak, retarded or hated.'

'I am sorry, my wife, if that example is inappropriate. Nevertheless, instances abound. Have you not heard from the catechist himself that his ailing heart was dissected and implanted with a new one by a medical team which included a man from a neighbouring village? Or have you forgotten that Umuike was once a village of warriors? They conquered their neighbours and expelled the inhabitants hence their enormous land mass. Interestingly, what the armed ancestors of Wanta hamlet could not achieve with their bows, arrows and dane guns, their illustrious lawyer-son has single-handedly achieved. Much of their lost farmlands have been recovered and he has sworn to continue to contest even the least parcel of land until everything is reclaimed. So, my son, I know you would want to be like the doctor, lawyer or...'

'Not Chief Nso. I detest him,' countered Sam's mother.

'You are right, father,' responded Sam.

'Then, we have toiled very hard to save for your education. I earn money from tapping palmwine, farming and petty trading. It is enough to fetch me more wives like my age mates or to buy new wrapper for your mother. But I decided to save it for you. I have decided to spend on your education. I never had the opportunity myself and that is why we are poor. You must obtain all the knowledge I missed. There is no doubt in my mind that it is the viable path to the top.'

Sam listened with rapt attention. His father shot a glance at his mother and chuckled. 'Take for instance, all the positions in the executive and judicial arms of government are occupied by educated men. The Queen of England granted independence, not to illiterates but to educated people. There is no illusion that education brings personal development and advancement, and makes the weak to become great and powerful.' In the light of this, three square meals for the family is henceforth a luxury. Every member of this household should forget about new dresses until we are through with your education. I am glad that your elder sisters will soon become women. By the grace of God, they will attract suitable men who will marry them and pay us more bride price.

'The childhood deficiencies of Chief Nso did not perturb the electorate when he took the podia across this country and delivered speeches eloquently. Therefore, my son, the benefits of education are endless and clear. They constitute the hub upon which life revolves. Your mother will give

4

you money for the next common entrance examination.'

'But I am still in primary five, father,' Sam reminded him.

'Yes we know,' responded his mother.

'Your teacher advised us to let you sit for the examination with primary six pupils.' She reached out and pulled him affectionately to herself.

'Do not worry, Nnadim, if you do not make it this year, you lose nothing. Rather, you would have acquired vital experience that will enable you to try again next year.' She untied the edge of the wrapper around her waist, ran her fingers along its edge until she found a knot at its tip which served as her wallet. Carefully, she unfastened it and brought out one rumpled note.

'Four or five years' studies are enough to get you a clerical job. It is only under this circumstance that you can transform the lives of people around you.' Sam's mother extended her hands while her husband watched. 'It is our mustard seed. No matter the vagaries of nature, it must prosper.'

***

Out of the forty-eight pupils that sat for the entrance examination into public secondary schools from his school, Sam was among the eight that passed. Dika, Chief Nso's only son, also passed. Sam's father took him to Umuahia to buy what he would need at school. It was Sam's first journey by car. Though he sat uncomfortably on his father's laps to create space for passengers who paid higher fares, he wished the journey would never end. The tarred road cut across rivers bridged with concrete slabs. He saw schools, churches, hospitals and other monuments that were spoken of in fairy tales by itinerant elders. He was surprised at the busy crowds of people at the town's market, and observed that all the stalls were rich. They had assorted items, unlike those in his village.

Gripping his father's hand, they walked down a lane of stalls until they arrived where clothes were sold. After trying two other places in search of a better offer, they returned to the first shop and bought some yards of white khaki and cotton for his school uniform. From there, they went to where sandals were sold. The shop owner brought out a pair of brown sandals that fitted Sam well.

'You know he is a small boy; give me something he will not overgrow quickly,' his father demanded.

Sam did not object, but he was not happy at his father's comments. They purchased a black leather belt and headed for the motor park to return home. Though, Sam had opted for secondary school education instead of tailoring, he was visibly excited as Dominic took his measurement to sew his school uniform.

Sam was hoping to leave home for the first time when his father told him that there was no money to pay his boarding fee.

'You would have to go to school from this house,' he pleaded.

Once again, Sam did not object. For three years, he trekked sixty kilometres to and from school, his legs wobbling inside his oversized sandals. He woke up each morning to a breakfast of pounded cassava with soup, and returned hours after school to a lunch of boiled yam with vegetables. His mother ensured there was something for him and his younger ones to eat.

Taking siesta was like a taboo in the family. Whenever Sam was caught sleeping after school, his mother did not

6

hesitate to spank him. 'You need to display the sort of vigour and alertness required of sons who help their families out. Your father and I cannot entrust our hopes in an indolent son,' his mother always reminded him. Sam continued to run errands at home and help in the farm to ensure that his school fees were paid promptly. He rarely had the time to play with his mates in the hamlet, but whenever he did, he was overwhelmed with joy.

Sam attended a missionary college reputed for its academic and disciplinary standards. He was attentive in class, studied hard at home, and had good grades. The first fifty positions in their class of two hundred and thirty students were known to be for those who had put extra efforts in their studies. The completion of his intermediate year was a turning point in his educational pursuit. He realised the need for more efforts to pass the West African School Certificate Examination in flying colours.

During the holidays, he sought for vacation job in order to save some money for his studies. Umuahia, a town about a hundred kilometres from his village, was his first choice to search for a temporary job. The impression the town made on him three years ago was not lost. Now fourteen and half years old, Sam gathered a few possessions into a plastic bag and barely sought his parents' consent before leaving for Umuahia. Sam had learnt of employment opportunities that exist in a bakery.

While there, Sam was faced with a difficulty. He lacked the necessary credentials for any job in the industry.

'Sam, my boy, you look agile and intelligent,' commented the director of Mountain Bakery.

'Thank you sir,' Sam replied.

'Are you a student?' asked the director.

'Yes, I am. I have completed my intermediate and will

proceed to the semifinal year when school resumes,' he said proudly.

The director shook his head in disapproval. 'You are already on the way to a higher position but frankly, I need those who will stay. I am sorry I cannot employ you.'

That was how Sam bungled his first interview. With these remarks, he patted Sam gently on the cheeks and returned to work. Sam stood still on the balcony outside, feeling dejected, miserable and confused as to what to do next. Some ten minutes later, a haggard looking old man, passed by. He was white with flour and wet with sweat. Sam thought the man could intercede for him by prevailing on the young managing director. He explained his predicaments to the old man but the man said he could not help.

Sam was more confident the next day when he stood before a proprietor of another bakery. He concealed his educational pursuit and portrayed himself as someone from a very poor family. He narrated his parents' inability to see him through primary school and how his mother compelled him to leave home in search of money to feed, clothe and educate his younger ones. When he was given the workers' register to write his name, he became convinced that his ploy had worked.

The bakery's workforce was divided in two groups. Each group had a miller, a baker, a supervisor and retinue of other workers. Night and day work alternated between these groups. Sam was assigned to Group A which was on evening shift that week. He waited anxiously as the hands of the clock ticked past the hours. At takeoff time, the proprietor of the bakery watched Sam's first day at work. Some of his colleagues who arrived earlier were around him too. He was introduced to some men he later learnt were group leaders. But for all his humility and enthusiasm, he received sneering remarks from the men, one of whom was old enough to be his father.

'Sir, this one is supposed to be sucking his mother's breasts,' one man said. 'At your age we had not thought of crossing the boundaries of our hamlets how much more coming to Umuahia alone, to earn a living,' commented another. The proprietor did not seem to take any interest in their remarks. He moved a few metres away and started discussing with his wife in low tone. The two men looked at each other and laughed.

'If at this age you are already interested in the pursuit of money, what would you do when you become old like us?' asked the dark, tall, muscular man. But Sam did not say anything.

'How old are you?' asked the other man.

Sam told him.

'You're exactly the age of my third child who is preparing for college.'

'What do you hope to do with your wages?'

'I think my parents need every bit of it for the upkeep of the family,' replied Sam.

'How many are you?' he asked.

'Ten children,' Sam replied.

The man's mouth parted in disgust. 'Why do some people bite more than they can chew? For no fault of yours, you have been turned to a slave early in life so that some other children can feed. I consider people like your parents ignorant and children like you stupid. Why don't you rebel against them and stand up for your rights? You may not change your fate but certainly, future parents will understand that child rearing entails much more than copulating at sunset,' the man continued. Sam looked away and started kicking an invisible object.

'Don't mind them,' the other man chipped in. 'They think that this bakery can solve their self-inflicted load of problems. Nobody here will tell this boy to run away when he encounters what it requires to receive forty naira a month.' These comments did not bother Sam as much as his churning stomach because he had gone without food the whole day.

Fifteen minutes to commencement of work, his employer's wife enquired from Sam if he was hungry. 'No ma, but I would appreciate some food if you offered me.' She walked briskly into the bakery's store and brought one big loaf of bread, sliced it into two, and used the same knife to collect butter from a giant container and spread on its surface. Sam received the bread from her and moved away from prying eyes to eat. At exactly seven o'clock in the evening, the supervisor introduced Sam to his job. He handed Sam a sharp knife, and demonstrated to him how he should cut a three-feet high dough mixed in a bath. Pointing to the milling machine, he instructed him to transport every chunk there. 'Do not hold the roller while it is in motion. It can crush your flesh,' he warned.

The dark, tall man who had been making jest of Sam, and who was cleaning and oiling the machine in preparation for milling burst into laughter.

'Where is the flesh to be crushed? It is his skeletal frame that he will lose if he doesn't take care.'

Again, Sam did not say anything. He did not even look at the man. Rather, he bent down and worked. His sweat-soaked shirt was white with flour, which reminded him of the old man he met at the Mountain Bakery. His sweat-soaked shirt gummed to his body. While he waited for the miller to signal for more dough, he ran from one end of the floor to another assisting others. Once he was caught walking to bring butter from the store, his supervisor roared in anger and Sam was shaken. Apart from these, the work had been smooth for him.

Trouble started when the amount of dough inside the bath reduced beyond his reach. Sam tried stretching fully to gather it from the bottom of the wooden bath and twice he nearly fell inside. Supplying the machines with dough was time consuming. In a bid to sustain the speed, he slashed his palm but did not report to anyone. He knew he had no experience, but was willing to impress his employers.

After twenty minutes break, the baker opened the electric oven with a long oak paddle, loaded it with alumnium pans of milled dough and allowed it to bake. Sam joined others in sliding the hinges of the pans which were stacked in a wooden board for storage. His superiors used rags to protect their palms from heat while doing so. Nobody gave any rag to Sam. And he did not ask for one. When work was over in the morning, his palms were blistered, his fingers ached and his eyes were swollen. But he was determined to work on.

The job was Sam's only hope of returning to school at the end of the holidays. He constantly calculated how many items his wages would buy for him, and imagined the amount of relief and pride his parents would feel for a son that faced challenges, and earned more money than the little they could get from their farms. This thought motivated Sam to regard the hostilities he suffered from his co-workers as insignificant, and maintained the positive drive in him.

Sam was troubled to discover that his employer usually retained, as a policy, half of each worker's wages each day. The policy was as old as the organisation, he was told. But Sam politely demanded an explanation.

'Workers are extravagant, and this always leaves them penniless. When they are unable to fulfil their family obligations promptly, it affects their attitude to work. So I try to ensure they have a reserve,' the proprietor explained. Sam could endure any adverse working conditions but withholding part of his stipend was outrageous and intolerable. He made his dislike for the policy known. But nothing changed. Reluctantly, he signed for and collected half of his wages and grumbled out of the office. Sam learnt from other workers that they had never drawn from the reserve. He soon understood that apart from exploiting the workers, the boss also uses the policy to tie down his key personnel. Sam needed to invent a ploy to be able to leave the work with all his earnings when it was time to return to school.

As soon as his vacation ended, he walked to his boss in his office and told him, 'You claim to care a lot about your workers' welfare. I am shocked that the agonies of my parents did not mean anything to you. I abandoned my home for Umuahia because I wanted to alleviate their burden. If my sacrifice did not make any difference in their lives, I have suffered for nothing.'

There was a disagreement between them. His boss flared up, banged on the table and spoke angrily to Sam. This is a strategy he had used successfully in previous negotiations with other workers. But he was frustrated by Sam's unyielding stand, which made him to give Sam till the following day to change his mind or risk dismissal. While he withdrew into isolation, some workers perhaps, sent by the proprietor, came to Sam to persuade him to apologise to the boss.

Sam was happy to be relieved of his job and paid all his wages the following day. He used the money to purchase a kerosene stove, a table clock fitted with alarm, a mattress, an iron bed and a pillow. He also rented a room in a building opposite his school compound and shared it with two other students. His once sagging performance at school soon improved but there were still necessary textbooks and materials he needed for the final examinations.

It became a routine for Sam to leave for Umuahia at the end of each session in search of a vacation job, while his schoolmates returned to their different families or enrolled in extramural classes. The second attempt was easier for him. His arrival at Umuahia coincided with the voluntary resignation of a friend he made during his previous trip. His friend was trusted by the proprietor of Sunrise Bakery to whom he presented Sam as a secondary school dropout, honest, hard-working and obedient. That was how he got a job with a family whose love and concern for his welfare exceeded known boundaries, and had remained indelible in his heart.

Before leaving for Kano, his friend, ensured that Sam was happy. He disclosed to James, one of his trusted former colleagues, that Sam was working to earn some money to enable him return to school. He appealed to him to assist in whichever way to ensure that Sam's mission at Sunrise Bakery was a success. Two weeks later, their boss concluded that Sam was a more effective, honest and resourceful salesman. He deployed James to the production unit, which worked all night, and assigned Sam to James' sales position. With this change, James lost the means of making more money from the company, and living extravagantly. Sam recognised that James was unhappy despite the fact that Sam's stay was going to be brief. It did not occur to Sam that James could later plot to discredit him and recover his post.

What served as workers' quarters was a three-bedroom house whose roof and wall were both made of corrugated zinc panels, nailed to wooden frames. It was erected on an undeveloped parcel of land in a neighbourhood of mainly senior civil servants and rich businessmen. The room which Sam shared with James served as kitchen, bedroom and dining room. They were not to cook outside their rooms. Anyone who stayed indoors on a scorching day would aptly describe the room as a furnace. At night, the roof and the iron panels emitted the heat accumulated during the day.

Sam and James could not keep their door open to let fresh air into the room because hordes of mosquitoes laid siege outside. The only remedy was to stay outside till late into the night before retiring to their raffia mat spread on a bare cement floor. It was on one of such nights when he abandoned the room to stay with mosquitoes outside that Mary, James' girlfriend, visited. Regardless of Sam's explanation of James' new schedule, she insisted that James promised to leave his duty at the bakery early to be with her that night. Hours passed, James did not return. Mary did not leave. At a little past midnight, Sam wanted to go to bed. Mary was unable to persuade him to remain outside any longer with her and she left. A few minutes after she had bid good-bye, she returned. Her residence was far and there was a blackout. She was afraid of the darkness that provided cover for armed bandits, rapists, witches and wizards. These were excuses she gave for her decision to sleep in the house.

Mary was twenty-five years old and had been a whore since she turned twenty. Sam was only fifteen and inexperienced in matters of sex. Mary hurried out of her blouse, and wears and joined Sam in bed. Her cotton wrapper stretched from her succulent and enticing breasts

14

down to her hip partially covering her nakedness. She snored heavily. She bent her knees and let them rest on Sam's buttocks. It was not long before his timidity and inexperience were reawakened. For hours, he lay wondering at her skilful seduction moves.

No healthy man could feel different with Mary. The time was four o'clock in the morning. Mary was amazed when Sam reached for his trousers and left her alone in the room, still wanting more. The next building was the bakery premises. Sam walked quietly to the van assigned to him as a salesman. Luckily, he found the door open and crept in for a brief sleep. Two hours later, the bakery owner aroused him from a deep sleep. He had been to the house at a quite unusual time of the day. He accused Sam of harbouring a prostitute. Sam thought that only an offensive posture could bail him from the trouble and did not hesitate to take it.

In a calm tone, he described how and for whom she came and why he had to prefer sleeping in a delivery van instead of their room. Raising his voice in anger, he deplored the inconveniences James had caused him and pleaded that the boss should warn him to desist from doing so again. The expression on his boss's face left Sam in no doubt that his alibi worked. It was a narrow escape from danger. James went on with his campaign of calumny. He disclosed to their employer that Sam was on a vacation and should not be trusted. The development made Sam to suspect that Mary was sent to trap him. However, these enhanced Sam's personal relationship with his employer and weakened James' reputation at Sunrise Bakery.

***

Another school year started in September; it was Sam's final year of secondary school education. He bid farewell to his boss, his wife, children and colleagues at the bakery. They made it possible for him to buy many expensive books and educational materials which otherwise would have remained beyond his reach.

The stage was set for the final assault on the great issue that took him and his peasant family years to prepare for. The year was 1980. Fear had been replaced by hope, doubt by certainty. He had revised questions dating back to five years and gone through the examination syllabus. He gave himself mock tests and organised group discussions to determine his preparedness to sit for the examination. What was left was a divine hand to lead him through. By the time Sam finished his final examination, he was convinced of success. He had prosecuted his studies with finesse and had the ambition to go beyond this attainment. But his family had no such resources to pay for higher education.

This was a dilemma. Between the period he left Madonna High School and the release of their examination results, he resisted the urge to travel to Lagos in search of job as did some of his schoolmates. He chose to be an auxiliary teacher of literature and economics in a commercial school. When results were released, Sam passed in division one, scoring alphas and credits in all the eight subjects. His determination and personal sacrifices had paid off but he still felt that his career had limited chances.

In January of 1981, he travelled to Yola with an uncle of his who had come home for Christmas. Months passed without him securing any job. He wrote to his parents:

My dear Parents,

I have not forgotten what you went through to ensure that I acquired education. I am aware of your hopes for a brighter future for the entire family as I have emerged triumphant. But it is disheartening to inform you, dear parents, that all attempts to secure a suitable job have been in vain. Initially, I thought my inability to understand the local dialect could be responsible. I toiled ceaselessly. Today, I am very fluent in Hausa yet my prospects of a gainful employment are bleak. Employers assert that I would not stay... and so have repeatedly hired applicants who do not have prospects of furthering their education. I have tried without success to tell them about my modest background. I think there is no feasible and enduring choice for me than to move on. I recognise the strain it is going to exert on you. I won't even blame you if you think I am crazy. But I am confident that after five years, the whole family will kiss the glamour of a new dawn.

Your son,
Sam.

Sam's parents did not only agree but also boasted that though they never envisaged a university level education for him, yet it was their responsibility which they would not abandon at any cost. To prepare for the spring entrance examination into universities, Sam accepted to teach at an institute of stenography in Yola. He opted for those subjects that were relevant to the course he wanted to study in the university. In addition, he made some money to augment the income he made from working as a labourer with a building construction company on Saturdays.

His first choice was law and the federal universities he preferred were located in the North and the West; he also chose a state university east of the River Niger. Admission in the law faculties of the federal institutions was competitive, hence the authorities were compelled to admit students on quota basis to reflect the federal character of Nigeria. It was a formula that tried to ensure that applicants from different states of the country had equal opportunities.

When the results were published, Sam scored three hundred points out of a total of four hundred. It was not good enough for an aspirant from his state of origin where many candidates scored up to three hundred and fifty eight points. Though the system allowed scores as low as two hundred and twenty points from candidates from certain parts of the country, he was not admitted.

Without resources, waiting to try again next year seemed an insane idea. Sam was in a hurry to climb to the top where he believed it would be serene and sweet. Therefore, he settled for a degree programme in business administration which was his second choice. Federal government institutions were substantially funded, and had all the necessary (educational) facilities. Tuition was free. Some of the undergraduates were on scholarship or paid stipend. With lots of money in their pockets, they carried out social and extracurricular activities within the campus.

The policy of equal representation of various states on every campus encouraged a blend of many cultures that would produce men and women who would be better disposed to the unity and progress of multi-ethnic Nigeria. However, it had done more harm than good to the national dream and aspiration. The disparity between the intelligent and ignorant had widened. Disaffection was common. Students and their lecturers experienced frustrations. Above all, applicants who were not offered admissions because there were more qualified candidates from their states, settled for lesser competitive courses. Whichever way, they felt the country had been unfair to them. The summary was that the gap which quota system set out to close became wider. There should not be quota system in harnessing the intelligence of the country's citizens.

Chief Nso was above the problem of quota system and lack of jobs in Nigeria. People like him had the resources, connections and power to secure admission for their children into any university. Neither quota nor the need to score higher points in examination into universities applied to them. While mere civil service jobs remained an illusion to Sam, Chief Nso would only drop a note to secure a plum job for his son in any oil company. But this was far from his plans for Dika. He sent him away from the demoralised and strike-prone lecturers. He sent him to the very house of western education, England.

As a way of protesting his disappointment, Sam left for a state-owned institution. Apart from the fact that there were still few students from other ethnic groups and cultures, state institutions directly contrasted with their federal counterparts. Tuition took a substantial part of the income of most parents and guardians. Library shelves were empty. Laboratories were mere extensions of the lecture rooms. Archaic computers were on display, only to be seen, not touched. Lecturers were overworked. Hostel facilities were substandard and insufficient. But, one thing was certain: admission was strictly on merit. Academic standard was very high. Students responded to lack of facilities by reaching out to other institutions and organisations in the state to gather materials and acquire more knowledge.

Finding his feet on the slippery terrain was not easy. Sam bungled his mathematics tests and quizzes repeatedly. The heat generated by mathematics was compounded by the fact that if he could not make it in his first year, the chances that he would make it in his second year, when he would have statistics to contend with, were very slim. No matter what grades he made in other areas, he would still not graduate until all compulsory courses were passed. In everything he did, the guiding principle had been to achieve the desired results first, and complain about the handicaps later. Failure to attain any set target was totally unacceptable to him. Otherwise, he would have attributed his problems to his family's difficulty in paying his fees and meeting his needs for books and food.

As he battled with his thoughts, one man emerged with a piece of advice which changed the course of events and established him firmly in the road to success. He was Dr. A. B. Ekwere, his lecturer on accounting principles and techniques. Dr. Ekwere said it was wrong to devote equal share of time to all courses. Sam was good in some and excellent in many others. Only mathematics constituted his Achilles' heel. Therefore, more time should be allocated to that which proved most insurmountable. He also enjoined Sam to meet his course mates who were very good in mathematics for further help otherwise, his graduation would be delayed.

The advice became Sam's magic wand. He did not only find it handy in studying mathematics and statistics but also in dealing with quantitative techniques in management and cost accounting which he encountered later.

It took Sam two years on campus to discover he could be admired by women, to be convinced that regardless of his skinny limbs, faded pair of cotton trousers, cobbled sandals and worn-out white shirts for which everybody knew him, he could hold his head high among his fellow students whose athletic bodies arrested the attention of the girls, or those whose pockets were filled with money which they could spend as it pleased them.

The discovery came at the beginning of another academic year when the Students' Union election was scheduled. Sam decided to vie for the post of General Secretary. His only opponent was a coursemate that was more mature and who belonged to many clubs on the campus. He came from a province that had the highest student enrolment and he, also, had enough money to spend on the campaign.

As for Sam, very few of the students came from his province. Therefore, they had no formal provincial association. The Rotaract Club which membership he had contemplated, required a huge amount of money that was enough to kill his zeal. In other words, he was not a member of any club. Despite all these, Sam thought that he was more equipped to serve the interest of his fellow students better than his opponent. He was certainly younger and hoped to turn age into an advantage. He demonstrated clearly in his campaign that a youth with a sense of purpose and radicalism was what suited students' unionism.

'There is no alternative,' he once said. Opinion poll showed that for every five students that knew Sam, only one knew his opponent. Compared to his opponent, his academic prowess was immense. His opponent used posters and billboards designed by professional artists and script-writers. Sam employed his oratorial power to warm his way to the hearts of students. He moved from one hostel to another and mounted the podia to get the students' support and votes. His manifesto was genuine and far-reaching.

Sam did not reckon with his opponent's strategy of organising his provincial association into a formidable voting bloc that went into an alliance with members of another provincial associations one of whose members was contesting for the post of president. The presidential aspirant himself had opponents from other smaller zones in the country.

Sam got wind of the deal and tried to pre-empt it but was unsuccessful. Yet, he remained undaunted.

The following day, votes were cast and counted. Sam lost to his opponent by only five votes. It was painful. However, he took it in his strides. He went to the winner's hostel and delivered his congratulatory message. He returned to his room and met Efe whose display of affection, sympathy and support for Sam during the election period was quite noticeable. So her presence was not odd.

'You deserved to win by every stretch of imagination. It is so appalling that an institution like this can succumb to the same mediocrity and mendacity that bedevil the country. You did not lose to your opponent, you lost to the power of money and sentiments. Whether they like it or not, you are my secretary.' These words were very comforting. They soothed his nerves in a unique way.

For hours, she stayed. People came in and left again. They talked about anything under the sun. Sam had not known much about her when she tutored him about those aspects of his behaviour which only a few days of public appearance could not have disclosed to her. She had taken interest in him a long time ago. Efe was tall and slim. Her complexion was so light that her friends and family nicknamed her 'oyibo' (white girl). She had long curled hairs and a set of white teeth with a gap which complemented her luscious large eyeballs. Her straight long legs and well proportioned body attest to the fact that long before she was born, essential vitamins had been fed into her system.

She was the only daughter of her parents who were federal government employees in Imo State. Her father, a director, and mother, a labour relations officer, no doubt, belonged to the upper class of the society. Sending her to a nearby university was a calculated attempt to keep her close to them, otherwise, the parents had what it required to secure her admission elsewhere. Her knowledge of Igbo language was smattering and the zeal to learn more was evident. Like most people from her ethnic group, Bini, she was liberal, accommodating and willing to venture into other cultures without herself making cheap.

Sam and Efe saw each other constantly for three days. Only lectures parted them. Efe was reluctant to tell him about her performance as a part-two student of architecture. He read between the lines and concluded accurately that she was well above average. He was captivated not only because of her concern for his welfare, her compelling wit, her love for him or her decent family background but because of the ease with which he related to her.

At the inaugural meeting of the newly elected executive council of the students' union, Sam was unanimously appointed editor-in-chief of the union's magazine, with the full rights and privileges of an elected officer. Efe volunteered to be a member of the editorial board and was later elected its secretary. People dubbed her Sam's secretary plenipotentiary. Her concern did not end there. She helped with the lecture notes he missed and made it possible for him to have three meals everyday. His wardrobe changed too. If stock would ever be taken of those who assisted Sam to complete his degree programme, Efe and her parents would sit comfortably in the front row. She spoiled him and enhanced his self esteem. Efe was his angel. She brought much needed sun to the winter of his life.

***

By the end of Sam's third year on campus, graduate unemployment had escalated. He still recollected that as a boy, his father told him that lazy men whither in starvation. Hope for happiness, financial success, fame and pride had disappeared. Education, it seemed, was no more the sure path to the top. Sam's family waited and hoped somebody would salvage the situation so that their dreams, wishes and aspirations would be fulfilled. Nobody did. No government rose to their rescue. Hardwork, honesty, conscience and patriotism became words that were rare in the mouths of an impoverished minority.

People who killed for money were honoured and given front seats in churches. Public servants who succeeded in looting the national coffers with impunity were reappointed by successive regimes based on their 'selfless' services to the nation. Conmen, drug barons, and arsonists were bestowed with traditional titles. They, and not the professionals his father told him about as a child, formulated fiscal and monetary policies to further serve their personal aggrandisement.

They dismantled national values and norms, and in their place, established national decadence, deceit and delusion. While other countries marched forward, they described Nigeria as Africa's giant. It could be an appropriate description if it was about population, or if the country had not been retrogressed by the same people who cheered it, and responded to the new culture with a fiendish glee.

The crux of the national quagmire was that as the

plunderers could not be beaten, it became inevitable to join them. That was precisely the dilemma of Sam's people. His family did not ask for political appointments in government or fleets of cars for their household or holiday resorts overseas. They did not clamour for posh houses with manicured lawns for their grandchildren or paid vacations. They simply expected that a family, which invested so much in educating their son be rewarded with a place in the labour market.

They were stupefied until Brigadier Ike Nwachukwu became the military governor of Imo State. As a special guest to Sam's annual graduation ceremony and the highest employer of labour in his state, he offered immediate employment to all first class graduates. The governor's gesture raised hopes and spurred those who would graduate the following year to work harder. He provided the only streak of light known to Sam during those dark moments. Sam had accumulated excellent grades in his courses and needed to maintain it throughout the two semesters remaining. His family members heard about the prospect of immediate employment for him after graduation and were delighted.

It was less than two months after his final examination when another military coup took place. Brig. Nwachukwu was promoted and redeployed. The hope for employment for Sam sank into a cloud of uncertainty. Some of Sam's lecturers to whom he made his anxiety known assumed that the policy had long been established, regardless of who held the mantle of leadership.

Sam and his colleagues converged from their various locations of primary assignment as National Youth Service Corps members for the 14 March, 1987 convocation ceremony. He was excited by the invitation to render a valedictory speech. There and then, he became a celebrity. Academic and non-academic staff wanted to chat with him. Old students pointed at his direction to new ones. His mates congratulated him too.

He hurried to meet Efe in her hostel. She still had one year to graduate. The months he spent without her seemed like years to him. Together, they sneaked to a friend's house where only the setting sun reminded them they had spent hours there.

They prepared for the convocation party organised by the students' union in conjunction with the student affairs registry. Sam was asked to jointly chair the occasion with the outgoing president of the union.

'Sam, you are very handsome in your suit,' Efe remarked. 'I hope other girls won't take you away from me tonight.' This compliment was unusual with her. It revealed her fears.

'But Efe, I owe everything to you. It's against my conscience to bite the finger that fed me let alone the one that is still feeding me. You made this moment possible for me. I shall be glad if the offer of myself to you always and forever will be enough as a show of appreciation of your love for me. The God of love will reward you abundantly.'

'Sam, you do not realise what a rare gem you are to me. If other women would meet with you and still be asking for more, I, Efe, am fully satisfied. You symbolise everything for which I pray.'

After three years of a serious affair, Sam knew Efe meant what she said. Hand in hand, they set out for the campus dining hall, venue of the party. A few metres to the place, he saw a throng of people. Out of curiosity, Sam and Efe moved closer to see what was going on. A brand new Mercedes Benz 600 SE automatic attracted the gathering crowd. Behind the steering was somebody who sat like a colossus. Beside the Mercedes was a glittering Porsche 911 Carrera Tiptronic. Efe whispered in his ears, 'Darling, it is Benson.'

Benson was the last child of his parents. His only brother studied very hard and with menial jobs, supported himself until he qualified as a pharmacist. Ten years after his departure from Nigeria, he returned to find out to his dismay that his four sisters had married without even a secondary school education. He swore that Benson would have all the education that their sisters missed. Later, he was appointed chief pharmacist of the federal ministry of health. His job included approving drugs supplied by companies for distribution to government hospitals and pharmacies all over the country. It also included ensuring the quality of drugs manufactured, imported and distributed for sale nationwide. He insisted on professionalism before the system corrupted him. Sub-standard drugs soon found their ways into the market. Suppliers to the government falsified their figures and got paid for qualities and quantities of drugs not supplied. He stashed some of his booty in foreign banks, imported the finest luxury cars for himself and his wife and bought a locally assembled Peugeot 505 SR for his aged parents. He presented a gift of Golf GTI car, worth twenty-three thousand dollar to his concubine, invested in real estate and the rest of his money, he allowed Benson to enjoy as much as it pleased him.

Benson was tall, broad shouldered and athletic. But these were not the only reasons why people were attracted to him. He was on a monthly salary enough to pay the salaries of five professors. His brother's fleet of cars was at his disposal. His ability to provide transport both to invitees to and hosts of parties within and outside the campus made it imperative to extend invitation to him. When he chose to organize a party himself it was with extravaganza and finesse. He was an unsurpassable womaniser. Women meant a lot to him only when he had not had carnal knowledge of them. Afterwards, he dumped them into his overflowing bin of 'have-beens'.

Benson donated generously to students' unions and clubs in return for publicity. Groups that missed his largesse were only those run by leaders who did not know how to flatter and pour encomiums on him. There was one area where neither his personal appearance nor his penchant for publicity could not hold sway – the classroom. After three years, he had accumulated too many carry-overs without any prospect of clearing them given another four years. Therefore, he was compelled to withdraw. While his counterparts studied for their final examinations, his brother procured a visa for him to study in Europe, a springboard, to the sky. He globe-trotted, from there to India, Thailand, en route USA and Nigeria.

On campus some students said he was doing well as a student overseas, others said he was in jail for rape, many more insisted he was an international businessman. Nobody was sure of Benson's position until he joined his former colleagues at their convocation ceremony. He was explaining the dynamics of the twelve-cylinder engine and rationalising the presence of his two hefty bodyguards when Sam and Efe thrust their way through the crowd to meet with him. Smiling broadly, Sam extended his hands to shake him. Benson responded with a cold grin as he extended his hands for a lacklustre greeting. There was no doubt that Efe aroused more excitement in him. Efe, one of the rare birds that eluded Benson's net, did something that had remained indelible in Sam's heart.

'Hi Benson,' she greeted and not caring for a response, turned and clung to Sam. Benson felt belittled.

From inside the hall, the microphone blared an appeal for all guests and hosts to come in and be seated. As they moved towards the hall, Sam said to Benson, 'Boy, you made...'

'I 'm now a chief and must...' Benson interrupted him.

'I 'm sorry. I did not know you have already earned a chieftaincy title.' Benson was apparently offended.

'Sam, with eight posh cars, a mansion on Allen Avenue, Ikeja, a guest house in FESTAC village, many hangers-on and a lucrative business empire that stretches from Europe to America and from Asia to Africa, do I need to beg traditional rulers to confer a title on me? Look, wealth is like pregnancy, which cannot be concealed. My wealth attracts attention and magnetises the wise and the foolish. My personal assistant had problems keeping at bay hungry and obscure traditional rulers who came cap in hand begging me to come to be honoured.'

Benson continued, 'I did not dismiss them empty-handed though. I gave them money. I'm investing in my political future.'

As they took their seats, girls fell over one another to get Benson's attention. He gave out his business cards which they pocketed as if they were a license to survival. Some of the girls who were more daring demanded to know in which hotel he lodged. Others promised unsolicited visits to his Lagos residence. Sam succeeded in pulling him out of his shell. They spoke like old schoolmates. Good times gone were recalled with nostalgia.

About Efe, Benson confessed, 'She is the only beautiful girl that I set out to seduce on this campus but failed. My money did not mean anything to her. You are lucky to have found a woman like that and she is fortunate to have landed the right Igbo son for keeps. Someday I will give up philandering and retire to her type of woman.'

When the master of ceremonies invited Sam to the high table, there was a standing ovation which was unequalled on the campus. But the record did not hold long before it was broken. It went deep when Benson joined them. Students, guests and even lecturers rose to their feet in applause. It took minutes before calm returned. If Benson intended to wreck vengeance on the society that looked down on him, he succeeded on a grandiose scale. If Sam symbolised academic excellence, Benson was the embodiment of financial success. The crowd went for him.

***

Early in the morning of 14th March, 1987, Sam went to the student affairs registry to retrieve his valedictory speech. He was sad to note that his call on Brig. Nwachukwu's successor to make good on the latter's promise of jobs did not survive the university's vetting. The officer who had the powers to make such alterations had ready explanations. 'Automatic employment for our best students is an example of government's responsiveness to our situation. We do not really need to put any more agitation before Nwachukwu's successor emulates him.'

The university's vice-chancellor rose to the rostrum and rendered a very emotional address. He lamented the shortage of fund which had hampered research projects and made administrative and academic schedules very rigorous for everyone. Sam delivered his brief speech. By the time the state governor concluded his speech, all the persons who had taken immediate employment to heart were wrong. Sam and a few others in his class were disappointed.

Once again, Efe was there to console. 'Darling, I understand how bad you feel but frankly, I am much more worried. I am not a labour pundit but suffice it to say that since the previous graduation ceremony, the government, with her several ministries and corporations, cannot generate jobs for ten first class graduates, only God knows what becomes of every other person.'

'I think the governor is either being insensitive or wicked,' Sam blurted out.

'Definitely, God did not bless you with so much energy and intelligence for nothing. It may take a little more time for His kindness and love to manifest. Sometimes, He reveals Himself beyond our comprehension. But He never fails.'

Sam had heard that type of sermon a thousand times from the pulpit but never from somebody as endowed with intelligence, beauty and resourceful parents as Efe. It was a great solace and a challenge to him. Outside, he posed for a group photograph with some of his colleagues. As usual, Benson took the centre stage. Others were Ugo, Grace, Susan, Osa, Simon, Izu, Emete and Betty whose diminutive size was further emphasised with Benson by her side. Only a member of the circle was missing – Yeru. He could not make the papers he flunked even in the resit examination and was told to repeat the final year.

On the 7th of June, Sam's year of National Youth Service ended with a colourful ceremony in Akure, the Ondo State capital. The year of respite from the demands of education had ended. Uncertain future, fending for family and self, and anxiety awaited him.

In August 1987, Sam boarded a bus for Lagos in search of a job. As the bus manoeuvred out of the chaotic urban traffic into the main road, Sam sat back and closed his eyes for a nap. Memories of the just concluded Youth Service flooded his brain. Soon, events of the past year took over.

'Excuse me,' he had said to Olaitan. 'Are you for the orientation exercise?'

'Which... which orientation exercise?' She asked.

'The 1986/87 August-tier orientation programme for National Youth Corps members deployed to Ondo State.'

'Oh, no. I am still in the secondary school and won't sit for the West African School Certificate Examination till another two years.' She replied with a smile.

Her white gown with black stripes and a black flat shoe with a black belt, her perfectly polished dark skin, trimmed hair, and tall slim frame set her far apart from other female passengers. On a closer look, Sam noticed her alluring eyes and pointed nose. Apart from her complexion, she resembled Efe closely. Sam chuckled as his palms became dampened. To save himself an embarrassment, he crossed his legs. When that was not enough to conceal the bulge between his legs, he slipped his hands into his pockets.

'How old are you?' Sam inquired

'Fifteen years last week.'

'What's a fifteen-year old Yoruba girl doing in the east of the River Niger?'

Olaitan radiated the same smiles that captivated Sam earlier. 'My father is a police officer in Owerri. Having spent the holiday with them, I am returning to Oruko Grammar School.'

'So you are from Ondo State?' Sam asked, clearly

excited.

'Yes. We have had youth corp members before. Perhaps you will be deployed to my school.'

'I will be glad to have such an opportunity but I consider the prospect very remote.'

'Why do you think so? Don't miracles happen?'

'I agree miracles happen. How can I explain that out of nearly a thousand corps members deployed to your state and with over a thousand places of assignment, I will be posted to where you and I wish. Moreover, I am a Business Administration graduate, not trained for teaching. I expect to be posted to a company.'

'Let me tell you, Sam. Ondo State hasn't enough industries for people of your type who aspire to do their primary assignment in offices. Competition for the limited places is stiff. It is not that I do not wish you well but I'm simply telling you the truth.'

Sam and Olaitan were still arguing and laughing when the bus arrived Benin City. Inside a busy filling station, all the passengers alighted for food. Together, they went for some snacks.

Suddenly, one male passenger hurried up to them. He shoved Sam aside with his broad shoulders and stretched out his hands and grabbed Olaitan's waist.

'Bisi, how are you?' the man said.

Sam was annoyed and sad. The urge to walk away was irresistible. He was a few metres back to their bus when Olaitan abandoned the man and ran after him.

'Don't touch me, you liar!' he spluttered.

'Listen, Sam. It is not my fault.'

'Whose fault is it then, mine? Liar.'

'I am not a liar, Sam, believe me.' She squeezed his hands tightly as they walked into the bus together.

Inside, she pulled him gently to her seat and started to explain. 'I do not have any business with that potbellied drab. In the morning, before you arrived, he was so menacing that I told him a fake name to set him going. Truly, I cannot touch him even with a ten-metre pole. Try to understand, please.'

The businessman did not give up without another attempt. When he boarded the bus fifteen minutes later, he walked to their direction and offered Olaitan a bottle of malt drink and some biscuits. She did not even look at the offer a second time before she rejected them politely but firmly.

They travelled for nearly thirty kilometres away from Benin City when Sam looked around and noticed that nearby passengers were sleeping. He placed his hands on her knee and started to rub away an imagined filth. When she did not object, he moved them gradually deeper into her barely covered warm and smooth laps.

'Do you remember your apparent reluctance this morning to accept my invitation to seat beside me?'

'Yes.'

'Can you explain your reason?'

'You were a stranger.'

'But now?'

'You are not.'

'Fine. It is by coming close to strangers that everything strange goes away. Again, every couple, whether married or not must have been strangers at the beginning.'

'I agree, Sam,' she responded feebly, her eyes closed, face creased, teeth tightened convulsively as Sam manoeuvred his fingers further until they reached her panties. He caressed her. With nearby passengers still sleeping and Olaitan not protesting, the fingers dug into her already wet body until she was trembling.

'Please...' Olaitan struggled to pull his hand off.

'So you are a virgin?' Sam whispered.

'Yes.' Her eyes opened and head leaned on his shoulders.

'You are bad,' she murmured.

'You are correct. I am not perfect. No man is perfect. The entire human race is a mixture of vices and virtues such that perfection is unthinkable. It seems there is nothing I can do about my vices some of which you have observed. They look irredeemable. My appeal therefore is that you embrace my imperfection. Put in another way, at childhood, I was impatient, thoughtless and stubborn. However my mother brought me up into a thoughtful, peaceful, tolerant and humble adult, not through intimidation or starvation but love. Now I am old enough to steer the boat of reckless youth into safe waters and ready to bear my cross alone.'

'Are you surprised I'm still a virgin?'

'Yes. Your personal appearance coupled with the promiscuity and materialism in our society make me not just surprised but shocked. I have found a treasure. I wish I can keep you forever.'

'I will love you, Sam,' she smiled.

'I will love you too.'

In his mind's eye, he could perceive that Efe was jealous, with a feeling of being betrayed. Sam quickly dispelled the feeling of guilt. He slipped his left hand around her neck and kissed her on the mouth for the first time.

They were still locked in each other's embrace when they arrived Ore. Her eyes were red and knees weak when they alighted. For minutes, they stood talking in subdued voices, ignoring yelling taxi drivers. With their composure regained, they were set to part to their different destinations.

With a promise to visit her at the end of his orientation exercise, Sam left for Ode-Aye, south of Ondo State while Olaitan sandwiched herself in a 504 Peugeot station wagon which headed out of the dusty garage for Oruko in the north.

Sam presented his call-up letter to camp officials and was duly registered. The following day, all the corps members were allocated platoons. Each platoon elected a leader whose responsibility included liaison with platoon sergeants and corporals to ensure successful implementation of the programme. General orientation course comprised drills, physical exercise, paramilitary training, lectures and leadership activities of Man O' War Bay type. Like most corps members, Sam initially found these activities hectic and developed painful joints and headache.

Lectures and discussions were held on a wide variety of national and local issues, including ideology, history, customs, defence, economics and government. Guest speakers were drawn from all walks of life. Major Nigerian languages were taught. Transport allowance was paid. The exercise formally started with a swearing-in ceremony. Camp activities, though routine, became less intensive.

Photographers had a field day. Confined to the camp, corps members lived a regimented life, obtainable only in military barracks. So a visit to the only supermarket in the camp broke the monotony. Nevertheless, a pass was given to those who wished to go out for religious worship. Occasionally, a small group of corps members were authorised to make a tour of Okitipupa and Igbokoda, the riverside and oil-rich areas of the state.

With only two hundred and forty female members, some of whom were married or belonged to religious groups that observed limited social interactions, the camp looked like

36

an all-male one. Sam was filled with nostalgia. He missed Efe and wanted to be with her again. Above all, he longed for Olaitan.

Eventually, the orientation exercise came to an end. Postings were published. Sam was disappointed that he missed the opportunity to acquire one year working experience. He was consoled with his posting to Oruko Grammar School, Akure.

Corps members packed their belongings and departed with their employers. It did not dawn on Sam what a wonderful time and friends he had until his only camp girlfriend walked to where he stood expectantly, hugged him for a long time and promised to keep in touch before she left with her employers. As their vehicle drove off, for the first time, Sam wished the exercise had not come to an end. The next time he saw her six weeks later, her elegant body was wrapped in Nigeria's national colours, ready for burial in Ibadan as a result of road accident.

'This is where corps members have been accommodated since three years. It is quiet and lifeless now because nearby residents have gone to work. I will send some students to come and clear the premises. Meanwhile, you can rest. Tomorrow, your assignment starts. I am sure you are going to enjoy serving here as your predecessors did but beware of students who are wont to causing mischief to unsuspecting strangers like you.' With these remarks, the beautiful female principal returned to her office.

The principal kept her promise. Four students arrived in a matter of minutes. When they had completed their mission, one of them who appeared to be their leader spoke to Sam.

'Sir, I live in the dormitory. I am the senior prefect of

the school. Any time you have problems with anything – cooking, sweeping, washing or shopping, send for me. I will ask any of the students to do it or I can always do it for you.'

'Thank you very much. Meanwhile could you please locate Olaitan Odudu for me? Tell her I want to see her immediately,' Sam requested.

'Okay, Sir,' she replied with a frown.

'Miraculous!' Olaitan shouted. 'Can you believe it that you are not only in our school but also a tenant in my father's house.'

'Miraculous, indeed,' responded Sam calmly as he embraced her. 'So, this is your father's house.'

'Yes. But no member of our family lives here. It is for rent.'

Nearly one hour later, she brought plantains, eggs, onions and tomatoes. 'I guess you haven't anything to eat hence I decided to bring these things,' she said as she went into the kitchen.

Soon, the senior prefect joined them. They ate together and talked till late in the evening. That night marked the beginning of a long intimate and risky affair with some of the students which nearly brought him in a head-on collision with his boss. Sam and the girls did not mind inquisitive looks. After six months of surveillance, the envious female teachers helped by their male counterparts armed the embittered principal with substantial evidence of the amorous and deplorable relationships.

When Sam entered the principal's office, three students and Olaitan were already on their feet like sheep for slaughter. The principal tidied her table, adjusted herself and broke the silence that pervaded the room.

'There were allegations of a clandestine affair between

some students and our corps member. I set up an investigative team to ascertain the veracity of these allegations, the students involved, and to recommend necessary disciplinary actions against the students and the corps member. The report has been submitted. Mr. Sam Ogemdi, you have been invited to ensure no innocent student is punished. The staff members here deserve to witness the proceedings.'

The senior prefect and two others denied any affair with Sam. One other student admitted an intimate relationship but blamed it on pressure from and threat of punishment by Sam.

'Can you recollect how many times you visited his residence?' asked one teacher.

'No, sir,' answered the girl.

'Is it true or false that on the 28th of January, you became violent when your classmate was seen departing from the corps member's residence early in the morning?'

The girl did not say anything. Apart from her head which dropped, she didn't show any indication of remorse.

The principal turned to Olaitan. 'Do you want to deny like your colleagues?'

'No, Madam. I can deny anything else in the world but I cannot deny my relationship with Sam. I met and fell for him before his deployment to this school. I had written to my father about him though I did not disclose the loss of my virginity to him. I do...'

'Loss of virginity to a passer-by!' shouted another teacher.

'Yes, Madam. I do not regret it." In tears, she continued, 'I have never felt this way for anybody before. I genuinely love him.'

Another female teacher hissed in apparent disgust and

said, 'you must be a sucker.'

'Thank you. But I love him. If love makes one a criminal, I am certainly one.'

'Were you aware your lover was dating other girls?' asked the principal.

'I was aware of it, but he treated me differently. He is not a predator. I am not a prey. I am not exploited or treated like an instrument of fun. He has continued to love me the way he did on board a Lagos-bound bus when neither the staff nor the students of this school had set eyes on him. His respect and tenderness for me are real and unique. I cannot deny him.'

'Supposing he impregnates you and runs away, what are you going to do?' the principal further asked.

'The last thing Sam will do against me is to abandon me with a pregnancy. He cannot do that to me, Madam.'

'Do you have anything to say Mr. Ogemdi? You are on trial.'

'I am not on trial. Olaitan is not on trial too. Love relationship between a student and her teacher is on trial. The outcome depends on one's viewpoint. But let me remind you that I had fallen in love with her before I became her teacher. I did not do anything to influence my posting to this school. Neither did she.

The questions are these: should we have carried on the relationship? Was it possible to put the lid on the fire of love because we were brought together by circumstances in this school? If any of you can feel so intensely, let the person go ahead and condemn us.'

The principal told the teachers and the students to vacate her office. Alone with Sam, she said, 'You disappointed me. Why did you condescend so low? Don't you notice all the admiring glances? Don't you think that many of the female members of staff are yours just for the asking? Are you not ashamed of being associated with these dirty riff-raffs, Mr. Ogemdi? What happened to your wisdom and sense of decency?'

'Why exactly am I standing trial, Madam?'

'I hope you don't misunderstand me, Sam. My word is only a piece of advice. You are not bound by it.'

'All right, Madam. Thank you very much.'

The following day, for over forty minutes, the school principal stood on the assembly ground and treated the entire students and staff to a vivid account of the story. Finally she decreed, 'Titi Osondare has convinced me beyond doubt that her appointment to the most enviable position of a senior prefect was a mistake. She led the team of mischievous and morally lax students to seduce Mr. Ogemdi. To cap it all, she mixed her immorality with penchant for lies. Therefore, Titi, Bose, Idowu and Iyabo are hereby dismissed from the school with immediate effect. The security chief has been directed to ensure that this order is complied with. Titi and her accomplices may be allowed to enter into this premises to sit for their forthcoming school certificate examination.'

The affected students started crying. The two security men quickly came and led them out of the assembly. Calm restored, the principal continued. 'Olaitan accepted her ignominious act with rare honesty and courage and swore to take arms to defend it. I am convinced that she is fully aware of the consequences of her action. Her age makes it imperative for me to intervene by informing her father about the development. I am making the necessary consultations to ensure that appropriate disciplinary action is taken against our corps member for his moral bankruptcy, misuse of female students, intellectual dishonesty and violation of the oath he took on assumption of duty. Let every student be warned that I will not hesitate to deal with anyone who has the effrontery to corrupt our system. Enough is enough.'

Though no action was taken against Sam, he felt sorry for the expelled students and looked forward to the end of his service year. His love for Olaitan did not diminish. It became more intense and quasi-official.

The end came. Corps members all over the federation started to handover materials entrusted in their care and say farewell to their hosts. He dusted his camp gear in readiness for the passing out parade and subsequent award of certificates.

Olaitan knew that parting was imminent but nothing was wrong with asking if there was hope of meeting again, when nothing, be it tide or time, could separate them.

'Sam, I want to know your plan for me, in fact, for our future. I love you. You came into my world and changed it forever. Perhaps, I am asking for too much.'

'Olaitan, dear, I am bothered about the future too. You have touched my heart in a special way. Your innocence, youthfulness, fragrance and sweetness make you special. I do not know if my head and heart will ever be free from the captivity to which you confined them from the first day we met. Honestly, I have never been so spellbound. Believe me. Please, believe me, Olaitan. Unfortunately, I have lacked the courage to tell you that my hands have been tied by an oath of blood I took while I was on campus. There is this woman. When I saw her, I thought I had seen the most beautiful and attractive woman on earth. There was no hint that I would ever meet someone like you. You may not be able to imagine the magnitude of despair beneath the love and joy you give me daily. The blood oath compels me to marry her or die.'

'No, Sam. There is no need for it yet. There must have been something special about her for which you submitted to the bond otherwise as smart and intelligent as I consider you, nothing else would have prompted you to do so. Go ahead and marry her.'

'And you?'

'I won't love you in the grave. It is only when you are alive and happy that my adoration for you will be meaningful. Marry your campus sweetheart but always remember me in your prayers. May I have somebody who would be so precious as you have been.'

'Don't let anybody know I have lost you. They won't understand that your life had been on the edge. Hence they would be right to have called you a passer-by.'

Sam looked at her and saw tears trickling down her cheeks. He pulled her closer to himself and was almost in tears too as he said: 'I understand the way you feel. Nobody deliberately loses an irreplaceable source of joy. But I have confidence in your future. You have brain, beauty and manners. You still have time on your side. If I ever have my way, I will come for you. Meanwhile, believe in God's benevolence. He taught us to love and surely those who love genuinely will be rewarded from His own abundance. I will continue to love and wish you well. I will never forget you.'

***

Sam was still thinking about the events of the service year when the bus arrived Onitsha. He missed Olaitan, her tears, anguish and plea. He found comfort in his teacher's comparison of a woman's love to the affection of a baby for a nanny who lures him to bath or sleep. To the baby, the nanny is prime. She is so invaluable that one worries about how the baby survives without the nanny.

But the baby rediscovers an enduring happiness in whoever replaces the nanny as if the nanny never existed.

He reassured himself that Efe was his God-ordained wife. Her love had stood the test of time and would endure throughout her life. Moreover, what mattered to Sam as he moved into Lagos in search of a job were not things gone but things yet to come.

He joined his newly married cousin at Orile, one of the slums of Lagos metropolis. The building comprised twenty-one rooms, three rows each containing seven rooms. Between them was a breezeway that served as a depository of some household items or kitchen for those who found the only kitchen distant or dirty. There were one pit toilet and a bathroom for about sixty residents. Workers rose as early as four o'clock in the morning to be able to take a bath or waited till evening if they could not.

Sam's cousin occupied a dingy room with his wife. After a very difficult day in the streets looking for job, Sam returned to have dinner with them and later retreated to his cousin's place along the breezeway, pulled a wooden bench close to the wall to ensure there was still enough passage for people and had as much sleep as mosquitoes and feet-shuffling passers-by would allow him.

One year after his arrival in Lagos, he had written two hundred and fifty-six applications for job, visited all government establishments, offices of multinational and indigenous companies without success. One interview was particularly remarkable.

A multinational company had vacancies for six trainee managers. From six hundred shortlisted applications, the selection was based on written and oral tests. Out of the fifty applicants who scaled through the first hurdle, Sam was number one. Susan and Osa, his coursemates were also successful. Five days later, they returned for the last lap. Sam had known a lot about eye-contacts in any interview. Among the panellists who appeared to wish him well, one was particularly outstanding. When the man asked if Sam had no other referees apart from his former lecturers and vacation job bosses at Golden Guinea Breweries Plc, Umuahia, Sam guessed the man was privy to some secret criteria for selection. Sam tried to find out why such persons could not competently vouch for his character. Another panellist promised to contact him soon. As Sam walked away, he developed goose pimples but was optimistic. He was still sure of one of the six vacancies.

When Sam went to find out why he had not been communicated, Susan and Osa were already trainee managers. Susan was mistress to one of the ministers. He simply telephoned the multinational's managing director to hire her. It was stupid of any right-minded chief executive to ignore a minister's order. The ever loquacious Osa boasted that the job was given to him, courtesy of his uncle who was the chairman of another giant industry.

Cases of nepotism, bribery and corruption were common and did not make any news.

Returning home, Sam decided to find out why the electricity authority, NEPA, with offices at Marina had not acknowledged any of his applications for employment.

'My uncle, the personnel director, wants me to see him immediately,' Sam told his secretary.

He had gotten accustomed to official protocols and red tapes. He had learnt how to crash through them. Without asking any question, she led him to the personnel director.

Sam thanked her and closed the door for a tete-a-tete. There was no trace of his trolley of applications. Sam was not surprised and did not want to waste that precious opportunity chasing shadows. To have access to the director was difficult and to find him in such a genial mood was rare.

'Though you specialised in business administration, yet I think you can fill one of the vacant accounting positions,' the director said.

Sam could not believe his ears. His heart pounded against his chest. He adjusted himself on the chair.

'Give me this opportunity, Sir. I will be loyal and hard-working. I will learn fast and accurately...'

'Well, you deserve it. You have the personal appearance, communication skill, confidence and tact – qualities that are essential for a career in management, which unfortunately are lacking in most of today's fresh graduates. Here, graduate employment is handled by a committee. That is the civil service rule. But I will bend it, employ you and present your file to them at their next sitting for approval. Your curriculum vitae is so interesting that I strongly doubt any of them will object.'

'Thank you, Sir.'

'It's all right. What's your state of origin?'

'Imo.'

'Jesus Christ!' the director blurted out in exasperation. 'Why is it that I have fantastic applicants from states whose quotas are filled. It pricks my conscience to turn people like you back to the streets whereas vacant positions exist to be filled. My young man, I have sympathy for you, as you can see, my hands are tied. It is indeed a pity I cannot hire you,' he concluded sadly.

He did not pretend to be interested in Sam's welfare.

He genuinely cared. Sam thanked him and walked away. His palms and forehead were wet with sweat. He was filled with rage at the obstructive quota system, rather than the helpless executive who would be risking his own job if he contravened the policy.

Out in the lobby, Sam waited for the elevator. From it alighted Simon, a schoolmate who graduated in engineering. They were seeing each other for the first time since their convocation ceremony.

'What are you doing here?' Sam asked.

'I'm a staff,' he quipped.

'You're lucky,' Sam hugged him.

'Do not say that, Sam. I'm waiting and hoping that someday, an engineering position will emerge on my state quota. Presently, I work as a clerk cum messenger. You could see that I went downstairs to collect these newspapers. Even the clerical job was not easy to come by. My family paid an officer here the sum of one thousand five hundred naira before it was given to me,' he lamented.

'It's better than nothing, Simon. At least, you can now afford to keep body and soul together.'

'No way,' he exclaimed. 'If it is hard for a fully employed engineer to earn enough money to meet the escalating cost of living, imagine how impossible it is when he is underemployed and takes home one hundred and eighty naira every month. If not the greater chances of moving upward by pressing buttons within, I would have concluded that the bribe was a waste... Before I forget, do you still hear from Efe?'

'Regularly,' Sam replied with immense pride. 'You know she has become part of my life. Her parents have been very helpful to me too. They have provided me with financial and moral supports.'

'I'm happy for you. Where did she do her primary assignment?'

'Maiduguri, Borno State. They passed out yesterday, she will be around soon.'

'Greet her for me.'

'Thanks. I will pass your greetings to her.'

'Have you stumbled on Benson since you came to Lagos?'

'No Simon. However, I am contemplating doing just that. Perhaps any of his business associates may be of assistance.'

'One is bound to locate big Benson in any of the five-star hotels in Lagos. Somebody told me he has executive suites to himself for months. Women struggle for his attention. He has always been generous with money but I am afraid he is a drug dealer. For fear of falling into trouble, I have maintained my distance. And will continue to do so regardless of my financial predicaments.'

As he was talking, Sam saw part of the caption of the newspaper which he folded under his armpit.

'Can I glance at the newspaper, please?'

Together they read: 'COURIER ARRESTED: BARON ON THE RUN.'

Line by line they read the details. The baron was Benson and the arrested courier was another schoolmate, Emete.

According to the report, Emete left Bombay International Airport, under circumstances still being investigated, with sixty-eight kilograms of cocaine. Prior to his arrival, Benson had procured the services of a senior customs official for an undisclosed sum of money to see the haulage through customs formalities.

Emete was already airborne when the senior official

48

learnt that the Area Controller of Customs was scheduled to visit the airport. The senior customs official telephoned Benson and suggested names of other officers who would be on duty and whose presence at the airport would not be suspicious.

Benson quickly located and started wheeling and dealing with them. Everything went smoothly until the half a million naira cash he had in the boot of his car was exhausted, yet there was still an agent of the airport authority to pay.

'This is not the first time you made a promise to us. As you did not keep those ones, you will also not keep this. Give me my own now!' The agent insisted.

When his colleagues noticed that he could not be dissuaded, they sneaked away one after another until he was alone with Benson. Meanwhile, the aircraft was already on the tarmac and passengers could be seen at the arrival hall.

Benson jumped into his car with a promise to return immediately. When he sped away, there was no doubt in the mind of the airport agent that he had fled.

'Others can make the money but I will not miss this opportunity to earn publicity and promotion,' the agent said to himself as he hurried back to the airport. Without observing official protocols, he left his check-point, walked briskly past the men of customs and nabbed Emete where, with his luggage, he stood apprehensively.

'God,' Sam cried. 'For importing cocaine into Nigeria, Emete may spend the next fifteen years behind bars.'

'That is it... desperation. Emete let his patience and wisdom desert him. His sun has set at noon. This is going to be a complete eclipse for a guy whose sense of right and wrong was incomparable. I think it is preferable to leave the shores of Nigeria for Britain, France, Germany, Italy or USA, enslave myself voluntarily for money than to risk even a day of my life in a Nigerian prison,' Simon said.

'Ah, do you talk about job specification? Manage to get across there, go to a farm, work as a factory hand, carry loads, sweep roads or houses. Make the hard currency and transform your life forever. Six months or at most one year on odd jobs in Europe is better than fifteen years in a jail. Do you know that because of the fluctuations in the exchange rate of the naira against other currencies, the stipend for doing such jobs for one year is bigger than a manager's salary for fifteen years in Nigeria? To add salt to injury, your country does not care about your life either. With some capital, I can start an engineering workshop. In the absence of any capital, if I have my way, I will do anything no matter how dirty, so far as it is legal. I know of three traders at Alaba market whose trading activities were falling apart a year ago before they left for Italy. Today, they have returned and bought houses and cars. They have moved from retailing to importation of large containers of electronics from abroad. The music has changed, Sam, the dancing steps ought to change too.'

They exchanged contact addresses and parted. 'Sweep... carry loads... nobody cares about your education.' The words resonated in Sam's head, as he sat inside the Orile-bound *molue* (passenger bus).

'My parents had toiled much on the farm. I had burnt the midnight oil. We had made personal sacrifices for good education. Today, it is a different story, a reminder of wasted efforts, a symbol of man's wickedness to man. I have fought every inch of the way to where I am today. One does not go to Europe from Nigeria on foot or by bus. It is certainly by air. There is no option other than to get the huge sum of money needed for it. No matter what happens, if I remain unemployed, God will cease to be my father. I will never worship Him again.'

The approach of Orile bus-stop terminated this stream of painful reflections. He alighted and trekked the rest of the way home.

***

'Sam, one girl came here and left this note for you,' his cousin's wife said as she picked an envelope from the table and delivered it to him.

The handwriting was unmistakably Efe's:

Darling,

Six months away from you seems a lifetime. I never realised how much of me you have taken with you until we found ourselves nine hundred kilometres apart. During the day, I thought of you. Doing so was the only thing that kept me alive. At night, I dreamed of all the times we had together, of all the tribulations you go through and of all my eternal commitment to your happiness and welfare. I talked about you to whoever cared to listen and adorned the walls of my bedroom with your photographs. Would it surprise you that I dropped my service kit at the doorstep of our Surulere residence and set out to this place in search of my jewel of inestimable value? Though you were not in and my body is aching for you more than ever, yet, if time be the only barrier, before you return to read this note, I will stay alive in my room until you come to kill me with your love.

Forever,
Efe.

Sam left immediately to see her, half walking, half running to the bus-stop.

'Now, I remember,' Efe said the following day. 'I saw Izu, your friend, while I stood at Stadium Bus-stop, waiting for a taxi yesterday. He was driving a 1984 Mercedes 200. In the passenger's seat was a woman old enough to be his mother. He introduced her to me as his bride. They even gave me a lift to Orile, up to the bridge from where he ran the risk of ditching his car. He promised to see you and pleaded that you should wait for him here until he arrives.'

'Why didn't you tell me yesterday?'

'I decided to keep it to ensure you have more reasons to be here longer,' She smiled.

'By the way, how did you make it to 30, Kabiru Street... trekked?' Sam asked as he stroked her hair.

'Yes, Sammy,' she replied. 'I did not even realize I had walked about ten kilometres until I was told you were away. But Sammy, don't you believe I will do anything, go anywhere just to be with you?'

'I believe you, Efe.' They kissed and finally ended up in bed.

Efe and Sam were having lunch when a black Cherokee Jeep came to a halt outside her parents' residence. It was Izu, always elegant. On campus, he was the Rotaract Club president. By virtue of that position, he gave Sam the club's brooch and song-book which Sam had not relinquished. Izu taught Sam the club's prayers and the four-way test and ensured he attended all the club's public functions. He could not be chartered for financial reasons. In return, Sam assisted Izu in research projects and assignments.

'Fellowship,' Sam greeted.

'Through service,' he responded as they embraced each other.

'Thanks for the lift you gave Efe yesterday'.

'It is a small thing, Sam. We all who studied with you love and respect you and we must be honest to say that you made our graduation a lot easier. You see, while we organised parties, you studied and went through all the libraries, got extra stuff, returned and shared them with us. Many of us would not have been so generous if we were in your position. You were good to us. Boy, in recognition of these facts, I have come to invite you and Efe to my wedding next weekend. The car outside belongs to my father-in-law, the former defence chief, retired General Ukadike Dawodu.'

'I thought the general with his family is living in Victoria Island. How did you get his daughter?'

'Sammy, it is not only military men who can plot a successful coup in this country. This is a carefully planned and perfectly executed coup. No blood was spilled, no heads rolled. Yet I hit the target,' Izu boasted.

'Could you guys please excuse me a bit,' Efe pleaded and left for her bedroom.

'I met a protocol officer of one of the members of the ruling military council at a night-club in Ikeja. I lied to the friend of my former fiancee that I saw the protocol officer glancing at her admiringly and advised her to tramp on him. Trust Lagos girls. She sashayed across the floor. In an effort to reach another man already known to her who sat behind the officer, she deliberately marched on the protocol officer's toe. She feigned a heartfelt concern for the officer's shrill cry of pain and even bent down to examine the damage. He told her not to worry and smiled to assure her he was all right. She strode back to us, her miniskirt revealing her thighs.'

'How could somebody fall for such a cheap prank?' Sam asked.

'Well, it worked. True to what I heard about him, he came over to meet me. I lied to him that she had a very wealthy industrialist who was dying to have her hand in marriage and so had turned a blind eye to any more overtures. I got him almost on his knees before I accepted to talk to her on his behalf. That was the beginning of our relationship. I started visiting his office and later his house. His opportunity to reciprocate my gesture came when the first son of Major-General Owuwamas hosted a party. He extended the invitation to me. Imagine those who were in attendance! All of them born with silver spoons in their mouth! I blended with them by all means. A greater part of the hunting was spent assessing the array of women critically,' Izu spoke almost in whispers. 'The general's daughter was more vulnerable. She is fourteen years older than I was and could not be described as very attractive. Man, I knew what I wanted.'

Raising his voice a little louder, he continued. 'She was attracted by my looks. After three consecutive visits to their home, the father demanded to know my mission. I told him I would like to get married to his beautiful daughter as soon as I secured a job. He swept aside the idea of waiting for a job and asked me to begin to prepare myself psychologically for the role of a husband. He has already given us a cottage in Miami, Florida, bought a mansion for us close to his estate and agents have been asked to find an exquisite summer house in Venice for our honeymoon.'

'What is the fate of your fiancee?' Sam asked.

'I think I deserve to have my head examined if I find

myself at the threshold of affluence, fame and power and instead of stepping in, I retreat to my miserable past and bleak future. Sammy, I cannot beat them, I am joining them,' he said with utmost finality.

True to his expectation, his wedding was deeply satisfying. Top brass of the military, the diplomatic corps, captains of industry and religious leaders were present. Prior to the wedding, Izu and his wife travelled to Spain for their shoes and wedding rings. Though there was no ring which attracted them, yet they were able to buy handmade crocodile skin shoes and a handbag, crafted by the legendary Mario Suza himself for the bride. Another bigwig in Nigeria had directed them to D'uomo, an internationally acclaimed shop near Vittorio Emmanuele II Park in Rome for the bridegroom's suit. But it was in Milan that Lenbini Boco rendered a design that stunned Izu and his wife. He made their wedding rings too. By Eurocity train, they arrived Paris. After two days of shopping and sightseeing, they left for London. At Juddi's, the bride's measurements, her choice of material and colour were taken. A computer-aided demonstration of the sewn wedding gown was made before they returned to Lagos.

The wedding was consecrated two weeks later by the archbishop of Lagos at Saint John's cathedral, Falomo. Unlike the reception, attendance to the mass was open to everybody. From the church to the military officers' mess in Victoria Island, the bride and bridegroom were escorted by a convoy of police and army special units. An army band opened the occasion after which highlife and traditional dance groups took turns to entertain the guests. Sheraton kitchen provided a range of catering services that included foreign and indigenous dishes. Many persons spoke eloquently about the bride. Sam was handy to extol Izu's efforts. For nearly two hours, a long queue of people wanting to give gifts to the couple persisted. Envelopes, cards and notes piled on of the table in front of the celebrants.

The bride's father presented keys of a brand new car and formally gave them a home on the Island. People were so carried away by the galore of colourful gifts and promises of assistance that the kerosene stove, wooden beds, mattresses, goat and some other pieces of gifts from Izu's parents were miserably dumped at the corner. Journalists and photographers had a field day. It was an opportunity for some people to renew old contacts and initiate or conclude business deals. By the time it was all over, there was no doubt on every one's mind that the occasion was a huge success.

'Izu's life can never be the same again from whichever perspective one looks at it.' Sam said to himself as he and Efe were on their way back to Surulere.

The newly wedded gathered their things and went to Murtala Mohammed International Airport. Aboard the aircraft with Izu and his wife was Betty. The trio sat together.

As soon as the plane was airborne, it was Betty who broke the silence.

'So, Izu, you did not invite me to your wedding?'

'In fact, Betty,' he explained, 'I had a very short time to prepare. But there was our Sam, who represented everybody.'

'Oh, yeah, that guy. What became of his girlfriend, that good for nothing bitch?'

'No, don't say that Betty. Efe is a very good lady. She accompanied Sam to our wedding and from all indications, Sam will marry her as soon as he gets a job.'

'So he has not secured a job yet whereas Susan, Osa

and many others are doing well as managers? The beginning of the day does not really foretell the manner the day ends. At school, he bothered himself so much that we thought he was graduating to take over as the President of Nigeria. Have you not heard that Yeru has been appointed special assistant to the governor of his state? All the people we thought won't survive are stars today while the Sams of this world are in the cold. I doff my hat for Benson. He dropped out of school. But it was not over for him. He established himself as a baron in international business. He would not have run into trouble if this hopeless military administration did not suddenly withdraw those men who protected Benson's interests.'

She continued, 'Do you know that his annual revenue was more than the budget of most state governments?'

'But where is all that now?'

'Benson is inherently extravagant you know,' Betty said. 'But he assisted many poor relations and unemployed peers and schoolmates. I owe everything I have today to his magnanimity. Beyond all this, he is making his mark again in 419 (a code name for duping unsuspecting persons by presenting them with tantalising deals). That guy has a viable brain and truly deserves all my respect.'

'How could Yeru be appointed special assistant when he has not completed his degree examinations?'

'He is well connected and that is what matters. The rule here is simple: follow what is, abandon what is supposed to be.'

Her voice started to rise in anger. 'When you arrive Venice, venture into adjoining cities during the day or night, Nigerians are everywhere, under rain or sun; be the weather cold or hot, they are the scum of the civilized world. I do not blame them. I pity them. I blame those who cast them into the wilderness. I blame those who lure them away from their mother's breasts even before they can learn how to write their own names. I blame our leaders.

For the avoidance of doubt, let me quickly point out that I do not hate Samuel. But I disapprove completely of his approach to his problems. His ideals are irritating. It is outright madness to presume that things will improve in this country in our lifetime. Honestly, this is my bone of contention with him.

Grace is another example of an adjusted person. Though she found life in Turin hectic when she arrived newly, today, she stays indoors and her girls make money for her.'

'What does she do?' Izu asked curiously.

'She is hustling.'

Suddenly the pilot announced, 'I wish to inform all passengers that in a few minutes from now, we shall be arriving Leonardo Da Vinci Airport. Please, remain seated and fasten your safety-belts. You are welcome to Italy.'

On touching the tarmac, Betty and Izu exchanged contact addresses and promised to follow up on the reunion when they returned to Lagos.

Izu's wife was still serene and warm to Betty regardless of her attacks against the establishment which her family represented. Her comportment was typical of an offspring of a public figure. Bitter criticism was inevitable. So they were always prepared for it.

'Pass my greetings to Grace,' Izu requested.

'Give my best wishes to Sam whenever you come across him,' Betty implored as they passed immigration.

Efe joined the bandwagon of the unemployed after graduation. With her beautiful body, it would have been a bit easier, but for her self discipline and devotion to Sam, she could not sleep with any other man even for a job. Above all, when there were vacant positions for architects and engineers, companies preferred men to women.

Her chances brightened when the Federal Civil Service Commission either by design or accident, short-listed her for a secretarial job. Pessimistic as she prepared for the interview, she emerged after a gruesome four-hour from the fourth floor of the federal secretariat complex Ikoyi with a letter of employment.'

'How did it go?'

'One of the panellists said she was my father's subordinate twenty years ago and would not hesitate to show appreciation for his concern for her happiness and welfare then. Others grudgingly fell in line after I had assured them I would learn to use the typewriter,' she declared. 'I have sympathy for professional secretaries who lost their jobs to an architect.'

'While you were there, I was busy praying for our success,' Sam said. They hugged each other and headed towards the bus-stop.

On arriving Lagos, Efe's father registered with the Federal Tenders Board. He had been consistently awarded contract to supply petty consumable items to various offices. Gradually, his influence grew. As part of the contracts awarded to him, he furnished some staff quarters, undertook electrical installations and renovated buildings. He was trusted with multi-million naira projects. He handled the construction of federal buildings in some states, including dams and bridges, resurfacing of roads and haulage of goods. He hired Sam, his prospective son-in-law, for accounting, taxation, quality control and general administration jobs.

Things moved steadily. Sam formally left his cousin's

residence and joined his future in-laws, but not without his cousin's objection.

'It is a taboo for an Igbo man to live with his in-laws no matter how rich they may be.'

'The culture neither gives me shelter nor food. It will be ridiculous if I allow it to prevent me from going to where I can find them' Sam said.

Eight months later, the neighbours of Efe's brother at Ire-Akari Housing Estate, Isolo, vacated their flat. Her father hurriedly paid for four years. Efe and Sam moved in with his prospective brother-in-law as his only neighbour.

Efe's father and Sam were acquiring and executing one public project after another. While the man felt safe, Sam was worried about the future. Political instability made contracts for public works the most unstable business in the country.

'This family enterprise deserves cushions,' Sam thought. He started gathering data and writing reports on long term plans. Cement, sand, gravel, iron and steel, corrugated roofing sheets, nails, nuts and bolts, ceramics and wooden frames represented eighty per cent of the cost of their projects. Suppliers had failed to meet either delivery schedules or specifications. The cost of such failures had been terrible. Manufacturers and distributors could grant credit facilities enabling the enterprise to store these items to meet its material requirements and sale to the public.

***

Efe's office was located on the Lagos Island. Because of the chaotic traffic situation there, she found it more convenient to board an Apapa bound ferry-boat at Marina. As soon as she disembarked, Sam was always there to lead her into their car and off they went through the expressroad to Isolo.

Sam could still recollect how it started. One evening, as they were approaching Iyana Isolo, he moved to the service lane. A *molue*, which was off-loading its passengers seven hundred metres away caused a traffic jam. Other motorists queued behind. Efe wound down the car's window to let in fresh air. As her eyes roved, she noticed a billboard mounted by a matchmaker. She stared at it and her lips parted with a smile.

'What is it, Efe?'

'Look at that slogan,' she pointed.

Together they read: 'WITH US YOUR DREAM FOR AN IDEAL PARTNER IS REAL.'

'And so?' Sam asked.

A debate ensued. Their idea of matchmaking and what constituted an ideal partner varied. They agreed it was a last resort for those who did not have the privilege of courtship. They also agreed that in a country like Nigeria, matchmaking had many disadvantages. There was no compulsion to carry identity cards or have definite residential addresses. The average Nigerian changed name as frequently as circumstances demanded and did not need anybody's approval to effect a change of address. A completed questionnaire was not enough to attest to a person's character or his claims of being this or that.

'For those who can afford it, long courtship is the most ideal way to understand a prospective partner,' Efe surmised.

'I think you are correct,' Sam agreed.

'If you think so, Sam, after half a decade, what stops you from proposing?'

The question caught Sam off his guard. He rallied round

to handle it.

'My dear Efe, there is not even a doubt in my mind that you were designed by God to meet my every need for a woman. From the first day I encountered you till today, everything you do or everything you say guides me like a star and assures me that to say 'I do' is imperative. Though things have improved considerably for us, I still feel insecure. I could not have expected more from God. But I simply need time to consolidate today's gains.'

It occurred to him that failure to disclose to Efe his anxieties and plans was a grave mistake. There was nothing as destructive in human relations as lack of proper communication. Almost at the gate of their bungalow, he stopped, turned to her.

'Truly, I love you and will marry you. It is my fault that you were left in the dark.'

'Then, why the endless waiting? Apart from me, the other child of my parents is a medical doctor. Moreover, my father does not see and confide in him as he does in you. My parents love you and take you as their son. Would my old man make money from his business and deny us a fair share of it?'

'Calm down. Let us get into the house first,' he pleaded.

Seated, Sam was more composed. For the first time, he told her of his anxieties and his plans to forestall future problems or reduce their effects.

'Then, you think I am so materialistic that unless you are stinkingly rich, a marriage with me won't work?' She struck at the chord of his resistance. 'You do not love me, you do not appreciate what I have gone through to be with you..' She started sobbing, the second time since Sam knew her.

The first incident took place the evening preceding his

convocation ceremony. Aboard a taxi with him from Owerri to the campus was his faculty's secretary. Before they could arrive at their destination, other passengers had alighted, leaving her and Sam in the back seat. She yawned, stretched her arms and kicked the air. Her silk skirt whipped up, exposing her thighs. When actions were not enough to convey her yearning, she used words to nudge it home.

Efe became the primary target of every man. She was almost everywhere looking for him. On a second thought, she returned to her hostel and waited till they met hours later. She wept like a baby. Since then, Sam had not been free to love another woman.

The tears that welled up in her eyes or every drop of it that rolled down her cheeks seemed to him thick and red. The sight of Efe in tears almost broke him too. On that second occasion, he cuddled her, wiped her tears away and took her to the bedroom. By the time they emerged, she had gotten everything she wanted and more.

'I will marry you. I will set off immediately to inform my parents,' he assured her.

The rest of the evening, he did not abandon her for his diversification project. They prepared dinner together, aired their views on an ideal family size. Though Sam did not mention his siblings, Efe knew it was a source of concern to him. She suggested ways of providing for them adequately without compromising her position.

There was still another cause for concern.

'Supposing your parents object to our marriage?' she asked Sam over dinner.

'If your parents had objected to our relationship, would you have married me?'

'My parents would not have opposed it. We are from the Mid West. We are more accommodating of other cultures. We are prepared to go to wherever our passion carries us. We cannot be compared with your people who are extremely conservative and dislike inter-cultural marriages.'

'Answer my question, Efe. If your parents say no, would you marry me?'

'Yes.'

'Supposing they disown you for it?'

'So long as you do not disown me too, I will always go for you.'

'Then, neither friends nor foes, neither poverty nor wealth, neither misery nor joy will stop me from marrying you.'

She came to Sam's side of the table and embraced him tearfully. Surely, he had calmed her aching nerves and quelled the anxieties that rioted within her. Sam set out to deliver an unforgettable conclusion.

'It was for your beauty and intelligence that I fell for you. In the process, I have secured a job, a car and an accommodation from your parents. Though without these things, I would have struggled ahead as I have done every inch of the way of my life. But they have made life easier for me and I am very grateful. You are indeed a blessing to me.'

It was six o'clock in the morning when they entered Lagos-Benin expresss road. Except for a few ditches, the journey was smooth and uneventful until a little after Ore junction.

'Stop Sam, stop,' Efe was visibly shaken.

He pulled up by the roadside, replaced a flat tyre and continued their journey.

'This is the land of my ancestors,' Efe said when they arrived at Benin City.

'Don't be cunning, darling,' Sam teased her. 'Just go straight and tell those your ancestors of what this sprawling city reminds you.'

'It was here that my parents gave birth to me over two decades ago. What else do you expect me to say?'

'Have you forgotten it was here you lost your virginity too?' They started laughing.

'My ex-boyfriend's father's house is situated along the first street on the right when entering Benin from Lagos. He was very handsome and intelligent. I gave him all my tender heart that I could have killed myself for him if he had asked me to please him. But I could not keep him to myself. The harder I tried, the more reckless his flirtation. Not even his friends nor his family thought I was right to insist on having him alone. On one occasion, he abandoned me at a party for another girl. I cried all the way to his parents. His mother told me, "his folks are like that. You are still a baby. When you grow up, you will learn to adjust to a situation you can neither change nor avoid." His father corroborated what his mother said. My heart was broken but gradually, I recovered and became wary of men until I met you.'

'Now, how do you feel?'

'You are an embodiment of all my dreams. I thank God for taking cognisance of my delicate nature and providing me a man in whom I feel very safe.'

Sam and Efe stopped briefly at a filling station for fuel, and food which Efe prepared in the morning. They arrived Sam's home when the evening sun was setting. His brothers were unloading the boot of his car which was full of food and gift items for everybody when his parents returned. Sam had been sending them money to meet their needs but it had been two years since he saw them last. Within this period, he had built a bungalow for the family, looked robust, comfortable and had a beautiful lady by his side.

There was a display of happiness by the people. A large turnout of guests formed within minutes. They all ate, drank and talked till late into the night. When the last guest left, Sam and Efe retired to bed. She summed it all up, 'though I studied among the Igbos, I never came as close to them as this. I have observed the way guests drank from one another's cup, ate from the same plates, left their half-filled cups for a visit to the toilet and returned to continue without fear of poisoning or things like that. I have noticed that almost everybody in this hamlet has shown up to celebrate your homecoming. Indeed I am captivated by this feeling of security and genuine display of affection. I love Nsu.'

***

Early in the morning, Sam's mother knocked gently at the door. 'Nnadim, it is daylight, wake up and get ready for church. You cannot afford to be late.'

As soon as she walked away, Sam turned for another round of sleep but Efe did not let him. 'Sam, wake up. We must go to church with mama and papa. I guess they would be proud going to church in their son's car.'

Efe was right. The dresses Sam bought for them fitted well and as the car glided down the dusty road to Saint Columba's Catholic Church, his parents waved through the window to as many faces as they could recognise.

The whole day was spent entertaining people. Children clustered around Efe. She shared sweets and biscuits to them. Elderly women and men jostled for money for tobacco snuff. Efe skilfully warmed her way into their hearts or so it seemed to be. So far, things had gone as planned. Later that night, Sam called his parents into their bedroom. Before then, he had considered a number of approaches and had settled for the one he thought would be more appealing.

'You are aware of the difficulties I had after my graduation. This lady and her family rescued me. To be sincere, I worked hard at school but my hard work and education would have been useless without the opportunities her parents offered me. I have known her for five years. We are presently living together.'

At the mention of that, his mother glowered.

'Well there is nowhere else I could have lived,' explained Sam. 'And after five years, my faith in her has become formidable. My love for her runs very deep and...'

'And so what?' his father demanded furiously.

'And so I have come to pay homage to you, to inform you that I am getting married to Efe Osamyime.'

'May my eyes not see my ears unless in a mirror. God forbid! Who in this hamlet has married a Bini woman?' Sam's mother roared as his father declared.

'Well, Sam, my son, it is not a taboo to have an affair with a woman without the consent of parents, but marriage is a different issue. It falls directly upon us to guide you through, the way our fathers did. Marriage is so highly revered that to abandon it to the recklessness and inexperience of two young people would be catastrophic. We have done our best for you and you have never disappointed us. Our ancestors will be bitter if we fail in our obligations, especially at this critical moment.' He paused and looked at his wife.

'Can I go to wake up Adaku?' his mother asked.

'No. Not yet.' Sam's father replied and continued, 'Efe is educated, beautiful and her family is rich. Fine. But when did wealth become a prerequisite for a woman's hand in marriage? How dare you trust a woman you do not know where she comes from? All this period of cohabitation has adversely affected your brain. You are only a shadow of my first son who left for Lagos two years ago. Your mother and I are still alive. Our people say that it is not only the dead whose bones can be stretched but the living as well. They also say that elders are never at home when a tethered goat delivers. You must have seen Adaku. She is the daughter of Edomobi who leases a farmland to us. Since you returned, she has fetched every drop of water you and your girlfriend use. She is well-behaved and will have good children for you.'

'Sorry to interrupt you, father,' Sam said with impatience and despair. 'What exactly do you want to say?'

'She has helped your mother on the farm and no doubt will make a very good wife.'

'Father, I do not want to sound disrespectful to you but I strongly feel that as the rhythm of a music changes, people on the dance floor must change their dancing steps too. Our circumstances today are not only different from yours but also more complicated. Our behaviour has definitely responded to these changes and complications. You want me to stay happily with my wife. You wish me well, no doubt. But it is wrong to imagine that I can abandon a woman who means a lot to me now. I love her and...'

'Did I not say you are sick. Is it a man's business to talk about love? Did I love your mother before I married her and have we not lived together for decades?'

'Nnadim,' his mother called softly, 'don't you see that your father is apparently bitter? Change your mind, do not make us an object of ridicule before our enemies.'

'I did not leave Lagos for the village to solicit your

assistance in finding a wife; I have found one. I am here to tell you as my parents,' Sam stressed. 'I must say that you are insensitive to my feelings and unreasonable in your demand. I am sorry I cannot surrender my right to choose a wife to your whims or the dictates of an obsolete cultural practice.'

'Do you hear the beast?' His father was furious. 'You do not deserve to be my son and you remain repudiated until you come back to your senses.'

Sam's mother was in tears when he left the room.

'Your parents had doted on you. You had always been very fond of them. The mention of my name has turned decades of cordiality into bitter disagreement, trust into contempt. Oh Sam, Sam,' Efe cried.

The disposition of his parents might have been a thorn in his flesh but Efe's anguish definitely was a dagger through his heart.

Sam continued to console her and reaffirm his position. 'I do not stand up against them for nothing. I know the road I am following. I know my destination. I have reached a point of no return. Even if the road is winding and infested with men who kill and loot, even if it is bedevilled with a desert, with you, I see my oases. With you my thirst will be quenched, my burden, lifted.'

Efe rested her head on his chest. The torrent of tears rolled uncontrollably down her cheeks on his shirt and amid it, she made her vows. 'I won't let you down, Sam. Even if the whole world despises you, I will not. I will be the world to you. I will devote all my life to you.'

The time was five o'clock. The second crow of cock had been heard. Another day was a matter of minutes away. Sam turned and looked at Efe, she had cried herself to a deep slumber. The tranquil body that lay before him portrayed the love and understanding within. He bent down, his forehead against hers, and kissed her lips.

'What is it, darling?' she asked.

'I do not want us to be in a haste back to Lagos. Begin to prepare.'

'Do not forget to leave the school fees for the children and some money for mama and papa,' Efe reminded Sam when she finished preparing.

Set to depart, she embraced every member of the family. She teased some and patted the younger ones. She thanked them for their hospitality. Before Sam's parents, she knelt down, her hands placed on Sam's mother's knees, and with voice quivering, pleaded in her fractured Igbo language. 'I am very sorry that my presence in the life of your son is not in line with your plans for him. After five years, it is no secret that I cannot live without him... I have not come to tear apart a family, nor to alienate a beloved son from his parents. I have come to contribute in my own way to the building of a family. I will always be loyal and respectful, please mama.' She struggled to steady herself. 'Do not reject me. Accept me for your son and I will be a grateful daughter-in-law forever.'

For all her plea, tears and sense of maturity, she received a deprecatory stare and pursed lips from Sam's father and mother. Sam passed his right hand through Efe's armpit and raised her to her feet. 'Let us go,' he told her. She waved and thanked everybody once again, seemingly oblivious of the disgust her presence evoked.

They travelled for many kilometres in silence before Efe broke it.

'Sam, there are two things I find irreconcilable. And the major problem is that I cannot take one and leave the other. Doing so will render me inhuman or mad."

'What are they?'.

She replied, 'I love and need you and will rather die without you. Nobody, no custom, nothing whatsoever will be enough to take you away from me. Mama and papa are absolutely opposed to our marriage. I know you love me deeply and will marry me. I need you and I care for their blessing. How to reconcile these odds is my dilemma.'

For a moment, he drove, speechless as if he did not hear her.

'Talk now,' her voice quivered.

Sam cleared his throats, 'Well, I had anticipated this turn of events. As I told you earlier, this is a struggle between the old and the new; between retrogression and progress; evil and good. I will only capitulate over my dead body. As long as the sun rises in the east and sets in the west, so will my resistance be.'

'This does not answer my question, Sam.'

'I have answered your question, but let me see if I can make it less ambiguous. I am confident time will heal the wound that had been opened. Does their blood not run in my veins? I am not giving in, not even an inch of concession.'

'Time in what way?'

'Let us go ahead and arrange our wedding. Perhaps in the next one or two months, I will send somebody they respect to go and persuade them. I am confident they will change their mind when they find out that I am not infatuated or under any spell. The humility and patience with which you conducted yourself deserve commendation. Things will sort themselves out with time.'

'Why do you think so?'

Sam replied, 'Though they are conservatives, they won't insist on those things that hurt and depress my feelings. They will succumb to the fact that you are in my life forever.'

71

'About repudiation, Sam?'

'It is a bluff. Have you not thought about the reason they chose Samuel as a name for me?'

'I think it means, "God has answered our prayer." '

'You are right. They gave birth to me after five female children. Now you can understand their joy when I was born. Since then, I have not done anything to their disappointment. They need me as much as I need them.'

***

Sam woke up to listen to early morning news, but heard martial music instead. Nigerians had experienced it several times that the significance was known very well. All radio stations were tuned to the national service, broadcasting from Lagos. He reached for the television. Apart from the national flag, there was no other image on the screen of the four stations in Lagos. There too, the martial music played. He shook Efe until she was fully awake.

'It is another coup!' he cried. Suddenly, the station came alive. A brigadier in the army read a list of grievances against the toppled regime, ordered the closure of all borders and imposed dusk-to-dawn curfew till further notice.

A day later, a new head of state and commander-in-chief of the armed forces was named. Before the end of one week, names of ministers and directors-general of ministries had been made public. The ruling military council had been reconstituted. Political analyst said it was a palace coup. Except the departure of one or two generals, it was just an old wine in an old bottle with a new name.

Nigerians were sceptical of the new regime. They were fed up with incessant military take-overs and yearned for a democratic rule. The feelings ran very deep but were suppressed. Nobody dared to air them publicly. Businessmen, speculators on government appointments, toadies and flatterers of public functionaries put up elaborate and lavish advertisements in various newspapers, applauding the new guys. Some traditional rulers paid official visits to Dodan Barracks (official residence of the head of the military junta). Nobody wanted to be left out. That had been the case with Nigeria.

A grandiose political map was charted. The administration did not intend to stay longer than necessary, Nigerians were told. A constitution review panel was set up and early local government elections were promised. The shrinking intelligentsia protested silently at the duplicity. The squalor in which the masses lived was unabated. They groaned under severe austerity measures.

To attract people's confidence in the administration and dispel rumours that corruption in high places had escalated, the government started clamping down on defenceless contractors.

Sam and his father-in-law knew that payments from government for jobs done involved procedures hedged about with red tape or outright insistence on kickback by officers vested with decision-making. Sam's father-in-law was among the contractors taken away by the state security service for interrogation.

Four hours later, he was allowed to return to his family. Next day, he woke up and started his usual business visits to the offices of the Tenders Board and relevant ministries. He made a non-refundable deposit of fifteen thousand naira to support a fresh bid for the construction of low-cost houses. He used the opportunity to see if payments for completed jobs could be expedited. His schedule was the same until three weeks later when he was taken away again by security agents.

Unlike the previous time, he did not return. He was charged for impropriety and economic sabotage. The assets of his company and his personal property were seized. His accounts were frozen. When these did not seem to be enough, the government extended its hands to the property of his immediate relations. Sam and Efe lost their only car in the process.

His son and Sam saw to it that lawyers were hired to defend him before the military tribunal. After two appearances, his trial was adjourned indefinitely while he was remanded in prison. The defence lawyers' plea that he be released on bail and his account unfrozen was rejected. A suit filed by them at a Lagos high court contesting the indefinite detention was also thrown out for lack of jurisdiction.

Gradually, days ran into months. Bills started coming in. Former employees and subcontractors became menacing. Sam's mother-in-law began to languish in pains. The absence of her husband was too much for her to bear. The entire family was not given any information as to his whereabouts. People who claimed to be law enforcement agents struck and ransacked the households at will. After months of outstanding legal fees, the lawyers wrote to inform the family about the withdrawal of their services. Seven months passed by. The situation deteriorated. Sam had his siblings and parents at home. There was his mother-in-law who was yet to recover from the trauma and whom he was duty-bound to cater for. There was Efe. There was a strong desire to deliver to her a shoulder to lean on, a refuge in times of trouble. The more Sam was distressed, the more she toiled to bring joy and hope into his life. She woke up earlier to prepare and trek to the bus-stop for the crowded molue, a bus she had never ridden. That was her routine five days every week with her meagre salary. To Sam, there was nothing consoling about their predicaments. But to Efe, there was something shakespearean. 'If the toad, so ugly and venomous, still wears a precious jewel on its head, I wonder why I cannot boldly claim that in this adversity, there are many good things for me.'

'Like what, Efe?' Sam asked feebly.

She beamed with a smile. 'I think I am trendier and healthier since I started walking two kilometres to the bus-stop everyday. Normally, I struggle to a seat located near a window in any bus. From there, I have a panoramic view of Lagos. I relish watching the Carter bridge in particular, as the lagoon sweeps slowly into the rumbling Atlantic. There are women with heavy luggage and babies strapped to their backs. There are others who sweat and shout themselves hoarse to sell one thing or another to uninterested commuters. A countless number of people roam about, in rags, without places to sleep or food to eat, without anything in this world they can call theirs or anybody to care if they die or live. As devastated as you think we are, my fellow passengers look at me with envy. My dresses, shoes, cropped hair, everything I have got draws attention. There are millions of Nigerians who would wish they are in our position. You are crying you do not have shoes to wear, go out and see people who do not have feet to wear shoes. You cannot but thank God for his kindness to us.'

Efe became the family's breadwinner. She recognised the fragility of Sam's ego and with alarming perseverance, massaged it. She cheerfully let her personal problems take the back seat. With tact, she showed her monthly salary before she kept it inside a bedside drawer where he had formerly kept money for their daily use. Sam only considered himself lucky to be blessed with such a woman.

***

'I must leave Nigeria for overseas,' he thought. 'And it has to be now.' He visited the Marina office of NEPA to see Simon. Somebody told him that Simon had travelled to Italy. He had been away for nearly eighteen months. Sam tried Simon's home address. His relations confirmed the story. Aboard a bus back to Ire-Akari, Sam's resolve to travel became stronger. At first, Efe would not take it. She toyed with several suggestions. Quickly, Sam explained their futility. They crumbled one after another. All her oppositions to the scheme caved in. It was a bitter pill. But for its promise of a remedy to their problem, it would not have been swallowed. Efe and Sam could object to each other's plans but when the objection was capable of causing a rift between them, the opposing partner switched-over and contributed to the perfection of the plan as if no objection existed. That day, Efe appraised Sam's mood and knew he would not be dissuaded. She teamed up with him.

Travelling to Europe in the '90s was not as difficult as recently. The requirements for entry visa were stringent but could be met. Sam succeeded to convince the officers at the Italian embassy in Lagos, that he was going to shop for his wedding. He was granted visa for a period not more than six days. Raising money for his flight ticket and basic travelling allowance was difficult let alone the substantial amount of money to justify his motive. They brainstormed until possible factors that would constitute impediments to the trip were eliminated. After all the travelling arrangements had been concluded, the couple looked forward to the trip with mixed feelings.

Efe assembled the personal effects Sam would need in Italy, including the gold necklace she gave him on his 25th birthday. There were two other items she enclosed which nearly blew up his emotion: the only perfume the two of them had used and his certificates. Sam objected to the inclusion of the perfume, arguing that there would not be a replacement for her.

'Like the necklace, this perfume personifies me. Every fragrance it exudes should remind you of me, of all the times we have spent together, our hopes and the promise to be reunited soon. You are no more free. Girls prowling like lions looking for prey won't know unless you tell them. These things will either by accident or design prod you to do so.'

'I will do your bidding. I will travel with it if it pleases you. Bear in mind that you are increasing my agony by contemplating that I can ever be unfaithful to you.'

'I do not intend to create that impression. Rather, I wanted you to know that the only thing you won't have from me is what I do not possess. If the perfume is so precious to me, that is the more reason I should let you travel with it, please.' Her insistence was strong, and in accordance with their tradition, he accepted.

Since he met Simon at the Marina office of NEPA, the idea of doing menial job in Europe had hung on him like a shadow. Sometimes, he coped by telling himself that it was not going to be true. Efe's support was earned by compromise. Sam was afraid of diminishing both her support and confidence hence he did not disclose to her that the certificates were useless. As she kept them inside a file and lowered it down the flat bottom of his bag, she raised her head and their eyes met. 'Darling, does it occur to you that Italians do not speak English?'

'Yes, Efe. They speak Italian. Learning it is inevitable.'

'Well, I trust you. I know you will cope.'

'Yes, I hope so, dear.'

When Sam was ready to leave, he went in to inform his brother-in-law who had done a lot to convince Efe about the need for the trip. He, his wife, Efe and Sam left by taxi for the airport. They went by the lift to the third floor, paid airport tax and returned to the departure hall to check in Sam's baggage. Rummaging through its contents, a customs officer found his credentials.

'It is necessary to advise you on the implications of travelling with your certificates since you claim to be going for shopping,' he told Sam. 'These documents are not expected of a shopper. Such carelessness can cost you all the money spent and dash your hopes on this first trip. If there will be need for them, your wife can send them later by post. With only a very small amount of money in your wallet, if they do not suspect you of drug pushing, they will accuse you of having made false declarations to the embassy. The choice is yours.'

Without travelling, the officer seemed to have a sound knowledge of Europe and America. He told Efe what Sam had strained himself to tell her without success.

The officer ensured that Efe went with Sam to the last security post. One part of him was eager to board, to discover what awaited him and to tackle it. The other was very reluctant to leave Efe behind. The intense struggle raged like wild fire inside him.

As it was wont to be, the desire to travel prevailed. They held each other for a long time until there were no more passengers outside. She kissed the collar of his white shirt with her lipstick coated lips. Her head rested on his chin. She mumbled inaudibly. Sam heaved her head up gently until she was facing him. Her eyes were bloodshot with pains.

'I'll be home after six months to wipe your tears and live with you forever. Bear it in mind that I love you. I respect you. I trust you. Nobody has ever earned these from me. Nobody will ever. This sets you far apart from the whole world.'

'I'm afraid it will be longer. Perhaps, a year or more. May the grace of God bring you back to me. My love is total. I have put everything, like eggs, into one basket. I have reserved nothing. Please, do not forget this. I will remain the way you leave me till I see you again.'

She stood there waving, waiting and weeping as Sam went on board a Rome-bound flight in the hot summer night of August 1990.

Chapter 2

Baptism of Fire

Sam was filled with joy when the police stamped his passport and welcomed him into Italy. It was a moment he would have wanted to share with Efe but the six-hour flight from Lagos had severed them thousands of kilometres apart. Some Nigerian traders he met aboard told him to follow them. Without asking questions, he obeyed. He had changed a hundred dollars for one hundred and ten thousand lire. From the money, they bought his bus ticket from the airport to Rome station, and to Naples. Sam knew their company was not going to be indefinite. Nevertheless, he was not prepared for it when they arrived Naples station and his guides simply pointed at a restaurant for him.

'Go there,' they said, 'this is a very popular joint for Nigerians. We are sure you can find your way from there.'

Travelling from Rome, they had passed houses that were far from elegant. Small industries stood miserably near few densely populated areas. Sheep grazed on green grass while shepherds sat under trees, away from the scorching sun. Farther from Rome, Sam saw dilapidated irrigation, and drainage systems and tomato farms overgrown with weeds.

The situation outside the station did not reduce his apprehension. There were stinking, homeless and mad people. Sam could count up to two at a glance. One dozed at a corner. His head slumping to his chin and saliva drooling from his open mouth. The other moved about, fiddling through the maze of discarded trash for food and cigarette. Green and red traffic lights bore no significance to pedestrians who meandered incongruously through the traffic.

Almost each car was peculiar as if dents, not registration numbers, were the vogue for identifying cars there. Some were emitting smoke like a chimney. Others had the boots, bumpers or fenders bashed or totally ripped off. Many more had lost their headlights. Those that had no such marks, were dirty. But one thing was common: the passengers did not seem to care. Apart from the presence of young men and women who could not be described as totally insane but as people who had been mentally and physically devastated and reduced to walking carcasses by drug abuse, Sam had not yet seen an outstanding difference from the home from which he was fleeing.

He looked at the direction that the traders went but they had disappeared into the crowd. Sam lifted his bag and set off for the restaurant. He avoided hailing taxi drivers and ran into a street overflowing with trading activities. A potpourri of hawkers, table-top shop owners, window-shoppers, pickpockets and passers-by crisscrossed one another. Gradually, the intensity of the congestion declined as he approached his destination. Sam stopped and looked carefully to ensure he was at the right place. Nearby, three gorgeous looking young Africans alighted from a 1984 model of BMW 520 that partially blocked the winding street which was already experiencing chaotic traffic. He could not believe his eyes. One of them was Simon.

They hurled at each other.

'How manage... how?' they asked simultaneously.

'He is my schoolmate,' Simon told his companions who shook hands with Sam and went into the restaurant. Simon took Sam's bag and they followed his friends. Passing through the bar, they went into the dining section. Simon requested a special table for only two of them. Sam appraised the young men and women at the bar. Though it was just twelve noon, yet he could not see through the mist of cigarette smoke. There were more empty beer bottles on each table than the number of persons there. The place was so boisterous that it looked like an extension of the commotion outside. Chain-smoking was not limited to men alone. Ladies had their packets of cigarette.

Nearby, people picked their teeth after a surplus meal of purely African cuisine. They gulped bottles of beer as if they had scorched their throats. Waiters came and left with baskets full of remnants. Conversations were overtly vulgar and loud but when voices were lowered, the things Sam heard were completely strange.

'So when did you leave Nigeria?' Sam asked Simon as he took his seat.

'A year and eight months ago.'

'Has the new government any credible programmes?'

'It is too early to say,' Sam replied. 'As a matter of fact, it does not take anything like that to become a military ruler. It takes only the barrel of the gun.' To avoid a situation that would remind him about the implications of the recent take-over on his family, Sam changed the conversation.

'Simon, you look great. I guess you got the engineering job nobody offered you at home?'

'Sam, if you ever came to work as a professional, you

are wrong.'

'But Italy is one of the seven most industrialized countries of the world. If...'

'Industrialised what?' Simon snapped, pounding his gold bangled wrist on the table. 'Well, just know that entry into the profession is iron-clad!'

'So how do you make ends meet?'

'We'll talk later,' he said as their order was served by a lanky waiter.

The manner unaccompanied ladies crisscrossed to catch the attention of Simon told Sam that he was popular and rich.

'Sam,' he looked at the direction of the last girl who left their table, "how do you see that dame?'

'In what sense?' Sam asked.

'Do you like her, to be precise?'

'Well,' Sam shrugged, 'she is tall enough but the discolouration of her skin is disgusting. Take a look at her face, almost blonde, her fingers and toes, black.'

'So, you cannot sleep with her if I fix her for you?'

'Simon, how dare you ask me this type of question? Have you forgotten that I am a one-woman man? Moreover, I left Efe yesterday, not only satisfied for now, but absolutely confident of my pledge to be faithful to her till we meet again.'

'Sam, you still carry your strict discipline. Efe was discounted when you boarded the plane for Italy. She was good, I admit. But she had served her own purpose in your life. It is only these ladies you see here who will determine what you will achieve in this country. When I arrived, I found them repulsive'

'Ok, she is a queen but I do not have any need for her now.'

Sam struggled to remain calm.

'These ladies have not been to our table only to greet me. They confided in me you look great and I think you are lucky to be admired by so many. Women here are more emancipated than those at home. Do not be shocked by their boldness. We are in Europe. I recommend the last one because she is kind and has a lot of money. She lives in a mini flat. Her most recent boyfriend has been thrown into jail for drug dealing. Since then, she has turned down many admirers. I am surprised she fell head over heels for you. Do not bother yourself about the imprisoned boy. If you play your card well, she won't have any time for him when he serves out his term. Just give to her what Efe has enjoyed for nearly half a decade. Go ahead, give her what captivated Efe and tell her your conditions later.'

Sam's eyes roved the bar, spotted the lady and looked her over. Another lady who sat next to her quickly noted his gaze and tapped her on the shoulders. Both whispered. Before he could dodge her glance, their eyes met. She winked at him and smiled. She was not as ugly as Sam had thought. A rich body lotion applied evenly and generously all over her skin could blend her face into an appealing complexion. But Efe had got him inside out.

'Another explanation for their keen interest is that they know you arrived from Africa, broke, homeless and with a tourist visa that will expire soon. My company communicates to them that your situation notwithstanding, they have a big meat for a prey. Moreover, you have the tall and strong look that drives women crazy. Believe me. They won't give up on you and they will catch you unless you run away. But who has ever run away from his shadow? The wisest thing is to cooperate.'

'Can't you stop kidding and tell me how I can make it

quickly and go back to Efe?'

'I will not withhold any important information from you. The problem however lies with you. I guess for a million dollars you will not accept to do what I will tell you now.'

'No, Simon. I am not ignorant of the labour market. Did we not talk about it in Lagos? Take me to mortuaries, I am ready to wash and dress up corpses for money. Or do we go to where I can be hired for other odd jobs like washing plates in restaurants, cleaning streets and roads? Boy, I mean I am ready for anything that earns money at the end of the day.'

'Sam, when we were at home and heard about these activities, we thought what a terrible cross to bear for our future. While we brooded over that, we came to confront the fact they do not exist to start with. If you happen to find one, you have found a treasure. Can anything be more heart-rending than this?'

'Are you saying that they are not available?'

'Honestly, one must be considered extremely lucky to get a cleaning job. Listen, only a few months ago, illegal immigrants were regularised. The lack of jobs here is acute and the chances of getting a job very remote. Armed with resident permits, many of them drifted to the highly industrialised and rich North in search of jobs. Unfortunately, news reaching us from there say that it is not a place for those who don't have resident permit.'

'So, what can I do?' Sam inquired.

Simon declined to answer the question inside the restaurant until they were together in his car a couple of minutes later.

'Boy, you recall my opposition to trafficking in illegal drugs. But when I came, there were no jobs, not even very odd ones. I was not as fortunate as you are to see female admirers. My family land was sold and my father's house was mortgaged to buy my flight ticket. I did not know how to tell them that the same Italy traders - former tenants in my father's house - who came and returned with great fortune could not provide for me as well. I contemplated travelling to the United States or Britain. It was like a camel passing through the eye of a needle. One day, almost frustrated and disillusioned, I met one of the two men that you saw a while ago. He took personal interest in me and taught me. Driven by desperation, I went for it. With a combination of luck, courage and ability, I have climbed from the bottom rung of the ladder to the top. I do not go into the streets peddling pinches or hauling the substance in my stomach or in containers that have false bottom. I have passed those stages. I send couriers who have good credentials and they are well paid. As soon as a consignment arrives, I dispose of it strictly on wholesale basis.'

'Simon, do you remember your dislike for Benson and all you missed for steering clear of him in Lagos?'

'Yes, I do. But man is not static. He is dynamic. He changes several times in his lifetime as his environment changes. I need shelter. I need the basic things money provides. I must get this money one way or the other.'

'How have you been able to elude the police?'

'I have told you earlier. It does not mean that the police are pushovers. No. Many of my friends are languishing in jail and some have been deported. I must point out quickly that I realised the consequences of my illegal deal. If the hunter learns to shoot without missing, the birds learn to fly without perching. I also take numerous precautionary measures ranging from telephone conversations to business deals. I am constantly aware of the risk I take and am always on my guard. Tension and drug trafficking are inseparable bedfellows. We have not only the police to contend with. There are deadly rivalries, mentally sick users, extortionists and conmen. It is highly infested with dangers.'

'Does it mean that those trader-tenants in your father's house trafficked in drugs.'

'In a way, Sam, I have found out that when they arrived, there was nothing to do here. No way to make a living without risking imprisonment. One of them left for Germany. With fake South African documents, he was granted political asylum in Munich, Bremerhaven, Dortmund and Wiesbaden. From each centre, he received a minimum of four hundred marks monthly. With the income, he was able to order for many kilograms of heroine from Latin America. Of course, you know that business grows. So from selling drugs to Germans, he extended his tentacles to Italy. The other person he left behind quickly became his agent here. Their revenue was so enormous that they moved into prostitution through war-torn Yugoslavia. Within months, it became the gateway to prostitution throughout Europe. Yugoslav visa was easier to procure for intending prostitutes. With help from such influential people, these women were smuggled into countries such as Italy...'

'Simon, there's something I've not understood yet. How do they lure young school girls from school into prostitution?'

'I cannot say exactly. But I am sure there are thousands of them, even married women ready to abandon their husbands and children to be here.'

'Doesn't the Vatican frown at this ugly development?'

'They can frown as it suits them, that does not bother the people involved. Some newspapers have described them as Black Mafia. Let me point out that there are other gangs that handle such human exports from Eastern Europe, North Africa and Asia. Wherever they come from, there is one common thing: they are still hustling. Just like drugs, prostitution is flourishing because it enjoys huge patronage. Mere frowns by the church cannot succeed where legislation has failed woefully.'

'Instead of drug peddling and exploitation of helpless poor women or any other thing which is immoral, it is better to go to Germany and declare oneself a refugee at many places and make more money. It appears neater and...'

'You are ignorant of the whole thing. To be granted refugee status by one centre is like the camel passing through the eye of the needle. Then think about what it takes to enjoy the same status at more than two or three centres at the same time. Nigeria is undergoing a crisis, hence we are here. Unfortunately, it is considered an economic one and does not entitle us to the type of status enjoyed by citizens of apartheid South Africa, belligerent Rwanda or fractious Somalia. You must not only furnish the centres with South African, Rwandan or Somalian documents but also convince them you are from there. You must prove beyond doubt that you are victimised because of your political belief or your life is at risk because of the raging war. Often, you need a lawyer to make these points. The applicant will be fingerprinted for proper identification. If the political reason for which you are granted asylum terminates sooner than expected, your status can be reversed. The police can come to the camp where you reside and deport you if you fail to leave after due notification.'

'If it is as difficult as you are saying, how did the trader acquire refugee status at four centres?'

'First, he obtained and furnished four acceptable identities. Then, he had the courage and patience, to burn the upper layer of his palms after each fingerprinting and

88

waited for it to heal again before presenting the next request. He was lucky to obtain his allowances undetected. In short, it takes a lot of things too numerous to mention now. Precisely Sam, behind every fabulous hard currency earned here, there are substantial risks.'

'About drugs, does the gain justify the risks and hazards?'

'Absolutely yes. It provides you employment. Though others may have been attracted to it by greed, I was motivated by the lack of reasonable jobs. The turnover is high. A little investment yields such a revenue that is breathtaking.'

'Don't you consider it wise to go home, use the proceeds you have acquired and establish the engineering workshop you proposed years back?'

'It is wiser to hang-on a little longer, Sam, and rake all the hard currency, as long as it flows.'

'At this stage, involvement in this business is induced by greed, not the basic need for employment.'

'But it is foolish to retreat into an engineering workshop, in a politically and economically unstable setting.'

'I am afraid you are lazy. You do not wait until you have amassed money before you begin to invest. This business is illegal and you cannot be lucky indefinitely.'

'Financial security does not necessarily derive from how much money we earn in the present but how much prudent investment we make for the future'.

'Do you know that there is an international law against laundering of drug money?'

'So, what have you been doing with your money; throwing parties and having a good time?' I have already seen your victims in the piazza. I have seen those wasted by your business,' Sam added.

'I know,' protested Simon, 'you are afraid of going to jail.'

'No. No. Without mincing words, count me out of drug pushing. It is against my philosophy to ruin people's lives in order to enhance mine. I may recover from physical imprisonment by the state but will definitely not recover from the imprisonment of my conscience.'

'What do you think about the girls? It does not carry any jail term and no life is at stake.'

'I think it is pertinent to know what this lady will gain for her money. I am married and will never abandon my wife nor marry more than one. Let us get it clear to avoid complications. I hate a dirty business.'

'Saaam. Your utterances indicate that you are destined for undue hardship in this country. What does it cost you to conceal your engagement to Efe, assuming you cannot leave her completely, lead on your new acquaintance and dump her when you are through. Marriage is not by force. When you are all right, give her an impossible condition or spin her a genuine yawn. You won't look far for reasons to boot a woman out of your life in this country. They are habitual liars. They are...'

'Excuse me. Supposing the lady is your own sister. She subjects herself to nasty things, makes the dough, dishes it out to a wretched man who eventually jilts her and leaves her with nothing, how would you feel?'

'There is only one reason my sister can be in this country - to study. It is over my dead body that she will find herself in this mess.'

'Does it occur to you that these women, no matter their atrocities, have blood and flesh like everybody else? If your collaborators do not see this scheme as bad, I, Samuel Ogemdi, do. It is the sleaziest thing I have ever known all my life. For God's sake, Simon, think about something different for me.'

'I do not run a company here where you can work as an accountant or manager,' he said sarcastically. 'I will take you to the White House. From there, you can go out every morning to hustle for work as a farm-hand. That is the best offer in the present circumstance.'

***

They departed the city centre and went through narrow streets. Simon pointed at monumental structures as they drove past them. After what seemed like hours of hobbling through a maze of alleys with undulating topography and skyscrapers whose paints were either rusty or peeled, they negotiated a curve, and burst into a major road.

'It is hectic driving through that zone but I prefer it to this major road which is known for its perennial traffic. There are police road-blocks too. Moreover, the station is infested with plain-clothed policemen. They take note of very strange persons. People like you who are arriving into Italy from outside the European community are of particular interest to them. They try not to embarrass innocent people by trailing only suspects until they find it necessary to swoop. You never can tell, some of them may be waiting somewhere to give us the searching of our lives.'

Sam was not in the mood for any discussion so he kept quiet. Not even when they descended a little slope and Simon said, 'the name of this place is Pozzuoli. It was here that Saint Steven was stoned to death.'

A kilometre after that city, Simon took another road on their left which led to a shoreline. Boats, ferries and yachts were anchored. Tourists and travellers mingled. 'One can sail to the island regions of Italy from here,' Simon said as they made further away from the city.

They passed through one riveting scenery after another which terminated awfully at a wasteland. They drove on in silence for several kilometres. 'Sam, it is important you mark this road. This place is called Licola. Take your left, go straight, do not turn left or right until you arrive at one of Naple's best holiday resorts. It has well tended forests and a lake. I had an appointment with one of my business partners and only called at the restaurant for lunch before I saw you. We cannot go to my house now.'

He looked at his time. 'I'll hurry to drop you at the White House and, may be, come for you when I am less occupied. Or you can always come. This road leads to Mondragone.'

Simon went through Lago Patria at break-neck speed until they arrived at the White House which was isolated from a residence cum restaurant on the east, and Qualiano train station on the west. Sam guessed it was from the white colour that the one-storey building derived its name. The top floor had two rooms, no windows. The doors had no cellar to protect them against rain and sun. They were in a state of decay. When there was heavy downpour, the rooms were filled with water. The residents stayed awake to battle the flood. The skylight leaked so much that a bucket had to be kept on the floor directly under it as a receptacle. A mattress was needed to support the door from falling on top of people when it was windy.

The ground floor had two toilets - one was often out of order along with a tap which was the residents' only source of water. It contained a room too. The room was exquisite. It boasted of a door, a window and portico which served as

92

a kitchen. It was occupied by the honourable president of the White House.

There was also a four-by-three metre house with corrugated roofing sheets on the premises. The wall was torn into two from the roof to the floor and vibrated with the passage of every heavy vehicle on the road, five hundred metres away. Many people evacuated and many more would not come near it because of the fear that it would collapse. The fear was not for the big boys. It was not only a residence but a cult of trendy, outgoing rich boys. The status symbol made every inch inside it a hot cake regardless that it was only second to hell. The popular side was a rotund concrete structure with a diameter of nearly forty metres. It had compartments that were transformed into rooms, partitioned with cartons and discarded wooden aluminium or steel panels. At the centre was a five metre deep rectangular, unsealed water reservoir and an open grassland that served as a football pitch.

The White House was an abandoned public works project. It was Sam's first residence in Italy, his first encounter with Europe. There were nearly eighty others whom it sheltered. The president thoughtfully assigned him to the popular side, with Richard, a born again, and Cento, a university graduate as his roommates.

They invited him to eat but he was not hungry. He watched as they happily consumed their dinner and talked about their exploits as they ate. Sam envied them. He wondered when he would adjust to the squalid conditions as they had done. The day had not been encouraging. Not even farm work was easy to come by. He pinched himself and felt pains. He was not dreaming. It was a reality. He had come to Italy to face another horrible ordeal.

Richard and Cento spared him a mattress and a stinking

blanket. With another mattress, they closed their door and put out the candlelight.

One hour after the light went out, Sam was still awake, his eyes staring blankly at the roof. While he struggled to come to terms with the fact that his fellow human beings had survived in the dungeon for months, he could hear Richard and Cento snoring away in deep sleep. He forced himself to sleep. Many more hours passed before he fell asleep. He had not slept for more than thirty minutes when a creature ran across his chest and missed his uncovered face by just an inch. Sam shrieked, prompting it to land on top of the pot of stew Cento had made. As he fidgeted, his roommates continued to sleep, unperturbed by the noise.

Sam woke up to daylight. Outside, some people collected trash and disposed of them. A routine that was strictly enforced by the president. Some boys, comprising mainly the big boys, played football on the green parchment at the centre of the White House. Everywhere, there was a hive of activities. A little queue of people wanting to use the toilet or collect water had formed. When Sam returned to their room, Richard was ironing his clothes. He had improvised a flat heavy stainless steel which he heated using a gas stove and rubbed it vigorously on the clothes until they formed a line. The procedure was repeated to achieve the desired result.

'You do not need these clothes on the farm?' Sam said curiously.

'No,' he replied. 'They are for church service.'

Americans stationed at various NATO bases in Naples and their dependents constituted members of The Bible Way Church. There were brothers Cleveland and Brown who came every Sunday, with an old green Volkswagen Combi Bus to convey those who volunteered to worship with the brethren.

Weeks later, Sam joined the congregation. Richard was more devoted than the rest of the new converts. As a pentecostal evangelist in Nigeria, he quickly embraced the faith. Some members who were eager to migrate to America saw it as an opportunity to achieve that objective. For Sam, it served to let off steam, to interact with English-speaking people, to move away from the ghetto and apple farms. It was good for his psychological revival so much that he started looking forward to it. He was never disappointed. Surely, people like brother Richard who went for spiritual succour felt highly rejuvenated too. But those who thought it was a passage to America were absolutely disappointed.

The rest of his first Sunday in the White House was spent learning Italian language, trying out shoes, trousers and shirts donated to him by old residents, for work. From five to nine o'clock on Monday morning, he stood in vain with over forty others at a strategic intersection of roads leading to major agricultural zones. White House residents nicknamed the junction 'Ama JK' - like a similar spot on Douglas Road, in Owerri, Nigeria. By the end of the first week, the horror of his new environment had started to subside.

Sam harvested tomatoes in Formia, and apples in Capua. And for three days at Aversa, he weeded an olive farm. For a total of five days, almost nine hours daily, he earned a hundred thousand lire.

The second week was better. Sam gained more knowledge of the language. Though not enough to know when to respond yes instead of no. That same week, a man on whose farm he had worked for two days, promised to hire him again the third day. Throughout the appointed day, he waited for the man at Ama JK. The farmer did not show up. He disappeared with Sam's wages for two days. When he returned to the White House and narrated his ordeal, he found out that he was not alone. Many of them had been swindled like that in the past.

On some occasions when he was not lucky to get a job; he returned home to write letters. One day, Sam decided to visit nearby ghettos: Buckingham Palace and Ave Blessed Maria. It was then it dawned on him how fortunate he was to be residing in the White House. These were buildings, four hundred years old, abandoned inside marshy farms. The inhabitants could be seen returning in the evenings with containers of water on their heads. It took them four kilometres to find a family that volunteered to let them fetch water. With shovels, they dug shallow holes in nearby farms which served as toilets. There was no playground or portico. There were no windows. Life there was miserable.

***

Sam returned to find out that about thirty per cent of his colleagues were at home, deep in merry-making. They were not bitter that they did not find any work as Sam often was. Somebody disclosed to him that it was a habit.

'What was their source of income?' he wondered.

There were stories of white men who came scouting for people to have sex with their wives, sometimes while they watched. It sounded like a tale to him until one evening. A car slowed down behind the president's side of the White House and blared its horns five times. Suddenly, a pandemonium ensued as boys who were around scurried out to a nearby bush. The only person that cared to explain the situation to Sam said it was *solo uno* (only once).

Two hours later, it was only he who returned gloomy.

He hissed and protested that Sam caused him the misfortune. He arrived late. The rest of the fifteen boys were happy. One of them was particularly thrilled. He was told that his missile was more effective than anyone known to the woman.

Solo Uno, as they were known, comprised an elderly man, perhaps in his fifties and a ravishing thirty-something year old lady. They came an average of six times monthly in different cars.

Inside the forest, the man stood on his knees with his trousers unzipped. The lady raised her gown over her back, bent down with her legs apart and buttocks protruding. The man handed out condoms and watched as the boys slipped them on to ensure that air was expelled to avoid rupture. She adjusted herself about three times before each round is over. Everybody that waited on line had only one go at her. She could stand as many as fifteen but never less than ten boys. With her mania contained and aching nerves soothed, she quietly got up.

She pleaded with others to whom she could not attend and promised to come again next time. With the man behind the wheels, she thanked the participants and left, leaving the boys exploited.

A similar incident occurred when two residents were picked up from Ama JK by a man to clean his newly completed house. It was a hundred thousand lire for each person, big enough for a week's work. The boys never anticipated that they would be presented with a woman to clean instead. One of the boys refused. To motivate the other to agree, he was given extra fifty thousand lire. A couple of minutes inside the woman, the man who stood stark naked and all eyes, pounced on the boy, yanked him away and made love to the woman until he was satisfied.

One case was particularly different. A friend of Sam's had been on a job for one month. A feat then. He always came home distraught. He had to trek a few kilometres every morning but that was not the source of his frustration. On a daily basis, it was traumatic for him, satisfying a fastidious male boss who saddled him with ten hours of rigorous work for a two-hour pay. He had to fend off his boss's wife who wanted to lure him to bed. A graduate and born-again, he did not know how to hold onto his concepts without compromising his employment. As if that was not enough, he had to contend with their homosexual and drug addicted son who at first, offered him his younger sister so that he could have sex with him in return. Outwitted and bitter, the homosexual resorted to the use of threat with a pistol. It was the prompt intervention of the boy's father to the worker's scream that averted what would have been a tragedy. The worker was admonished by the old man for exposing his muscular chests. Sam's friend learnt that as well proportioned frame could entice women, it could also provoke men. He resigned that day and forfeited weeks of outstanding pay.

One evening, Sam returned to find his roommate slumped in bed. His hand was bandaged. Cases of injustice like this were rampant. Ignorance of the justice system, insufficient knowledge of the language and lack of resident permit prevented action.

At the end of one month, Sam had saved five hundred thousand lire. It was neither safe in the White House nor possible to keep it in the bank. Some of his colleagues went for baggy knickers where they concealed their savings. They slept with it and when they were bathing, the knickers were hidden away from any possible intruders into the bathroom..

As the savings increased, they gave them to tourists or businessmen returning to Nigeria for delivery to their families. Other residents chose to keep their savings with friends in Italy who were regular and could not be deported. A few others dared sticking to their savings as long as they could. Whichever way, there were always hazards.

News of inflation in Nigeria, the collapse of banks and government's inability to come to the rescue of depositors were rife. In Italy, large amount of cash with an illegal immigrant attracted the police on drug control. Explaining to them that all the pieces of furniture, cooking utensils, dresses and shoes found in the White House were picked from dustbins or that some good spirited Italians brought gifts of food and drinks, while the residents only needed to procure cheap chicken, spaghetti and tomato sauce from the supermarket was not always acceptable. Nonetheless, Sam opted to keep his savings.

The big boys were an exception. They bought fashionable dresses and shoes for night parties and brought cartons of beer home for relaxation. There were only two persons who owned cars, a rickety FIAT 128 and a smoke-puffing FIAT 500. The president was one of them. For five thousand lire he could be hired to go and refill exhausted cooking gas cylinder. The depot was not far away from the White House. It was located inside a bush. It was run by a black boy. He was paid well but was under instruction to run for his safety as far as his legs could carry him on seeing law enforcement agents or to risk abandonment in prison if he was apprehended. He neither knew the name of his boss nor his residence.

Summer ended, autumn set in. Individuals, religious organisations, especially the American Baptist Church at Lago Patria and The Bible Way Church donated kerosene and heaters. Richard and Cento had one in their room. It was useless heating a room that was more or less an open space. As soon as the gas that came with these donations finished, the heaters were abandoned. Residents slept under a pile of unlaundered blankets. The marginal improvement the third week was encouraging.

A man from Sam's hamlet who was an employee of an international organisation had been contacted. He presented an English and Italian language text to Sam. As the months passed by, he earned Sam's respect and trust which remained intact until years later when he squandered the money Sam gave him for safe-keeping. Exactly thirty-seven days since Sam arrived Italy, he ceased to be a farm-hand.

As usual, they waited for work at Ama JK till a little past nine o'clock in the morning. There emerged a white Mercedes Benz 190, a car not mainly used by those Italian farmers. A robust man sat behind the wheels and a boy on the passenger seat. They stopped in front of one Evans and spoke. Evans was dazed by the outburst of Napolitan language. Before he recovered, Louis and Sam who were nearby, dived for the rear doors of the car. He needed only two persons. Evans was left to nurse his wounds. Louis was a week older than Sam in Italy. But accompanied by his dictionary and language book, Sam was better in the language. The young schoolboy on the passenger seat was the man's son.

With the aid of Sam's books, he informed Sam and Louis of a company job. The driver was visibly apprehensive. He avoided trunk roads. From one desolate street, he ran into another until they bumped into the rough-surfaced and busy Nazionale delle Puglie.

Albaflex Snc was a family company. The driver was

married to one of the daughters of the late owner, Ruongo. Apart from Franco and Giuseppe (he was later convicted for the murder of his estranged wife, Loredana), Sam and Louis were the only non-family members. Luisa's brother was married to one of the owner's daughters. So she could not be described as an outsider. The eldest son of Ruongo, Carmine, oversaw the general management, logistics and sales. His younger brothers, Ciro and Paolo worked on the floor like anybody else.

Neither Louis nor Sam had a technical background. Louis however, did well on welding test. Sam's performance was very shoddy. With welding glasses on his eyes, he could not see his targets clearly. There were other jobs to do. Many finished products needed to be loaded into a delivery van. There too, Louis surpassed Sam. He became worried that eventually the employers might go for Louis.

Sam's chance came when they joined Luisa on the assembly line. She worked with such speed and accuracy that they could not equate until they left the services of Albaflex. Louis was actually awkward and impatient in fitting together small components and parts. In subsequent months, a regular telephone call from his friend in town saved him the boredom and fatigue. When there was no call, he retired to the toilet for minutes to smoke cigarette. In the evening, the Ruongos invited Sam and Louis to a corner of the floor. The burden lay on Sam to negotiate very favourable conditions.

His books proved invaluable. Ciro did what the young boy did in the morning. He undertook the translations. Sam started from the roof while the Ruongos chose the floor. They negotiated until they reached an agreement.

'For how long will our stay last?' Sam asked.

Carmine pointed at Franco and said he had been there

for years and that so far as they were hard-working and well-behaved, they could be there as long as they wanted. Sam and Louis waited in front of the post office at the station every morning for a ride to their place of work with any of the Ruongos.

Coming from the White House to that place posed another problem. Transport, though a necessity was a pain in their neck. It took a chunk of their income. So when it was possible, they evaded ticket controllers.

The Ruongos were God-sent. Insufficient farm work due to approaching winter, waiting endlessly at Ama JK for work that was not forthcoming was no longer of any concern to them. Sam and Louis had lunch with their employers on Saturdays in their family house at the city centre. Homely Nuncia, wife to Luisa's brother, was often around. There was another Ruongo daughter who came occasionally too. Always there was the family matriarch who supervised the cooking. It did not take Sam long to believe she was the fountain from where her children inherited their heartfelt sympathy for the downtrodden.

For a change, Nuncia and her husband invited them for lunch on Sundays. Ciro and Luisa's parents, the Aquinos, were there. Luisa never was. Her tall and gigantic father once left them with some fine winter coats. Carmine was surprised that Sam did not accept his gift of a second-hand BMW 316. The reasons were obvious. Maintenance cost was too much for his income and even if it was not, he had no resident permit to effect change of ownership.

He and Louis mounted more pressure for an accommodation as the winter was about to set in. The pressure intensified when the local authority gave the residents an order to vacate the White House or be forcibly ejected. The efforts the Ruongos made to relocate them before the deadline proved futile.

Many of the residents went about their normal engagements. They reacted to a reminder of the quit notice by packing their possessions but still hoped that their ejectors would back-pedal. Alas, they were wrong. They woke up on the cold winter morning of 16th December, 1990 to a large number of police in anti riot gear, local officials and representatives of Caritas (a charitable organisation).

Their president was nowhere to be found. A reliable source told them that he heeded the notice, armed with his working permit and left for northern Italy. The occasion demanded a leader, a mouth piece which was readily found in Frank. He understood Italian language even better than the run-away king of the White House. Frank was sipping from a bottle of beer as he walked in the midst of adversaries and sympathisers. Though he spoke soberly, yet there was something irresponsible about his manner. Sam thought that even with a million angels by their side, ejection from the White House that morning was a *fait accompli*. He was right. The officials were patient until the residents removed as many junks as they could. Uncertain where next the tide would carry them, they wept for the loss of those fine gas heaters donated by some religious groups.

With everybody out of the compound, and while the police watched, carpenters and bricklayers erected a gate. The man from Caritas entered his car and drove away, defeated and sad. A moustached fatman emerged. In their presence, he jammed the gate with a massive key, thereby sealing the White House from squatters forever.

One never knew how valuable one's possessions were until he lost them. Some of them broke into the abandoned

Anambra ghetto which, one year earlier, witnessed a gun attack on its residents by unidentified assailants. Some squeezed into congested Buckingham Palace. Many more joined their friends in Ave Blessed Maria.

The American Baptist Church offered an emergency relief to eight persons. They were kept in the well-ventilated, warm, tidy and clean basement of the church building, provided with every basic thing until the eighth day when the last person fully recovered from the trauma of ejection and left for Padua.

Sam telephoned the office of his kinsman. With a not-surprising green light from him, Sam went and waited outside his house until evening when he returned.

His house was a two-bedroom flat and he was still a bachelor. For the first time, Sam found himself alone in a real room. But he still missed the White House. His new residence was far away from the nearby station and bus-stops. He woke up as early as 4.30a.m in the morning and returned not earlier than 10p.m. He spent a minimum of eight hours everyday in transit. His kinsman occasionally provided him with transport to the nearest station. At home, food was many times better than what he had known. Drinks were abundant. Nothing was free; he was not under any illusion about it. To drink entailed owning up the replacement. Sam badly missed the freedom the White House allowed him to live according to his income, without constituting a liability on anybody or compelled to live above his means.

Sam worked hard at nurturing a cordial relationship. He would rather save nothing than default in honouring any of his financial obligations to his host. That way, they lived harmoniously for six months before Sam left for Padua.

While Sam struggled to make things work at home, the job security which they took for granted became shaky for reasons of poor turnover. Louis and Sam were laid off for days without pay, and at times, for a whole week. The harder they worked to sustain the confidence of their employer, the earlier they were sent home. Actually, there was a pile of finished products awaiting buyers. It was imperative to accept the explanation the Ruongos gave for the incessant lay off.

With Giuseppe in jail and Franco, an indispensable spray painter, still on the job, Louis and Sam were the only outsiders and easily became the pawn in the organisation's retrenchment agenda.

The first indication that Sam's numerous problems were increasing came in March 1991 when they were asked to go again. Two weeks later, he was recalled. Louis was not. A family member had taken over his position. Without his company and confronted with a possible loss of job, Sam became withdrawn and depressed. The first time he had been so demoralised was when his employer indicated interest in sending him to Nigeria with a container load of laboratory equipment. Sam contacted I.N. Venantius Nigeria Limited, the prospective buyers and sellers in Nigeria. The prices and conditions of sale were negotiated. The revenue was compared with cost, insurance and freight. There was no doubt the venture was lucrative. Time and energy were spent. Telephone bills were incurred and hopes raised. That the idea was aborted did not hurt him as much as the fact that nobody cared to explain the reason to him.

Another family member displaced Sam three months after the departure of Louis. Due to his raving, he was given two hundred thousand lire in lieu of notice. For two weeks, he remained indoors. His life had again been dealt a blow.

Some of his White House colleagues who had resident

permits drifted to Milan, Modena, Treviso and other northern cities in search of work. Others, who were irregular, settled in Padua. They employed themselves by doing *vu compra* (hawking wares from door to door). The news he heard from those who passed by his place of work about their experience in the course of soliciting for patronage was heart-rending. He detested *vu compra* as a means of survival. But with his job down the drain and the prospect for another uncertain, Sam had no choice than to join in the race.

He arrived Naples Campi Flegrei train station one hour thirty minutes before the departure of the 8.25 p.m. train to Udine on the 28th of June, 1991. After nearly one year of commuting to work, eating and drinking with Napolitans, Sam had made considerable acquaintance. He would miss their genuine friendship and every good thing they symbolized. It was not his fault. The search for the golden fleece had to go on. The weather was very hot. Instead of the waiting-room, Sam stood outside. Simon drove in. He came to drop his girlfriend who visited from Rome. Since the first day, Sam had not seen him. But he had not forgotten the name he gave Sam that first day for security reasons. Sam adopted the name and was known by it. Even his kinsman, gradually got so used to it that alone in the house, he addressed Sam as such.

'Billy!' Simon cried, dashing out of his car.

He flung himself at Sam. 'How are you? Oh Billy, I feel ashamed and guilty that I have not kept my promise to come over to see how you have been coping. Anyway, I have been on the run.'

'What happened?' Sam asked.

'When my boys arrived from Pako, all the men of calibre came with their cash to buy. Then the police struck with a precision that drug business in this town had never witnessed before. The quantity of drugs was colossal. Flushing it through the sink was impossible for lack of time. Eight of my friends are behind bars and everything I have saved is gone. The work permit I obtained in 1990 is gone too. Among those arrested included a pregnant woman, and two men who were AIDS carriers. The three persons have since been let off the hook.'

'AIDS carriers... Your friends?' Sam was obviously stunned.

'On paper they are carriers. In Italy, pregnant women cannot be imprisoned. And those infected with that terminal disease cannot be prosecuted. This is the law. Sometime ago, when they started robbing banks with arms, the Italian public cried out for a review of their immunity. The outcry has waned nonetheless. These my friends had the foresight to obtain medical certificates that listed them as carriers prior to their arrest.'

'So, they are not carriers?'

'They are not.' Simon started laughing.

'You can as well enjoy the same privilege by obtaining a similar certificate,' Sam told him.

'It's not possible. Only Italians who are well-connected and rich can get a qualified and duly registered medical personnel to append his signature on such false document. Law abiding citizens will quickly get you arrested for merely suggesting such an act. I might have risen very high in drug business but today, I think, I had not earned the trust of my colleagues so much as to be introduced to the doctors in our employ.'

***

Sam lost weight. Of course only few persons would share his experience and still remain robust. But to see Simon so emaciated was touching. To Sam, the moment was not right for recriminations.

'How did you escape?' Sam asked.

'I was mistaken for another person. One of my clients, Orlando, sent his car to a mechanic for servicing. The mechanic rang my house when the car was ready. Orlando was busy. I had always trusted him with packing my drugs in the right measures. I decided to go and pick the car before the mechanic closed for the day. I tried the lift but for fifteen minutes, it was still occupied. I decided to use the staircase. On the ground floor, I met three men in mufti. They greeted me appraisingly.

As the condominium had witnessed a surge of guests before, I was not alarmed by the presence of three Alfa Romeo 75 Twin Spark, FIAT Tipo and other cars. When I was returning from the workshop, police cars with sirens blared ominously past me as they sped towards the direction of my house. I became afraid and stopped at a roadside telephone booth. My fear was confirmed when a policeman responded to my call and told me to come. I fled with nothing. It has been months since the incident and I have been in hiding. They swore to pursue, arrest, prosecute and jail me. This is not a bluff Billy. I have a premonition they will catch up with me sooner or later. I heard that one of my friends had volunteered more implicating information about me and had opted to act as a prosecution witness in return for a short jail term. Once, I had the opportunity of sneaking out of this country for the Balkans with false documents. But I could not pay the owner of the documents, so he took them away. Honestly, Sam, I am confused. Life is over for me without money, or work permit and my freedom.'

His eyes were filled with tears when he pointed at his

girlfriend and begged Sam to thank her for providing him financial and moral supports. 'Without money, the range of my friends has shrunk to a mere handful. Those who ate from my coffers, now brazenly shun the sight of me.'

Crying over spilt milk, or dwelling on the past, was not for Sam. He liked to confront the present, draw from the past and look to the future. Guided by these precepts, he advised Simon not to cave in. Sam gave a summary of his activities for the past one year to Simon. Neither of them knew who should console the other.

Sam's case was different though. He was not a wanted criminal and had not owned as much as Simon had. Sam missed nothing. 'You don't miss what you don't have,' Sam later told himself.

Regardless of the burden on Simon's shoulders, he still cared. He racked his brain in an effort to remember any of his colleagues in Padua who would receive and assist Sam on arrival but no name came to his mind. Padua was not for his type. Sam was not perturbed about who would receive him either. Cento, Louis, and Jude were there.

'I will give you Grace's address and telephone number. She is doing fine in Turin. If you have any need of her, ring her up. You are great, Billy. She will be at your beck and call. Turin is not very far from Padua. If you ever see her, pass my love and good wishes to her. Do not tell her what has become of me. The last time she came to Naples for shopping, she advised me as you did a year ago.'

They shook hands. Sam boarded the train with Simon's girlfriend.

Chapter 3

The City of Saint Anthony

It was almost six o'clock in the morning when the express train made the seven hundred and fifty kilometre journey to Padua. With the help of an African immigrant, Sam learnt that he should wait for his friends at a piazza on Via Fra Sarpi where they traded wares every morning before departing for various destinations. They arrived an hour later. There was no washing or bathing for Sam. He could not miss a steaming plate of rice sold by food vendors. Even then, he had no time to eat. He took the food along to eat inside a blue FIAT Ducato. There were ten passengers and the driver, Moses. Most of them were known to Sam in the ghettos or apple farms of Naples. Cento saw to it that he learnt the names of the goods packed in his bag for sale. He also taught Sam the prices. Before they arrived a town in the province of Treviso where the team worked that day, Cento had left Sam wondering if he was a graduate in education or business administration. He tasked Sam to memorise all the names of the sixteen items and to identify ten of them at sight. Moses encouraged Cento to show Sam how to get closed gates and doors opened; how to engage the attention of even the most indifferent, how to arouse their sympathy and interest and how to twist and transform these emotions into sales and revenue at the end of the day. Many years afterwards, Cento took the credit of guiding Sam through the nitty-gritty of *vu compra*.

When the time came for Sam to practise what he had learnt, Moses boosted his morale and let him off right inside a busy city centre. Moses gave the time he would return to collect him and pointed to the place he was expected to be. There was nothing left for the commander to do. Off he went. Sam looked left, right, back and front. There were people everywhere. No shelter. No place to hide. He was nervous and sweating. He realised he was an obstruction to pedestrians and ducked out of their way. About a hundred metres away, Sam saw an elderly woman, seated inside a shop. She was mending an underwear. She was his ideal refuge. She bought an item from him. The fear and shame were gone.

Sam quickly defined his target: people who were alone in the premises with the entrance gates ajar. Next, he went for a younger woman. She refused but he could not take no for an answer. He culled from the lessons acquired not long ago. He pleaded and outlined the special features of his wares. Unknown to Sam, the man who stood and watched from the balcony of another building across the street was her husband. He came over. 'Valeria, why don't you want to buy from this *poverino*? You have been buying from others or is it because I am at home today?' Husband and wife started laughing.

'I know he is poor but there is no money in the house to buy from everybody,' she said.

Her husband prodded her to buy something. She went for the most expensive item, a packet of three fine, high quality T-shirts in pure cotton which suited the hot weather.

It enjoyed a rock-bottom price of only eighteen thousand lire. In addition, the couple gave him extra two thousand lire for coffee. The next person Sam met was a handsome young man who was cleaning his car outside their beautiful one-storey home. Sam joined him and chose not to rattle the man immediately with his rubbish. He genuinely admired his car and his macho look.

'You are handsome. I am sure you can have as many wives as you wish.' He was elated and laughed.

'I have only one.'

'If I were you with a fine car like this and such looks, I will marry as many as I can lay my hands upon,' Sam pretended he meant it.

'We don't do that here.'

'Where do you come from?'

'Nigeria.'

'What is your name?' Sam decided to be on the offensive otherwise the discussion might lead him to a one-way tunnel.

'Mario.'

'I am Billy.'

'Billy Ocean of America?' Mario asked jokingly.

'Are you a student'?

'I am Billy Ocean of Africa. A student. I am strapped and decided to hawk these wares for house rent and food,' Sam lied.

'What are you studying?' he asked.

Sam was aware his graceless and disjointed Italian grammar disqualified him from any claim to scholarship. 'I am presently studying Lingua Italiana and will proceed to the university soon for a degree in engineering.'

Mario left what he was doing and came over to see what Sam had for sale. If Sam let him search for what to buy, he might choose an item that cost very little. Obviously, certain family members were vested with specific buying decisions. If there were doubts about who would buy pants, T-shirts and stockings for Mario, there was no doubt that the purchase of car polish would be without any interference from his mother or wife. So, Sam brought out the can of spray and moved straight to the car bumper and demonstrated its efficacy. The demonstration left him in no doubt. With ten thousand lire for the spray paid, Sam thanked him and left.

At the end of the day, members of the team rendered account to the driver and risk bearer. He took sixty per cent of the revenue accruing from sales from where he paid for the goods, insurance, tax, fuel, repairs, and other miscellaneous expenses. The remainder belonged to him. Sam's sales that day was not as much as that of the first six persons but it was more than his friend's sales and quite enough to motivate him.

The time was eleven-thirty in the night when they reached Via Forcellini 186, the place that would be his residence for nearly four months from that day. The bus had hardly stopped when his colleagues rushed to buy food. Their business with Moses which started when they boarded his bus in the morning, terminated as they all bade him goodnight. Once again, Cento was there for Sam. He secured enough food for two persons from the vendors. The food was cold otherwise it was delicious. They washed hands at the tap and went upstairs.

The building was a disused elementary school. The accounts about how it was converted into a hostel were conflicting but a more probable one was that the local authority volunteered it in order to pull away homeless African immigrants from the train station. Initially, the residents were few. The place was orderly and tidy. However, as ghettos south of Italy crumbled and the quest for greener pastures by all and sundry intensified, the approximately ten-by-eighty-metre one-storey building had a minimum of five hundred inhabitants. The building was divided into large rooms with six-spring beds. Each of the six-spring beds had two occupants. All the spaces inside the rooms were filled. At night, there was no free foot space on the gangways and staircase. Some parts of the toilet served those who had no place to put their mattresses. There was a committee which saw to it that a monthly rent of forty-five thousand lire was collected from each person, that sanitation met the standard stipulated by the health authorities and that there was general discipline.

But the reverse was the case. It was difficult to say whether the residents deliberately evaded payment or that the committee members colluded with them or that those vested with the authority to make such collections were ineffective. Nevertheless, it was an act of bravado to avoid payment of rents. The toilets were very dirty, inadequate and often put out of use by the use of newspapers instead of soft tissue papers. Free-for-all fights involving the use of bottles that got on-lookers scampering for cover were common. The physically powerful and wild held sway like a god. Those who were not endowed with muscles and stamina dared not raise their voices very loud or they were quietened with broken ribs. To dare and defeat a notorious bully was met with ovation. It was another jungle.

The room where Cento stayed was exceptional. It was not as crowded as the other places. It had drunkards, scoundrels and mischief-makers. It also boasted of many mature and enlightened men who knew how to avoid or lure them to a war not of fists but of wits. For Sam to bulldoze his way into such a circle was difficult but not impossible with Cento who gave him a foothold by introducing him as his guest. When one Mr. Rex, the room captain convened a meeting to announce that Sam had overstayed his welcome, the members effortlessly bent him. From that day, Sam became one of them.

Nothing of value was safe. Things, from the ordinary to the precious, could be lost. There was movement to and fro, up and down almost all night. As congested as the place was and as thoughtless and heartless as some people were, stepping on legs and arms by passers-by was rampant and it often sparked off brawls. To be able to bath before going out in the morning entailed rising as early as four-thirty when most people had yielded to fatigue and when there was still warm water in the tap.

The noise, menace and nuisance within, soon, exploded into the neighbourhood. Neighbours complained about naked bodies and cars abandoned at their entrances. They protested against rancorous motorists who kept them awake at odd hours. These were genuine grievances but the barrage of protests did not peter out until they included allegations that were utterly false and malicious. The residents were accused of habouring women and dealing in drugs. Soon, the municipal police stepped up patrol to check the obstruction of traffic. Food vendors were made to be more responsible. They were made to collect aluminium foils, plastics and papers abandoned by their customers into dustbins provided by the government.

By the time the state police intervened in the problems of Via Forcellini 186, Sam knew their days there were numbered. Whatever grouse he had against the hostel, with water, electricity, toilets, heating system, it was better than the White House. No matter the commotion which the residents experienced on a daily basis, to Sam, there were no such obligations as when he lived in Lago Patria. He felt less stress. There were very frustrating moments doing *vu compra*, moments that sharply contrasted with his first day experience. The job brought them right into the homes and lives of people who nurtured strong prejudice against foreigners in general and blacks in particular.

An instance was in Trestina, during the first quarter of 1995 when Sam went to work there with four of his friends. Three of them were in Umbertide. One was in Trestina. The arrangement was that Sam would collect the fellow in Trestina, Mr. Ikuku, before others. Still recovering from the pains of ribs fractured in an accident in the course of his work, he sat inside the car he had managed to buy in the parking ground of Sidis Supermarket, as Ikuku passed by only a few minutes to Sam's appointment with him. So, when time was up, Sam drove the kilometre stretch of shops without seeing Ikuku. He drove round in vain for eight times. Late for his appointment with the others, he left to collect them. All of them returned to Trestina. By then, all the shops were closed. Sam inquired from those who cared to listen but nobody saw Ikuku. He telephoned their houses in Padua. Ikuku had not rung yet. They departed for their dinner in a nearby restaurant. After dinner, the incomplete team joined the trunk road, E45, for Fina filling station where they waited anxiously and made more telephone calls. It was two o'clock in the morning when Ikuku tapped at the wet glasses of Sam's FIAT 131 TC. He was shivering, cold and tired.

They quickly made room for him inside the car. It took him minutes before he was composed to narrate his ordeal.

'I was concluding my day when I arrived at a shop near the train station that sells car accessories and walked in. The shop owner who should be in his early fifties did not even allow me to drop my bag on the floor let alone present him with what I was selling when he rumbled 'Go...go...go...' My plea for audience was like pouring fuel into fire. He strode out of the shop. I reached for the double sash door when he jammed it and got me trapped inside with my finger bleeding from injury. From there, I saw when you drove up and down looking for me and I was still locked up until the patrol police he invited came. I was taken to the police office. The complainant joined us later and immediately rolled into the commandant's office. I was still clutching my injured finger when the police recruits and corporals invited me into another room for interrogation. I was fingerprinted. One hour thirty minutes to midnight, I was set free with a note to go to the foreigners' office in Perugia for the completion of other formalities. By then my finger had stopped bleeding but was still susceptible to infection. Nobody cared. Trains and buses were no more available but a motorist pitied me and helped me to a larger and busier train station where I hoped to stay till later in the morning when you will come for me. Unknown to me, it was the type that was vacated and locked at midnight. For almost two hours, I had stood outside, cold, hungry and confused about where next to go when a very kind man volunteered to bring me here.'

'The command of Trestina is not wicked. We have been there over a dozen times. Are you sure you were not rude to the shopkeeper?'

'Look at what Billy is saying. Did I make the hundreds of kilometres from Padua to here to make trouble and return with my wares unsold?'

'Why did you not request to call Padua, at least to quell our anxiety and save yourself some of the inconveniences?'

'Call! Ah, they didn't allow me access to any telephone.'

The refusal of the police to allow Ikuku access to a telephone or give him a chance to present his side of the case before his accuser was not strange. Some members of the police force, however, were kind and sympathetic to the plights of illegal immigrants. They even bought some items from them when they were met buoyant. But they could not be relied upon for fairness in any dispute involving a door-to-door selling immigrant without a valid stay permit.

It was during one of such fits of dejection that Sam decided to telephone Grace in Turin. He chose the time all employees were supposedly home from work. He had not called her since Simon gave him the number. So, he was relieved when he tried the second day and a girl told him that she was sleeping and would not take any calls. For fear of violating the instructions given to her, she did not attempt to wake her up. Sam understood and thanked her without disclosing his identity. The third time, he got her. She was extremely excited. A telephone card of ten thousand lire was exhausted, yet she begged for more. Her joy was genuine. Sam concluded she was not like most women who had a penchant for avoiding anybody known in Nigeria. From that day till when he visited two weeks later, he telephoned her daily. He was alarmed by the joy he too derived from doing so. Since 1987, they had not seen each other. So, they were eager to meet again.

Grace was well off. A two-bedroom flat, alone in one room and her three girls in another. Television sets and VCRs in all. Everywhere was sparkling, tidy and free from cigarette stench. The food was superb. The most delicious Sam had tasted in Italy. Grace's girls were very respectful and caring. They called him uncle. Sam had his bath with a brand new towel. When he finished, there were two new pyjamas and housecoats to choose from. Grace was good in bed. But she could not have her way every time. Sam insisted on using condoms to her dismay. She contended that all the times in Italy, she had been sleeping with men using condoms and deserved a feel of the real thing. 'Do not assume that a person of the same complexion or cultural background or a neighbour is not prone to AIDS like everybody else. There is need to practise safe sex constantly.'

Grace was humbled. It took his experience in women and managerial ability to calm her nerves, restore her confidence in herself and to eliminate her fears of rejection. He would not have succeeded if he were in a hurry to enter her. For almost one hour, they talked and played.

'I have never had it so many times since I came here,' she confessed. 'I did not believe I could achieve it with condom.'

'Are you saying that you do not achieve orgasm with your clients?'

'No, Sam.'

'So you do not enjoy sex?'

'Certainly not. Enjoyment is not my motive for whoring to start with. I simply pretend to be enthralled so that my clients can achieve orgasm and leave amicably.'

'Does it not hurt if you feel so dry below?'

'It does.'

'Yet you go through the same punishment everyday?'

'Punishment indeed. I like that word. However, I use medical lubricants to make intercourse less painful.'

'Now you see that arousal is more of the mind. We should not allow superstition to expose our health to incurable infections.' Sam told her as she expelled air from another condom.

She described *vu compra* as very humiliating and the hostel as a despicable place to live. She suggested that Sam should join her in Turin. The proposal resembled the ones those ladies presented to him through Simon.

'What am I going to do here without a work permit?'

'My girls spend one hundred thousand lire daily on transport to and from Corso Regina where they work. Even then, some of these drivers are often drunk or get carried away, there have been accidents resulting in injuries and deaths. We have come here to search for what to eat and not to be disabled or carried home dead. I can provide you a car and you can pocket the hundred thousand lire instead. In addition, I will meet your basic needs for food and shelter at no cost to you.'

'Food, shelter and easy income for me at no cost?'

'Who can leave Africa, give up dignity and honour, walk the streets of Italy, stay single, keep an educated handsome guy at home, meet all his sexual, financial and social needs and yet want nothing in return? What a smart idea put together to pluck me away from Via Forcellini 186, make me highly vulnerable and finally confront me with her hidden agenda. By then, refusal to do her bidding will spell terrible consequences for me, Sam thought.

To her he said, 'I need the money but the job is not appealing to me. If I had wanted to do it, I would not have come as far as Turin. It is against my conscience.'

When she found out that no amount of pressure or logic would convince Sam, she came up with a better idea. She suggested that he could go to Naples, buy shoes, sandals, belts, trousers and shirts in bulk, return to Turin and sell them in bits to women. Prices of goods were lower in Naples than in the industrial city of Turin. She even promised to put up the capital necessary for a sound take-off.

Unlike most women who drank alcohol, chain-smoked cigarette, loud and aggressive and wore gold, Grace was in a class of her own. She was a teetotaller and had never smoked before. She was tranquil and respectful; gorgeous in dressing and demeanour. She had plenty of money without the pomposity of her contemporaries. Her skin had not lost its natural glow to cosmetic make up. With her modulated voice, the inexplicable was explained; the indefensible defended. She was a victim of circumstance. Suffocating from want and hunger because of unemployment after graduation, she could not resist the temptation to come to Italy.

As soon as she fully paid her *igbese* (money paid to sponsors to obtain freedom), she stopped walking the streets herself. Rather, she procured girls who were paying *igbese* to her. She still hoped that someday, her stay in Italy would be legalised so she can seek a decent job. Indeed, Grace was different. She had qualities that well compensated her flaws. Sam had been bound to Efe. He was not free to fall in love again. He would only be courting trouble by consenting to live with her. Grace knew about Efe as his campus sweetheart and thought it had faded like most adolescent affairs. Unknown to her was that only time stood between them and the solemnisation of their marriage. Once again, she deserved to know that Sam did not reject her but that his hands had long been tied.

'No woman who comes across you would wish to let you go. The search for greener pasture in Italy is not as easy as we thought at home. It is even worse for men. Though women go through very dirty experience, yet there are many of them who have made, in only a few years, more money than men could make all their lifetime in Italy.

You are endowed with a lot of intellect. Considering the fact that it may take you decades before you can go home again, I do not think that you require any one to advise you on what line of action to take,' she sermonised.

'Grace darling, if it were for my own sake, perhaps, I would not have come to Italy. But for her sake or more appropriately, for our sake. I thought I had the opportunity to harness my potentials, make fortune and go back home. Unfortunately, life, so far, has been a nightmare. But I will overcome. I will eventually go home.'

'I hate to say this about a woman who is not here to defend herself. I am a woman and I know the way our minds work. I am sorry if you find what I am saying offensive. Efe forgot you for successful Nigerian men as soon as you boarded the flight here.'

'If trusting her makes me a fool, let me be. If believing that she will continue to be there for me makes me dumb, let me be. Help me to keep my promise to her.'

Sam had no doubt that Grace would take necessary measures to avoid unprotected sex with strangers but did not think so about her girls. She had told him that how they hawked their bodies was not her business. What mattered to her was her *igbese*. They could be easily enticed by an offer of huge sum of money. Sam called the girls when his departure was due and started to tell them the story of Dika.

***

'All of you are aware of Chief Nso who has served in every administration since independence. He needed a son to save his marriage from collapsing; a son to inherit his name and ill-gotten wealth when he died. Initially, his wife went about the task with the assistance of her mother-in-law. After an unfruitful effort, the old woman gave up hope and started persuading her son to marry another woman. However, instead of abandoning her, he chose to pursue the goal with her. Together, they consulted the best gynaecologist, fasted and prayed fervently to God. But when the next child came, it was a female.

The chief was undaunted. They exploited many more avenues. Among them was a visit to the famed Ube shrine, abode of the goddess of fertility. Many couples had attested to the credibility of her powers and the virtues of her magnanimity. Hopefully, Chief and Mrs Nso made the one kilometre trek through the most winding footpath to the bottom of the valley where the shrine was situated. They performed all the rituals which included presentation of gift items and washing of feet with water infested with worms and lava. But it did not matter to Chief Nso or his wife who could face more horrible things in order to have a son.

'Eventually the chief priest led Chief Nso and his wife further downward the valley... Half way, he instructed them to wait. He alone could make the remaining journey into the restricted territory of the goddess. A few minutes later, he returned and joined the couple

'I have consulted our great mother,' he said.

They ascended a distance of three metres. He pointed to a spot barricaded with red and white pieces of cloth. 'Go into that altar. Meet your wife with all your might,' he instructed Chief Nso. As the couple began to go, he added, 'Our great mother is watching. She will give you a son but do not forget her.'

'Never! Never!' Chief Nso and his wife promised.

When the rituals were over, the chief priest warned, 'be careful, the child will give you an inestimable joy, and the joy may give way to unfathomable anguish if you do not protect him from enemies.'

When every door seemed to have been slammed against them and even their prayers to God appeared to have been stuck half-way, Mrs Nso made up her mind to run away from their matrimonial home. She dropped a brief note for Chief Nso.

My dear husband,

My parents, brothers and sisters objected to our marriage twenty years ago. So also your own relatives. We went ahead and married. From that moment, you have been everything to me. I didn't mind until recently when you and I became too cold to comfort each other. It is not your fault. Perhaps, it is not mine. But definitely fate is not in our favour. There must be a son to be your heir. This son I cannot provide. May be, another woman will succeed. If she ever does, I will rejoice with you. To make it possible, I am leaving the house forever for an unknown destination. My children are not aware of my flight. My request is that let a little kindness be spared to the eight of them I have got for you. Let whoever is taking over my place know how much I love you and let your appreciation manifest in the female children I am leaving behind. Bye.

'She gathered a few of her possessions, a handful of jewelleries, many wedding photographs and some money into her box, locked it and waited to decide her destination. Incidentally, she woke up the next morning with fever, and headache. She reached for her analgesic and returned to bed. Her maids invited her later for breakfast. She had no appetite for it. Her mind was on the plot. After only two spoons into her mouth, she started vomiting violently and uncontrollably. Her husband quickly invited the family doctor

124

who accompanied them to the hospital. To her greatest disbelief, she was three months pregnant.

'Six months later, she delivered a handsome baby boy at a private clinic in London with four specialist doctors around to attend to mother and child. Chief Nso registered the birth in London. The child was named Gini-Di-Ka-Nwa (Nothing is like a child, a male one certainly in this case). For convenience, the registration officer at the birth registry sought and obtained permission to shorten the name. So the child's birth certificate bore Dika.

'Dika was the Nsos' spring of life. He sustained their marriage. He returned smile to their hitherto gloomy faces and enthusiasm to his father's pursuit for wealth and authority. He made the uneven, even and changed retrogression to progress. He symbolised a new lease of life.

'At the age of eighteen months, Dika's father hired for him the services of well-trained teachers of English Language, Mathematics and Current Affairs. Not long after the exercise started, he began to exhibit substantial understanding of the white man's language. His narratives were vivid and imaginative. His memory proved highly retentive.

'Three years of age is quite ideal for a child to seek and obtain formal education,' Dika's teachers said.

His mother objected vehemently at first. She rather suggested that more teachers be hired. Chief Nso consulted his friends among whom was Elo Ude, a renowned professor of guidance and counselling. The professor advised that Dika needed to socialise with other children. He added that the quality of education obtainable in the country then did not fit Dika's status. He recommended a prep school in London; the world's first class prep school.

He was afraid Chief Nso's money might do little or nothing to secure admission for Dika as it was on record that no black child had ever been offered one.

'Bucks Institute was located on Queen's Way in Central London. It was bordered on the East by Bond street and on the West by Shepherds Bush. Hyde Park and Nothing Hill Gate shared its southern and northern borders respectively.

'The preparatory school which also incorporated higher school curricula charged thirty thousand pounds per session but recommended the sum of one hundred pounds a week as living allowance to a student from his parents. The school started in 1764 first as a place where patriotism was inculcated into young men who were sent out as missionaries, explorers, navigators and traders. Later it included as its objectives the training of sports men and women in various sporting activities for export to the rest of the world. By a special act of parliament in 1860, it was transformed into its present status and renamed after Mr Berlin Bucks, Britain's twelfth century highest advocate of formal education. It was for children of heads of government in Europe, millionaires, kings, queens, movie stars, scientists and professors of international acclaim.

'The school's population did not reflect the huge investment in it by the British government. Only five hundred pupils were on roll of which the number of girls nearly equalled that of boys. Dika's citizenship of the United Kingdom, his father's enormous wealth and his astounding intelligence earned him a place.

'Security at Bucks was formidable. As a rule, before a higher school pupil left the school, an application was made. The pupil's destination was either telephoned or visited personally to ascertain if the visit posed any risk to the safety of the child. If the application was approved, a police orderly was assigned to accompany the pupil. He carried with him a movement note which the host of the pupil completed and returned through the police. The note stated the arrival and departure times. When a pupil was visiting a place different from an individual's residence, a museum, for instance, it was up to the police orderly to complete the note and as well make a resume of the pupil's mission.

Persons, whether matrons, patrons, or nannies were properly identified and drivers who were not residents were issued with a pass before they could go into the school compound. On their departure, they were made to sign out too. Visitors were rarely admitted and those who had the fortune of access into the compound were compelled to pass through gates mounted with sophisticated metal detectors and then interrogation. Things went extremely well according to the elegance and tradition of Bucks Institute until Dika was in his second year in the high school.

'Despite the tight security in and around the school, kidnappers managed to get hold of a son of a Saudi Arabian sultan billionaire. The circumstances of the kidnap defied even the Scotland Yard. The kidnappers demanded a ransom of one hundred million pounds sterling. When the sultan was informed by the British Ambassador in Saudi Arabia about the incident, not even promises of a crack down on the kidnappers by heads of intelligence in America, France and the whole of Europe could dissuade him from succumbing to the whims of the abductors. The ransom was left in the place specified by the abductors. Two days later, the prince was picked up on Heathrow Airport Road in West Kensington region, drugged and almost blinded. Letters were dispatched to all parents and guardians whose children or wards were schooling at Bucks informing them about the incident and the efforts made by the government to ensure that it did not happen again. The same letter pleaded that parents should discountenance any reports by communist newspapers and magazines that security in that school was porous. The letter was belated as Nigeria's High Commission in London had already visited Dika, spoken to him and relayed same to his father. Chief Nso was agitated. He arrived London the next day and procured his son's release from the school hostel and put him in a ten million pounds posh house in the heart of Victoria.

'The house enjoyed sophisticated electronic security gadgets and a deployment of security men from Scotland yard. One served as an orderly and accompanied Dika every time in his car to anywhere. The other security agents took care of the house on shift basis. The other members of the house were a female steward and a female cleaner. These staff were well paid and adequately motivated. That year again passed remarkably well. His studies witnessed record improvement, having made the best result in literature, geography and mathematics.

'At first, the chain of command was clearly defined and relationships were almost formal. Nevertheless, formality was gradually dismantled. The servants started to dine and wine together with Dika until a new security man who replaced an old one inadvertently betrayed others. In the presence of Chief Nso, the new security agent requested that food be served. Chief Nso felt humiliated. Upon investigation, he found out that the security agent's predecessors and some domestic staff used to dine with his son. The chief was so bitter that he reprimanded the security agent, sacked other culprits with immediate effect and employed a new set of staff within two hours.

'One morning, Dika's cleaner went into his bedroom

to do her usual job. It was a public holiday. After completing her duty, she deliberately left behind a pornographic magazine she smuggled into the house. Dika retired to his room after breakfast and found the magazine. Initially, he wanted to ignore it but the cover photograph was very enticing. Before he knew it, he was devouring the magazine page after page.

Suddenly, the cleaner knocked on the door and without even waiting to be asked in, dashed into the room and met Dika with her magazine. 'I am sorry to intrude on your privacy, Mr Dika, I forgot my magazine here. I don't know if you could permit me to have it?' she said.

'I am going through it. Hope you do not mind coming for it a couple of minutes later?' Dika replied.

'It suits me, Mr. Dika. Invite me to have it when you are ready,' she said and reluctantly left the room.

'Ten minutes later, the cleaner returned to the room and went straight to Dika's bedside. She pleaded, 'Dika, I am scared of the prying eyes of these Metropolitan boys (referring to the police). I wouldn't want them to find me here. Please, let me have it quickly.'

'You mean to have the magazine?' Dika inquired.

'Mm...' she responded and sat on the bed.

As Dika did not complain about such an effrontery, she drew close and suddenly snatched the magazine from him.

'It is enough, Dika,' she murmured.

'Their eyes met. Their pretences crumbled as they saw in those eyes the assurance that no one else would know. From that moment, it became a regular affair.

'The stewardess who least expected to find a cleaner with the master, came to invite Dika one morning to his breakfast and stumbled on them. The cleaner pleaded that Dika should allow her to join in order to avoid a possible blackmail. Dika had no objection. So every night, he slept with both of them with each beside him. The ages of the two women were thirty-eight and twenty-nine years respectively. That he could satisfy their lust and eventually leave them exhausted fired his drive further. The older lady was a budding television star when her career was rocked by a sex scandal between her and a married clergy man. The younger lady was a high school drop-out. She had been a call girl before the opportunity to work for Dika. She had never been engaged in a decent job before and forged all the documents that earned her the job.

'As Dika continued to grow, it dawned on him what a balance between his father and mother he made. He had his mother's beautiful face, kindness and concern for the welfare of others. From his father, he inherited a towering frame as well as courage. Dika also had a touch of his father's business zeal without a dime of his craftiness and self-centredness. Beyond all, Chief Nso's rare intelligence manifested itself in his son.

'The only aspect of Dika's personality which had no biological explanation was his insatiable desire for elderly and sexy-looking female celebrities. His studies did not suffer in spite of his shortcomings. He continued to do extremely well. Every hour he wasted womanising, he made up with two hours of his sleep. It did not surprise Dika's lecturers or the university authority nor did it take his coursemates unawares when he, having made the best academic performance, rendered the historic valedictory speech on behalf of all the graduating students – white, yellow and black. His admission into the reputed doctorate degree programme of the university at Ox was automatic. But he turned it down. He wanted to join his country men and women in preparation for what his father wanted him to be; not in England but in Nigeria.

'At home, Dika came face-to-face with abject poverty. Roads were dilapidated, hospitals were mere consulting clinics, schools and universities were ill equipped. Beyond Victoria Island and Ikoyi, children roamed the streets naked, hungry and without any hope of going to school. He was baffled by the gap between his family and the average Nigerian. Like Chief Nso's nemesis, Dika resolved to exploit his father's resources to improve the living standard of the masses.

'He launched Education Endowment Fund for talented but poor people. He vigorously lobbied and secured free primary education for all. Assisted by some European missionaries and indigenous medical personnel, he established family support programmes which gave virtually free consultation and medicine to pregnant women and children. But to enable families provide for themselves and escape from poverty, he formed a cooperative society which secured loans from banks and other financial institutions and disbursed them to its members according to their business needs. These contributions were like urine on scorched earth when compared with the magnitude of problems surrounding him. He was not deterred, he continued to work to alleviate the sufferings of the poor.

'It was clear to him that only the position of president had the resources and authority to make a far-reaching impact on the lives of everybody and hoped to go for the elevated position in the future. In the interim, he appointed directors of transparent integrity for his people-oriented programmes and decided to return to school for his doctorate degree. A couple of months into his doctorate degree, he started having plenty of night sweat. It was so much that he had to change his dresses twice at night in

131

order not to wet his bed or embarrass himself before his girl friend by waking up with sweat-soaked clothes.

'As the situation was not ameliorated, he installed a more potent air conditioner in his bedroom, that was enough to chill the life out of a normal human being but his condition did not improve. Within two weeks, he had lost tremendous weight. Initially, he weighed eighty-six kilograms but astoundingly netted only seventy kilograms at the end of the period. His weight and body temperature moved in opposite directions. While the former nosedived, the later skyrocketed. Simultaneously, he developed fever and catarrh. While his doctors thought he was suffering from influenza, he battled helplessly with persistent diarrhoea and general weakness of the body. Dika contacted many medical doctors in Nigeria, they diagnosed one ailment or another but he remained incurable.

'Witch doctors and herbalists came into the scene. The same ritual that characterised his birth began to repeat itself. Spiritualists were invited. They attributed his sickness to the evil machinations of witches and wizards. Sacrifices were offered but the crown prince's condition degenerated. He was now a walking skeleton. Nothing was known, seen or heard of in Nigeria that could rescue him from the brink of despair and the grip of death. There was money but there was no man throughout the length and breadth of Nigeria who could take as much money from Chief Nso and save his only son. There was no man who could sustain the smile on the faces of Nigeria's poor and oppressed.

'Chief Nso and the man whose daughter Dika would marry – the president of Nigeria, arranged that Dika be admitted into the most reputed specialist hospital in New York. Quickly, an Air Force plane was mobilised for the journey. Dika's two physicians, his father, who could not be dissuaded, and his immediate elder sister accompanied him. Among them also were two top plain-clothed security agents. He had heard much about the hospital. There was hardly any sickness the hospital had not handled effectively. It was expensive. Patients of terminal diseases like cancer had had their life span prolonged. There had been very successful transplant of heart, liver, and kidney. Dika concluded he would come back to Nigeria very healthy again to carry on with his philanthropic work and education. He also hoped that eventually he would marry the president's beautiful daughter.

'The chief medical director of Galloways Medical Centre spoke with Dika's physicians, appraised his medical records and finally asked him a few questions before they recommended that he should be isolated. Chief Nso objected vehemently to this directive.

'Chief,' the doctor said, 'it is in your interest that we be granted a conducive atmosphere to give your son the attention he deserves. We promise that granted this atmosphere, you will be able to see him soon.'

'Reluctantly, Chief Nso agreed. Dika could imagine the anxiety and fury that welled up in his father's heart. Chief Nso wished he could ameliorate his son's anguish. They reached for each other's hands. The grip was firm and then an embrace, a prolonged one too.

'Do not worry, papa. Soon, I will be well again,' Dika consoled his father.

'You can have anything you want as soon as you are discharged,' Chief Nso assured him.

'I know you love me, papa. Greet mama for me and express my gratitude to the president.'

When Chief Nso was about to leave, Dika remembered something and said, 'Papa, please, ensure that the cheques

133

in respect of the Foundations' subventions are signed promptly.'

'I will do so my son. Bye,' Chief Nso promised and walked away.

'Dika's blood sample was taken by a senior laboratory technologist. The blood was put into a bottle and corked. His name was boldly written on a small proportion of the label, the technologist took the bottle to a centrifuging machine for processing and testing. Barely four hours later, the laboratory technologist returned to the consultation room. He presented a note to the chief medical director. Sweat began to gather on the doctor's oblong face. The technologist's fingers were visibly fidgeting. A couple of minutes passed before the chief haematologist came in and studied the result. He made a very brief note on the result sheet. Together with the technologist he left the room.

The medical director walked into where Dika was isolated. 'Are you gay?'

'No doctor,' Dika replied.

'Were you having unrestrained and unprotected sexual intercourse with multiple partners?'

'Yes,' Dika chuckled. 'I have met a lot of movie stars, actresses, singers and business baronesses', Dika paused. The doctor beckoned on him to continue and he did. 'I have regarded it not natural to wear condoms when I make love. To that extent doc., I have been unprotected.'

'The doctor further probed, 'Has anybody known to you been similarly sick before?'

'Certainly no.'

'You have AIDS,' declared the doctor.

'Contrary to the doctor's expectation, Dika remained calm except for his probing eyes which urged the doctor to go on with the death sentence.

'The disease has as its headman a virus. This virus has gained access into your body through sexual intercourse and after a spell of incubation, has multiplied and spread to all facets of your body through the body cells. There are militant cells in the body which are constantly waging war against diseases. Unfortunately, yours have been attacked and destroyed by this virus. Consequently, your body has been exposed to a lot of infections, illnesses and cancers, especially kaposi sarcoma which is a rare anaemic infection of the lungs. The presence of the virus also accounts for your chronic diarrhoea, night sweat and severe loss of weight and stubborn swelling of the lymph and glands. Soon, Mr Dika, other infections of the disease will surface. You might have your memory impaired because your brain might be susceptible to damage.'

'So, am I going to die?'

'Well one thing about this infection is that it is incurable.'

'So, I will die?' Dika asked.

'Not really. You need drugs which can hold the virus at bay though the drugs cannot destroy them. AIDS is incurable. The drugs can prolong your life span. But they cost a lot.' The doctor said.

'How long can I live?'

'It is difficult to say. It depends on your system. Some sufferers have had as many as three years but some as few as weeks. In short, I cannot say precisely now.'

'The only help you can render to me now is to give me writing materials. There are people who must hear my story that they may be saved.'

'I am at your disposal, Dika,' the doctor said as he walked away.

'Weeks ran into days and days gave way to hours. The life of Dika, the crown prince went in bits, every minute that passed. His fingers had shrunk and vision blurred. His brain responded to his incoherent heartbeat, worked only when there was mild pounding on his chest and blacked out when the pounding died. The components of his total body system were at loggerheads with one another. Running nose and terrific pain arising from damaged kidney and liver made sleep difficult and life impossible.'

'Jesus Christ!' one of Grace's girls shouted.

'So Dika finally died?' asked another.

'Yes, he died. Dika succumbed to AIDS regardless of his father's wealth. It was too late for him to learn but not for you and me. The essence of this long story which some of you perhaps already know is not to show you the way to heaven but to remind you about the existence of land mines as we live well on earth. The wealth you accumulate or your sacrifices for loved ones at home will be meaningful if you go home alive and healthy. AIDS is incurable. It is not limited to any colour or race. It is among homosexuals and heterosexuals alike. The only way to guard against this scourge is to stay safe. Resist the urge to make money by meeting your clients without condoms. A word is enough for the wise.'

'Thanks, Uncle, for the advice,' responded the girls.

After three days, Grace could not persuade Sam to stay. She packed all the brand new apparels he used in his bag. A taxi arrived and together they went to Turin Porta Nuova station. She went and purchased a return ticket for Sam. Her hands were trembling when she appealed to Sam to accept a gift of five hundred thousand lire. She was very happy when Sam accepted the offer but that was not enough to conceal her disappointment. They waved persistently to each other as the train ran its serpentine course until they were out of sight.

Grace gambled and lost but some of her proposals still lingered. Instead of black women in Turin, Sam targeted black men in Padua and with in-depth knowledge of Naples, he left Padua by a low fare midnight train. He arrived in the morning, shopped for goods from discount stores, made arrangements for future supplies and was ready to return to Padua by the next low fare train. Sam did not need to look beyond his door step for patronage. Nearly ninety per cent of Nigerians in Padua were resident in Via Forcellini 186. Within hours, all the items he put up for sale were gone. Some paid cash instantly. Others promised to pay when they returned from work and they did. Some of his customers started indicating colour preferences or specified sizes and designs. From such people, he insisted on payment upfront and slightly marked-up prices. He ploughed back some of his profits.

Gradually, he started going to Naples every week. It was on one of such trips that he met a lady from Mestrino. They sat inside the same couch from Rome where she boarded till Padua where both of them alighted. Luckily, Sam still had the telephone number of the hostel. In return, she gave him hers before they parted for different destinations. In the evening, Sam was still occupied, recovering debts and delivering special orders when Ivana rang. She had not lost the same sense of humour that made Sam wish to see her again. It was only his concern for callers who would be trying in vain to reach other residents of the hostel that moved him to let her go.

She kept her promise to call again the second day. Three days later, when Sam had sold substantial proportion of his wares and ran less risk in the event of theft, he dumped the remainder into the luggage-room at the train station and visited her. She was near a car park, waiting, when Sam alighted from the Vicenza-bound bus. As she led him hand-in-hand into their premises, she informed him that her parents were racially inclined. 'They are stupid and ignorant. All human beings are the same whether white, black or yellow. Isn't it true, Billy?'

'Yes, the colour of our skin should not subject us to prejudice,' Sam responded.

'Leave everything to me. I will handle it,' she assured.

Her father was sitting outside their home with a coffee table beside him and a glass full of locally brewed wine. Her mother tended flowers in the garden. Her father's face lighted with a smile as if a lost friend was coming home again to roost. The mother headed towards the terrace to welcome Sam.

'Meet my friend, Billy. He is an Americano.' She stated.

It seemed to Sam as if he were stung by a bee. He instantly remembered the story of a person who went about telling young Italian girls that he was an American. One day, at a popular night club in Vicenza, one of the girls met another American who requested to be introduced to him. And this dialogue ensued.

'You are an American, right? I am from Georgia.'

'Oh yes, I am from Canada in America. Happy to meet you, brother,' responded the impostor.

Though Sam knew his geography well and would not be so ignorant to describe Canada as part of the United States, yet he considered it safe, patriotic and wise to be identified as a Nigerian than to parade himself as an American. Ivana's mother came over and embraced him. The father motioned to the chair nearby for Sam. All of them except Ivana who asked to be excused and went into the kitchen, settled for a conversation.

'So, you are an American?' Her mother inquired as if

she did not hear her daughter properly. It was an opportunity to iron things out and save any impending embarrassments.

'I was born there by an American mother and Nigerian father. They are separated. In fact, they were not legally married in the first place. My biological mother was very busy enjoying herself and had no time for me. My father had a lot of it and after his studies, took me along with him. On attaining the age of maturity, I opted for Nigerian citizenship to please my father.'

'I see,' chipped in the father later. 'Now that things are hard in Italy and harder in Nigeria, if I were you, I would have chosen America.'

'You are right. But my choice is one certain way I could reward my father for all his concern for my welfare. If he had abandoned me as my mother did, I won't be alive today. Nigerian citizenship is my cross and I will bear it till the last day of my life.'

'Oh my God,' shouted Ivana's mother. 'You are very intelligent and in charge of your life. Do you hear him Andrea?' She asked her husband.

Their excitement when Sam was introduced as an American had to do with preference but certainly not out of racial prejudice. This Sam discovered by the time the evening ended.

'Ivana, I have noticed that you have been very happy since you started seeing Billy. Your father and I have no objection if you say he suits you,' her mother said after one of Sam's subsequent visits.

'He is exactly what I want, mama.'

'Therefore, I do not want to see Desmond or Solomon here. I do not want a deluge of Fred's telephone calls either,' her mother further requested.

For Sam, Ivana wasn't exactly what he needed. She

had little education and no skill. No income of her own or latitude of freedom as she was provided for by her parents. Her golden blond hair and shapely body had earned her a lot of Italian men. But without the right comportment, the right men fled, leaving behind memories of have-beens. Running out of time in a very conservative society where most relations that culminated in marriage started at infancy and often between families that had enjoyed years of relationship, Ivana went after immigrants but she was indiscriminate about it. By the time she came into Sam's life, she had lost count of how many of them she had befriended. That way, her dotting parents had had to intervene on several occasions to save her from ruin.

Unfortunately, the man she considered right did not see her as appropriate for anything beyond a platonic affair. Sam's chance to quit came on the 13th day of October when Via Forcellini crumbled. Only those who had stay permit and demonstrated they were doing regular work were left behind. No matter how much sustenance one derived from *vu compra* before the law, it was not employment. Only a handful of persons were spared. Ivana went with the tide.

Chapter 4

Victim of Circumstance

Sam telephoned the Gadibas, a couple he had met while doing *vu compra*. They invited him to their home in Ravenna. For weeks they worked on all the contacts known to them. On the fourth week, it paid off. Sam was offered a job by Systems Marketing Srl as a trainee manager. The company was planning to tap the resources of Nigeria's one hundred million population. It jumped at the opportunity of training and appraising a prospective representative before dispatching him to combine ethical marketing with the arm twisting necessary to make it in Nigeria. The firm's personnel director and Sam went to the Foreigners' Office for work permit. He was told by the female head of the office to return to Nigeria and wait until he was sent a letter of invitation to present himself to the Italian embassy in Lagos.

The personnel director thought it was simple. 'I will rather go back and get the letter prepared so that he can travel with it.'

'No,' replied the woman. 'First, advertise the vacancy in any newspaper. If after three months a suitable candidate is not found, you can approach the ministries of internal and external affairs and the labour office who will give you enabling documents to commence overseas job search. Your taxes must be fully paid and the facilities you have for accommodating the employee when he arrives must be inspected and confirmed to be of the same standard available to Italians of equal status.'

'So, there is no way we can get this poor young man to work? I mean, we shall be grateful if you can save us this red tape by issuing him the easier-to-obtain work permit as a rank and file. What matters to us is the knowledge we impart and not the job title,' the personnel director pleaded.

'Absolutely no,' she said. 'Follow the procedure stipulated by the government. It is fair for the employee and safe for you and me. If you are caught for under-employing an immigrant, you will face a serious penalty.'

The Gadibas were ready to provide Sam with the ticket to return to Nigeria but just then, the personnel director called and informed them that his company had backed out. Their reason was simple. They could not foresee any tangible and legitimate cause to turn down thousands of qualified Italians if an advertisement was made and applications began pouring in. The Gadibas were very sad that their efforts had not paid off and that Sam was leaving without any work or home.

'However, I will overcome,' he assured them with a smile as he stepped into the cold street on the 29th of November, 1991.

Geo, Franc and Law were waiting for him outside Ferrara station. Law came down from the passenger seat so that he could enter into the back seat of their BMW coupe where Franc sat. Sam adjusted a bag that stood on his way and settled for a thirty-kilometre drive to his new residence. Geo, behind the wheels, negotiated the bends with one hand and with the other, whipped cigarette ash into a receptacle by his side.

'Please, switch on the heater,' Sam pleaded. Others started laughing.

'It does not function. That's why I'm smoking to keep warm. Do you care for a stick of cigarette?' Geo asked.

It was Sam's turn to laugh. 'There is no proof that cigarette shelters anybody from the harshness of winter.'

They debated the advantages and disadvantages of smoking. Geo, the only smoker among them supported it. At the other end of the spectrum was Franc. He insisted that cigarette companies provided employment to a few compared with those who were disabled or killed by cigarette related diseases. Sam thought health authorities were right to insist on warnings of the dangers on every label. Law thinks people owe themselves a duty and should fulfil it before they expect any obligations from the government. The arguments were genuine but neither side appeared decisive. They were still immersed in it when Geo left Modena Road for a five hundred-metre stretch of untarred road. The car wobbled under the strain of the road's bumpy and wet surface until they arrived at Via Traversi 2. Sam clambered out of the car. Together all of them climbed the staircase to their room. Except for a giant bed and pieces of personal effects, the room was barren. They went into the kitchen and prepared dinner. Sam refrained from asking many questions. There was plenty of time for him to find out everything he needed to know.

When he lay in bed and covered himself with a blanket, there was no doubt in his mind that once again, he had come to a better place. He quickly put at the back of his mind the frustrations he encountered in Ravenna and was still thinking about Efe when he fell asleep.

In the morning, Sam came to appreciate more deeply where he found himself and for years, he remained grateful for the foothold Geo, Franc and Law gave to him where, by a combination of physical combat, manipulation and luck, he found himself in the third vacant room before christmas, free of rent charges.

The house was located nearly three kilometres from the city centre. There were no entrances to block or neighbours to disturb. The nearest signs of life were ceramic industries, seven hundred metres away. It had two duplex flats. Sam was told that the wealthy owner built it for his newly wedded son. His daughter-in-law spent only a few nights there and disliked its isolation. So they moved. Ever since, the owner had been giving it out to immigrants for a modest price. Those characteristics the young woman hated were the ones that endeared the dwelling to the new occupants. Occupying the other flat was a Nigerian couple who did not pose any threat. Sam's hosts shared their own flat with another Nigerian - Tony.

There was no other honest means of survival except *vu compra*. Everywhere, it kept them employed. D. Due Srl which later went bankrupt by mismanagement and bad debts, came from Padua to supply them goods. From there, they went to Carpi, Modena, Reggio Emilia and Bologna. Some outings were good while some were awful. Without a choice they still looked forward to better days. On one occasion, Sam climbed the skyscrapers of Carpi. For three hours, not even a single person had opened his door for him. When he was almost giving up hope, a family opened their doors and cheerfully welcomed him into their home. They offered him food to eat and water to drink. They did not strut about like most persons. They were very humble and soft-spoken and their purchases of thirty thousand lire worth of items, unlocked other flats and wallets. Sam later heard from their neighbours that they were members of the Jehovah's Witness. As if others had been challenged to defend their Catholicism, everybody bought generously. Those who declined to open their doors initially, joined too and before he left that building, his hope for the day had soared.

Only weeks after his arrival, he went into partnership with Tony. At the core of this relationship was a second-hand FIAT 127 which they owned jointly though it was registered with the name of Tony because he had resident permit. With his assistance, Sam opened his first savings account with Banca Popolare dell Emilia. They sent for three other Nigerians from Naples including the younger brother of the man who sheltered him at the collapse of the White House. All of them worked together using the car with Sam as the driver and Tony the guarantor of the credit allowed them by D. Due Srl.

Finale Emilia is a small town. Mail men, gas sellers, motor mechanics, supermarket clerks, and even insurance agents knew them by names. The patrol police could not claim not to have noticed their conspicuous presence. Things went very smoothly.

The only thing that worried him was that Efe had not written him. For months he had made unfruitful efforts to reach her Ikoyi Federal Secretariat office. He had long given up trying to write her with their Ire-Akari Housing Estate address. Could it be that Grace was right when she said that Efe had long given him up for money bags? What really happened to his indomitable Efe, Sam could not imagine. The only persons who could help to find out were the same family members that rejected her. Unsure of the cause of her silence, he did not want them to learn of it before him. Assuming the reason was an awful one, privy to only him, there could be chances of reconciliation and forgiveness. But if it got known to them, managing the damage could be difficult if not impossible. They would laugh at him. They would be very right to have rejected her with impunity. He had not made the fortune for which he left Nigeria. Based on the daily income from *vu compra*, Sam thought he should be able to save some money, cut his trip short and return home in six months.

Meanwhile, there was a university chemistry student whose family lived in Colombaro, near Ferrari plant at Maranello. Her relationship with Sam which transcended buyer-seller relationship was enhanced by her pleasant character and ability to speak a bit of English Language. Sam became so fond of her that when he dropped his friends at Spilamberto, Castelnuovo and Castelvetro, he hurried to be with her for as much as one hour. Often she phoned in the evenings when Sam must have arrived his Via Traversi residence to say good night. One Thursday evening, she called as usual. Towards the end, she told Sam that he was invited to join the family for dinner on Sunday. She also hinted going to a night-club together in future. There was an apparent suggestion of a gradual departure from their platonic relationship to a romantic one. So he really looked forward to the dinner. Sam was filled with joy when two days later, he woke up to a bright Sunday morning. She had not known him for wealth but he decided to appear smart. He scrubbed his car until it was glittering. He washed his clothes until they were sparkling. He did not stop ironing until all the lines were prominent and stiff. There was no more preparation to do. Only time stood between them.

The preceding weeks had witnessed an increasing tension between the couples in the other flat and another couple who were the previous occupants. As it degenerated, Tony was involved. So also another man who lived at Casumaro, a neighbouring town. All of them had resident permits, spoke Italian fluently and had graduated or were studying for various degrees for nearly a decade. They were titans; nobody dared intervene when they clashed. Any of their kinsmen who appeared stubborn easily fell in line when they threatened to invite the police.

That Sunday, 12th of April, started like any other day of badgering. Sam was busy preparing for his date. Unaware of the twist outside. A violent scuffle had resulted in the invitation of the patrol police by their neighbour. The police had arrived before she came up and advised them to run away. With military despatch, the police came after her, moved into all the rooms, searched all the cavities to flush out everybody. Outside, all assembled. Eleven persons comprising residents and guests.

They separated the legal residents from illegal ones, sent a radio message for an additional vehicle and bundled five illegal immigrants to their office. As in most cases, the police did not ask any questions about the mangled doors and shattered windows. The frowning and bruised faces were equally ignored. The warring parties were abandoned to settle their own differences. One of the officers, Christian, took photographs of the five immigrants with an amateur camera inside the commandant's office. The other officer, Emmanuel, assembled materials needed for fingerprinting. More men joined them. They were very shoddy and it reflected on the time it took to complete the exercise.

At about eight o'clock, four hours after the arrest, two police vehicles swept into the barracks at Finale Emilia and scooted them to Mirandola police station like criminals. When they arrived Mirandola where only few officers were on duty, two police men took charge of them at the lobby while they waited for a superior officer who was away. The lobby was barren. Not even a single seat was there for them. The two orderlies rejected their request for chairs which lay vacant inside the waiting room. There was no dinner, not even a slice of bread or a cup of cheap bottled water. The tired and hungry among them sat on the bare floor. The rest stood on their feet with the hope that a superior and humane officer might notice the subtle protest and provide seats.

At midnight, came a rotund man whose Italian language was corrupted by his local dialect. He did not care about those who sat on the floor or those who had been standing since four o'clock. He took the file prepared by the patrol police in Finale Emilia, asked the immigrants a few more questions and started typing their expulsion order. Finished, he went upstairs through the lobby and got the orders signed and stamped. When he returned, he asked them to append their signatures one person after another. The time was two o'clock in the morning, Monday, 13th of April, when every protocol was observed. The expelled immigrants were free to leave the police station into yet another uncertain future.

The police turned down their request for telephone to contact their kinsmen at Via Traversi. They refused to provide them transport or to allow them remain inside the cold lobby till later in the morning when there would be public transport. With assurance rather of having called a taxi for them which was waiting outside, they tricked them out of their premises and slammed their door.

Franc was wearing only a T-shirt. Others had very light dresses which suited the weather when they were taken away from their residence. They did not realize how cold it was until they stepped into the dark and wet city centre. There was nobody at home to take their call. The city centre was desolate. No train. No buses and taxis, absolutely nobody. Their jaws clattered against the cold wind. Their nose dripped and could not be wiped with their frozen and stiff fingers. The cotton shirts tuck to their skins. Hands were sheltered inside pockets, and clasped against their chests that trembled with their hearts as they lurched towards the porch of a shop. The expelled immigrants picked small doormats from nearby shops and sat on them and then heaved the spacious one they found at the shop behind them in the direction of the wind. That way, they subverted its incursion and stayed alive till three hours thirty minutes later when they rose. It was nine-thirty in the morning when the five finally made it back to their residence, hungry, weak, sick and depressed.

Finale Emilia was small unlike Padua or Naples. It could not provide cover for anybody wishing to run away from the law. While the affected persons charted their next course, the Finale Emilia police bombarded them with late night visits. Before the 27th of April, when their fifteen days of grace expired, they made a total of seven visits.

'Boys, do not say that you are unaware of the contents of the expulsion order that had been served you. It is in your interest to pack your bags and leave. Failure to do so will warrant us to escort you to the airport without any further notice.'

They had the resources and authority. A critical assessment of the enthusiasm with which they initiated the expulsion process left no one in doubt about their resolve to pursue it to the end. Something had to be done. One of them who merely visited from Ravenna left. He disclosed that he had never seen a situation where illegal immigrants had been so hunted like a criminal. Oliver, younger brother of Sam's kinsman in Naples, and one other person opted to return to the South. Franc and Sam decided to take refuge at Piazza Terranegra in Padua.

With their fingerprints and expulsion order already in the data bank which was accessible to any police station, their stay depended on luck. Perhaps there would not be time to pick their personal effects or withdraw money from their accounts. Should the dreaded happen, Sam needed a reliable person who would send money to him while in Nigeria. In this regard, he had an account with his kinsman. When Oliver was ready to return to Naples, Sam entrusted one thousand dollars unto him for the contingent account with his brother. The following day, Oliver called to inform Sam that he lost the money to unknown persons.

'Under what circumstances?' Sam cried.

Oliver rambled from one incredible scrap to another. He had not finished piecing together the incoherent account when Sam accused him of ingratitude, betrayal and blatant robbery.

'I spent money and time to transport you to Modena, seven hundred and thirty five kilometres away from the sleazy ghettos of Naples; for nearly one month, I paid for the food you ate and the water you drank; I lost my goodwill with some occupants of Via Traversi to earn you a free accommodation; I sacked very resourceful and hard-working salesmen from my car just to encourage you to struggle for survival as others. You saw what I went through for every lire I had and you know how bleak the future is for me. Nonetheless, you still deem it fit to rob me of my hard-earned one thousand dollars. Oliver, it is over my dead body!'

'Wait, Billy. Excuse me. Cool down, let me explain to

you. I told you sometime ago about one rich Nigerian broad in Naples who had been very elusive. She was right there at Naples station when I landed. She hurled herself at me and said I looked gorgeous. Honestly, Billy, I was overwhelmed by her sudden change of attitude and moreover, I have eyes on her money. She will trust me with a chunk of it if she holds on to her new impression that northern Italy had enriched me. So, I suggested we should go to a restaurant. To mesmerise her, I pretended I did not know which part of my bag I kept the lire needed to settle our bills. In the process, I exposed the dollars with me. From there, she took me to her house for the first time. She responded to every advance I made. Boy, it was at the peak of the affair, that another woman came and demanded her rent. Believe me, she started shedding tears. She was without a dime. Before I realised it, I had given out five hundred dollars to the woman. I made love to her only once. When her excuses could not stop me from asking for more, she said some sticks of cigarette would be necessary to rekindle her zeal. She was tired to go out so I went with my bag still in her house. When I returned, I was puzzled by the haste with which she tidied everywhere. "What happened?" I asked her. She told me that her Italian boyfriend sent a message that he was on his way. She said he is violent and carried guns. She took me to a hotel, requested three days of lodging for her and me and promised to be back as soon as her Italian boyfriend departed. Billy, I could not bear it after the first night. Without any telephone in their house, the only means of contacting her was a visit. I rang the doorbell. Some other lady whom I had not seen before shouted from the window of the fifth floor of their six-storey building that she had gone out and left a message that I should stay till four days when she would be back.

After the third day, a staff of the hotel came into my room and said, perhaps I would like to extend my stay. I said yes, and reached for my bag to pay the equivalent in dollars. The remaining five hundred dollars was gone. I cannot say categorically whether I lost the money in the hotel or in the lady's house.'

'Oliver, I am not interested in this palaver. Deliver my money to your brother and I am coming to ensure that this is done immediately,' Sam banged the telephone.

Oliver's brother was indoors with his girlfriend whom he later married when Sam walked into their Naples residence. Sam had not said anything when the man disclosed that Oliver had already reported to him the loss of Sam's money to thieves aboard a train.

'Do you believe this story?' Sam snorted.

'Billy, my dear, I did not accompany him so I cannot find any other plausible explanation.'

'Well, Oliver knows what he did with my money. I would not have spent more money coming here if I am not determined to recover it from him before going back. When you welcomed me into your house and cared for me, I did not rob you. To reciprocate your kind gestures, I had taken him into my life. I have suffered inconveniences and made sacrifices. But I will tell him that this is the last time he will do that to anybody. I am leaving immediately to look for him. I will either come with my money or you should be prepared to arrange for the transportation of our corpses to Nigeria.'

'Billy, if I were you, I would not react differently. Accept it if I say that his story is believable. You know what efforts I have made to help Oliver. He has continued to be a disappointment to me. However, I beg you to give him time to restore the money. I guarantee that he will pay and if he defaults, hold me responsible.'

The fiancee promised that she would see to it that her fiance kept his promise. A few months later, Oliver fled Italy. Nearly a year later, his brother reneged on his promise to pay and his fiancee did nothing.

Sam used the visit to Naples as an opportunity to assess the prospects of returning to reside there again. Anambra ghetto had replaced the shelter provided by the White House and it was flourishing. The faces of the occupants were strange. The few he spoke with lamented the dearth of work. However, some of them were hopeful that with the advent of spring and summer right on its heels, every cloud had a silver lining. They were right. The peak period for farm-work was a short distance away. Like most ghettos, the environment was dirty and infested with flies. Water was very scarce. Only those who could reach Mama's former house could be sure of enough water. Whatever the promises summer held, in the ghetto, Sam looked like a stranger. It was not for him again, he vowed.

On his way back, he met Sandra. She worked as a cleaner with Ferrovie dell Stato. She was two years younger than Sam. Her physique was stunning and epitomised the devotion with which God created the Italian woman. She dropped out of secondary school and had no vocational training. She did not inherit anything from her father whom she remembered with spite. She knew Italy's billionaires by their first names and their life history though she had not met all of them before. She was one chick that loved affluence and was bold to say so. She held unto her cleaning job as a drowning person would grip a straw to remain afloat while she shoved her exquisite frame from one corner to another hoping that it would land her the big one.

It was another case of misfortune when she met Sam.

He told her he was working as a truck driver.

'What a tedious job! They don't have time for their families. I do not like it," she protested.

'But I do not have a family to miss. Even if I stay in Germany or France for weeks, does it make any difference? I will always come home to meet a lonely house.'

'So, you are free?'

'I hate to say it. I am not married.'

'What is the big deal about it?'

'I hate to say I am not married because I saw the best woman whom any husband could be sure of when I could not afford ordinary food for a household let alone rents. Hence she left, perhaps into the kitty of the rich and corrupt who are responsible for my woes. Now, things are improving but good girls don't exist any more. Or could you be the reincarnate of my lost love?' Sandra smiled. 'Do I look like her?'

'Yes, Sandra. Your curled hair, large eyeballs... leave me wondering if you are not her twin.'

'Is that so?' She giggled like a child.

'I am sure of what I missed. I am aware of what I am seeing. But it is too early to rejoice until I travel to your heart. If beneath this ravishing body, exist congeniality, warmth and freshness, nobody could be luckier than you and me. I will create an indelible mark in your life.'

Sam visited her house twice. On the third occasion, when the end of his fifteen days of grace drew closer, he told her the truth. 'Sandy, I am a truck driver in the figurative sense. A truck driver moves about from one city to another. His vehicle is his house. If it collapses in transit, all those things he cherishes in this world go down with it. He has people who love and care for him. It is because of them he chooses to stay away and it is for the same people still that he misses home. It is necessary that I tell you the truth."

'So what are you?'

'I am a star which cannot twinkle in the sky. I am an eagle which cannot fly because its wings have been clipped with steel. I am well armed to conquer the future but until then, I belong to the present and I am nothing.'

'I beg your pardon?'

'I am a graduate, a doctor if I were an Italian. I am hard-working and determined to succeed. Since two years I have been here as an illegal immigrant. Securing a job is impossible. I have had opportunities to deal in hard drugs, make it or go to jail. But I have resisted the temptations and settled for *vu compra*. The income has not been great but it has been better than nothing. I would not have bothered to tell you if after two visits I considered this affair a fleeting one. You are sweet and earned my confidence and affection in a short time. But if you want to throw me away like shit, I won't blame you. Only few women have the patience for a poor, tomorrow-may-be-better man. If you accept me today, I will utilise every available opportunity to make you proud in future.'

'Billy, before I met you, it had never crossed my mind that I would someday sleep with a black man. And all my prayers had been to have a wealthy man who can spoil me with luxuries. But all these transformed into fantasies when I met you. I have had brief affairs with rich and powerful men. Truly, it was with you I fully felt happy. I won't leave you, Billy. True.'

She might have stayed but Sam was already in troubled waters and she lacked the maturity and resources to rescue him. While he battled with his impending move from Finale Emilia to Padua and the spate of problems created by his new nomadic life, he had less time for her. Her patience and zeal became strained too. Gradually the relationship fizzled out.

On the eve of 27th of April, 1992, Sam packed his belongings into his car and was almost in tears when he entered the main road. If it were before, the Concordia and Panaro ceramic industries, a few metres away would have reminded him that he was arriving home. On that day, they seemed to have felt his anguish. There was neither the smoking furnaces nor the movement of night workers. Neither the wind nor the birds broke the atmosphere of stillness and gloom. If nobody missed him, nature did.

Chapter 5

Terranegra Indeed

Centuries ago when sub-Saharan Africans were confined to the safety of their forest region and when the various republics that made up today's Italy were on the heels of Christopher Columbus to the new world, not Africa, a town square had been named a black land. Whatever inspired the name could not have been more meaningful than what had actually become of the piazza and its environs today. Sam joined Trunk Road A13 in Ferrara and driving at sixty kilometres per hour, headed to the same square that had provided refuge to the homeless and hungry. For the squatters, piazza Terranegra and Via Forcellini were different but inseparable. Though the hostel had long been relieved of occupants whose stay in Italy were illegal, yet it remained the only address for them to receive letters from their families and friends in Africa and all over the world.

Police in Marche, Umbria, Toscana and Emilia Romagna knew well that almost every illegal immigrant on foot with bags of wares dangling on his shoulder came from there. Food vendors still brought food there every evening except Sundays. At night, the legal occupants smuggled out plastic bottles of water with which their illegal kinsmen stood at the dark corners of the building to wash with. That way, the hostel was still an integral part of their daily lives. The difference came when darkness descended and the glass doors of the former elementary school were shut or on Sundays when everybody was resting.

Piazza Terranegra was about five hundred metres from the hostel. There were two bars. While the clients of one bar were mainly blacks, whites constituted a greater proportion of the clients of the other. Apartheid, you would say. But it is not. The other attended to every one regardless of race or social status. The immigrants' preference for Paolo's bar was not accidental. The proprietor was knowledgeable in customer psychology, armed with a great acumen and patience. He spoke English language and mimicked a number of Nigerian languages particularly Igbo. He stocked items which met the unique needs of the immigrants and not only what he found convenient to sell. He took into cognisance their cultural background. He attended the weddings of some Nigerians and was always there when they mourned dead colleagues. His bar was available for meetings of town or cultural associations. He did everything to attract black immigrants and more to retain their patronage.

On a typical summer Sunday, nearly two hundred of the immigrants, legal or illegal could be at Terranegra. It was an occasion to initiate new relations, renew lost contacts, and rekindle sagging ones. For some people, it was an opportunity to relax after a week of tension and work. Many others used the chance to buy shoes, dresses, food items and drinks that didn't exist or were rare in local shops. Buyers were as many as sellers. To them, it was their own day of work. When the festivities of the day were over, there were people who stayed behind, night after night.

They slept in cars and buses anchored at various corners of the piazza. They stocked them with everything they needed on a daily basis. Sam still had his dual purpose FIAT 127. Of all the persons who begged to share the sleeping spaces with him, there was only one whom he preferred more than others because he did not snore or make the type of noise that could make sleep hard for him.

They rose every morning for the station to clean their mouths, use the toilets and wash their bodies. When they became too many for available facilities at the station, and travellers were kept waiting for minutes, the staff of Ferrovia physically barred them from using their facilities.

The station piazza was their next destination. Between seven and ten o'clock in the morning, serious trading activities took place. Manufacturers, suppliers and agents brought pants, stockings, handkerchiefs, medical plasters, toiletries and many other items. They bargained hard and finally paid cash or promised to pay at the end of the day. Food vendors and immigrants enjoyed a symbiotic relationship. None existed without the other.

With their stomachs and bags loaded with food and goods respectively, they trooped out by buses, cars or train to work. Sam used his car and, unlike in Finale Emilia, worked alone. He operated an independent account but the proceeds were nothing compared with when he was in Finale Emilia. Going back to Nigeria in the immediate future became increasingly uncertain.

From Terranegra, he forayed into the green hills of Vicenza. When he allowed it to lie fallow, Rovigo became a substitute. Not because of its economic strength but rather because of the activities of its police. A lot of colleagues had either lost their wares to or been fingerprinted by the police and served with expulsion orders. Consequently, many of them had fled from there. Others thought the zeal with which the police implemented the law in Rovigo created business opportunity for those who could dare them. Sam went there because for weeks or even months, he had worked without any events. On the few occasions that he came face to face with the patrol police, he was simply advised not to make trouble or fight whoever did not want to buy. Good times, like bad times, were not forever.

One afternoon, after trekking from nine in the morning till one-thirty in the afternoon without any encouraging result, he retired to his car to rest for a couple of hours. Not long after, Alesandro and Ugo swooped on him. The former was robust, already balding and twenty-three years old. The latter was slim, tall, handsome, innocent-looking and only nineteen. While Alesandro searched Sam's car, Ugo stood battle-ready. Satisfied there were no items of interest, Alesandro began to interrogate him. Sam raised his head and saw that Ugo's gun had been lowered. Sam explained the hardship besieging him and begged them to see with him as many of their colleagues did. Sam's plea fell on deaf ears. They collected his driver's license and took him to their station. The commandant, Brigadier Vitale reflected the mood of his boys. Regardless of Sam's appeal, he sent him away with a written invitation to appear again the following day. There was no written declaration that he withheld Sam's license. Aware of the consequences of driving without a declaration, Sam refused to vacate his office until the officer wrote one for him.

The following day, Sam returned, homeless, emaciated and nostalgic. With his morale at its lowest ebb, it would not have mattered to him if he were escorted to the airport with a flight ticket from the state. Otherwise, no illegal immigrant with claims to mental sanity and emotional serenity would deliberately walk into the lion's den which Rovigo Foreigners' Office by then symbolized.

Inside his car, there were fine pairs of trousers and shoes to change into and some money tucked away in one of the dresses should they decide to do their worst. The brigadier handed him to the Foreigners' Office and left. Ugo, who accompanied the brigadier, did not leave until he had shot a glance that tinged with apology and friendship. He and Sam did not say anything to each other but Sam grinned to assure him that he understood what happened. He had simply executed the job assigned to him. And in Sam, there was no animosity against Ugo.

The much dreaded female commander of the Foreigners' Office travelled. Her subordinates took charge. Sam was taken upstairs and fingerprinted with an efficiency and precision induced by skill and constant practice. Finally, his license was released to him with a letter of invitation to the office after one week. Normally, such letters were destroyed promptly. It was horrible to be associated with one not honoured. However, Sam intended to keep the appointment. Since his sack from Finale Emilia, life had never been the same. He had had it very rough but drug dealing or trading in women did not still appeal to him.

Some time in May, a few weeks after their departure from Via Traversi, the squatters at Terranegra were awoken by a dozen or so supposedly well meaning police. They went from one bus or car to another and gathered them together before an elderly plain-clothed police chief. From the White House to the hostel, it had never taken arrests to evict squatters so they trusted and waited to be addressed by the man whose demeanour was fatherly. Alas, they had been tricked. Seconds later, a battalion of officers surrounded them. Others positioned themselves at strategic places.

Instantly, except one person who was regular and let off the hook, they were hurled into vans and taken to the provincial police headquarters.

The lack of decorum in dealing with Sam and his compatriots was not strange. So it did not matter that for hours, they were left standing inside the lobby. More so, when those who had money could buy coffee, tea, milk and snacks from an automatic vending machine to fend off hunger and tiredness. It took the callousness of a superior officer to enrage them. He ordered the five hefty recruits and corporals who guarded them to deny them further access to the machine. Among the immigrants, two or three enlightened minds put heads together. In a muffled tone, using pidgin English, the consciousness of the timid and indifferent was quickly aroused to the unfairness of the directive. What would have been a confrontation with the police was averted by the dynamic and ebullient president of the Nigerian Community, Bob Okoye. After meetings with various police chiefs, he came and delivered an eloquent and soothing speech.

'Securing your freedom to work honestly for what to eat, unmolested by anybody has been paramount on my mind. I may not alone and instantly convince the authorities to issue you work permit. But I have consulted the relevant officers and have been assured that so far as you conduct yourselves peacefully and steer clear of criminal activities, the police will turn a blind eye to your illegal status. Denial of hungry and tired imprisoned illegal immigrants access to a food vending machine does not deserve to be taken lightly. It is inhuman. Believe me, it is the decision of only one or few persons. And, of course, you should not expect all Italians to be comfortable with your presence in their midst. However, I want you to know that there are more persons

162

in this office whose love and sympathy for us are more obvious and must be cultivated. In this light, do not resort to physical confrontation or squabbling with people who lack the authority to change your fate.'

'Why can't we deal with the bastard now so that next time he will not treat his fellow human beings like animals?' shouted some people.

'Is this the way Italians in Nigeria are being treated?' asked others.

The president replied, 'All your questions are pertinent. Your situation has been my concern too. That is why I scrambled from bed to come here as soon as I was informed of your arrest. It is in pursuit of the answers to these questions that agitate your minds that I have been into every office that matters since I came. I crave your indulgence to leave and trust me with obtaining redress using diplomatic means at the decision-making level of the Foreigners' Office. Finally, submit yourselves to be fingerprinted, not for the purpose of deportation but identification. Afterwards, you will be free to go and buy delicious food from your favourite food sellers. There is practically nothing I can do without your support. Heed my advice so that all of us shall be around to continue the struggle.'

From that moment, the detained illegal immigrants started cooperating with the police. True to the president's word, every person who was fingerprinted was free to depart. Sam drove to the station, passing through Terranegra where the arrests were made six hours earlier. There were practically no blacks at the station. Everybody had gone into hiding until the fate of their arrested colleagues was known.

The encounter had hardly subsided when the police struck again at Terranegra, two weeks later. Early risers had seen them, twice more than the previous number, fully combat-ready. Commotion ensued. People ran helter-skelter in search of safety. They were pursued and apprehended, some bleeding, others bruised, all of them gasping for breath. Nobody was physically assaulted but the drive and professionalism with which the police plucked them out of their holes coupled with the contortions of their faces, left no doubt on their minds that they would be bundled to Nigeria.

Once again, the presence of the Nigerian Community president comforted them. Though he would not stop police resolve to deport them, yet with him, a very good legal battle or horse trading was certain. They believed that somehow, he could save them from the brink of danger and he did. After high level consultations, those who had been fingerprinted before were set free. Then others went through the ritual one after the other.

The funereal atmosphere that befell Terranegra two weeks earlier intensified. That evening, few persons came to roost. The population decreased further the following day. The exodus did not stop until fear coupled with impending winter drove the last squatters out. Some left for filling stations on the trunk road. Others located to new hideouts at public parks. Many found refuge by the banks of a canal. The incessant police raid on Terranegra marked a new dimension in the life of the average black immigrant. The quest for flats and other basic amenities was deep. A trend that continued till today.

Temporarily, Sam sought a parking space for his car at the premises of a building occupied by three Nigerians at Via Italo Bordin, Cadoneghe. What it involved appeared simple to him: he arrived when it was very dark and flattened the seats of his car to sleep. In the morning, he waited until there were signs of life inside the house before he went in to wash his face, mouth and left without any other obligations on the occupants. Unknown to him, what appeared simple was indeed a burden on the residents. Two days later, one of the three occupants accosted him at the door and blasted his presence in their compound.

'Do not ever come here again,' he warned.

Sam was short of words. His fingers quivered with embarrassment.

'I'm sorry,' he said.

The other occupants whom he had known from Naples and who granted his request to stay in their premises were in their rooms. They did not come out. Many days after his disappearance, they did not ask what happened when he saw them. As Sam entered his car and drove away, his eyes were for the first time full of tears. 'Life has messed me up. Perhaps, I had made a mistake to have ignored the offers made by Simon on my first day or Grace not quite long ago,' he murmured to himself.

Sometimes free or at others for a fee, the few legal immigrants contracted houses from landlords on behalf of the illegal ones. With six or more persons in a three bedroom flat for instance, money could still be saved at the end of the month. The colleagues with resident permits were also handy for effecting change of ownership of cars. Gradually, more business activities sprang up. From hawking foodstuff, cosmetics, shoes, dresses at Terranegra on Sundays, supermarkets, restaurants, bars, beauty salon and boutique were located near the train station. Shops that competed with and eventually supplanted D. Due Srl were either owned wholly by Africans or jointly with Italians. From the same Terranegra rose people who afforded posh cars and cellular phones, whose determination and drive to succeed economically, attracted male-hounding females from Rome, Naples, Genoa, Milan, Florence, Turin and Mantua. They came in large numbers that later, they were as many as the males.

People who moved to other cities soon returned. *Vu compra* was their main stay. It provided them employment, income and independence but it would never have been so without the black man's piazza, indeed, without the understanding of the people of Padua and the police who preferred *vu compra* hustling immigrants to drug peddling ones. Sam's encounter with the police in Rovigo was on the heels of the turmoil in Terranegra. Three days to the appointment with them in Rovigo, somebody brought two letters recovered from a heap of abandoned mails at Via Forcellini 186. One was from his parents, the other from Celestine, his schoolmate.

His parents expressed their gratitude for his contributions to the upliftment of the family. They informed him that his younger ones were doing well in the university and requested money to enable them prosecute some projects. Celestine in his letter, made a graphic representation of the state of decay of public institutions at home. Life and property were not safe. As if that was not enough, he hinted that he would be without a job soon.

Celestine was the luckiest of the 1986 set. The bank where he served as a national youth corps member retained him. After two years, he rose to the rank of a manager. The banking and oil sectors were the two most formidable guarantors of employment. But recently, most banks had been eroded like houses built on sand, Celestine noted. Too many unsecured credits were granted to dubious businessmen who used them to acquire wives and concubines or vanished with them into the thin air. His colleagues had earlier been relieved of their appointments. He was assigned to the debt recovery unit for only half of his basic pay. The future was uncertain. His plight was further aggravated by the birth of his first child. He envied and considered Sam lucky to have left the shores of Nigeria early.

The contents of these letters reflected the prevailing views of overseas by people at home. There was no story Sam could spin to convince them that the views were erroneous. Before morning, he had resolved to persevere. He mapped out new strategies and tore into shreds the appointment with the police. He never stepped into their area of command again. With the increase in the immigrants' incomes came changes in tastes. They went for fashionable reptile skin shoes and belts. With a little amount of money, Sam visited an importer friend in Caserta, bought some shoes which he sold as soon as he displayed them at Terranegra. The margin was encouraging. He went for more. Eventually, he shoved aside *vu compra* and devoted more time to attending to the luxuries of his trendy colleagues.

On one of his trips to Caserta, he visited his kinsman. Sam was unsuspecting when the man asked him the price at which he was supplied shoes. Sam told him. He also answered that he was making quite enough to warrant the effort. However, when the man went further to request that his wife should be supplying shoes to him, Sam found himself suspended between the deep blue sea and the sky. It was difficult to break up with an existing supplier whose performance rating was superb, who had confidence in him to the extent he was given credit facilities, and ready to replace unsold stock. This was somebody with whom he practised wheeling and dealing. On the other hand, it was difficult to say no to the man who sheltered him when he needed one most or whom he trusted with part of his savings.

Dealing with his kinsman would be like fighting with his hands tied behind him. But on a second thought, he left the man to hijack his business. The wife's first supply was good for the cost price. The second was different. Until then it would not have crossed Sam's mind that his kinsman could brazenly exploit his respect and regard for him. The colours of the shoes were drab and in absolute violation of Sam's specifications. The prices were marked-up by twenty per cent without any prior notice. Sam found himself in a tight corner. He complained about the colours and the cost price. To the first, his kinsman, not his wife replied, 'Another dealer who came earlier and paid cash selected thirty pairs.' To the second protest he answered, 'The rising cost of British pounds sterling has made these items very expensive in London. I think your profit margin is enough to absorb the increase or you can push up your selling price.'

Sam knew his rights and obligations as a buyer but while he strained to save their relationship, the man had a field day talking tough. He paid one third of the cost and reached an agreement with him that unsold ones would be returned for replacement, that was the only concession he made. He did not go down on the prices. Sam remembered his previous supplier with nostalgia. She would not have tried such cut-throat business practices. There was the impression that a good salesman could sell even a dead body. Sam canvassed, cut prices, fell on towering goodwill and yet less than one third of the shoes were sold. In violation of their agreement, and in furtherance of his stance, the unsold supplies were rejected for replacement.

'Do whatever you can to sell them. It is your business

and not mine, let me tell you,' his kinsman said coldly.

The shoes were still in the boot of his car without any hope of recouping cost plus expenses when the man gave him deadline to pay for the outstanding cost of the shoes.

'But the shoes are still in the boot of my car,' Sam lamented.

'Well, you should better consider your three thousand dollars in my custody gone. I cannot wait indefinitely for you.'

As if that was not enough, he reneged on his pledge to pay should his younger brother fail to restitute Sam's one thousand dollars.

'But this is contrary to your pledge when your brother was still in Italy?' Sam reminded him.

'It is not binding on me or my wife. You can send your family in Nigeria to go for your money. I have no obligations to you.'

That was how those Sam trusted most liquidated his business and kept him longer in Italy, six thousand kilometres away, from Efe. That was how lack of resident permit subjected him to the whims and caprices of heartless men. The era of doubt and low morale had gone. Sam had vowed not to give in to odds and handicaps. He had sold his FIAT 127 and bought a trendier and bigger Alfa Arna. He returned to *vu compra* stronger than before. In addition to himself, he got four of his friends on board. They sold and received commission. They were doing what he did with Moses two years earlier. The difference was that Moses used a bus while he used a car and sold too. Modena and Rovigo were no-go areas for him. With his friends, he went to Ascoli Piceno, Macerata, Ancona and Pesaro.

They were often away from Padua for three or fours days after which they returned to replenish their stock or worked locally for the rest of the week. When duty took them to Grosseto, Pisa or Florence, they were away from Tuesday till Saturday evening. There were shops in Prato where they replenished their stocks and continued from there to Bologna. Sam was cost conscious and result oriented like an astute businessman. They travelled all night at the beginning of the week to the farthest of their zones of work for the week and wound up at a location near Padua on Saturdays when they were exhausted and their bodies ached. The routing was planned to eliminate expensive and unproductive movements.

These were not the only considerations. Certain zones were juicy and irresistible but risky. The commanding police was known for wicked, inhuman and frustrating tendencies towards them. They were inclined to the confiscation of wares, cars or imposition of heavy fines and even seizure of cash found on illegal immigrants. Saturdays were ideal for such zones. By then, stocks had depleted and revenue remitted to Padua through the post office. The risk was minimum.

Their meals alternated between purchases from supermarkets in the mornings and food well prepared by inexpensive restaurants at the end of the day. Restaurateurs who were used to them would acknowledge that their orders were a deviation from what obtained in their restaurants. It was Sam's task to negotiate with the managers. Even before such managers suggested it, Sam would say that it was okay if all of them were cramped at one table instead of two or three. Disposable paper napkins were preferable and only water was served. To be apt, they went for whatever cost less.

In exchange for these austerity measures, Sam insisted that the quantity of spaghetti or macaroni should be large and that tomato sauce must be abundant. Big bottles of beer purchased cheaply from supermarkets and hidden inside Sam's car constituted their appetiser before the meal and the right liquid afterwards to wash it down. Only those who met their demand for large quantity of food saw them again. Those who went further to combine quantity and quality occupied unique places in history.

There was only one occasion the team slept inside a hostel. It belonged to the Catholic Church in San Sepolcro, province of Arezzo. For only ten thousand lire a person, they were allowed lodging and very big and nutritious meal. They kept to themselves so much that they were surprised when one month later, the management could not accept any group from Padua. The cost of checking into a pension elsewhere was too much for them. Again, they did not have the necessary documents stipulated by law for admission into any hotel. Therefore, whether it was winter, summer, spring or autumn, Sam's car provided them shelter until they returned to Padua. Not every spot was suitable for parking. They found filling stations most favourable. There were toilets for personal administration and bars for breakfast in the morning. However, it must be the type that operated twenty-four hours and whose manager or proprietor was sympathetic to their plight and courageous to hold at bay night patrolling police. Sometimes, such places were many kilometres away from their destinations the next day.

Experience had shown Sam that police could work twenty-four hours to combat crimes but less urgent cases like the menacing *vu compra* immigrants were kept till eight o'clock in the morning. The police erected road-blocks and scouted for dusty old cars with non-indigenous registration numbers and with foreigners as passengers.

To elude them, the team woke up early and passed such road-blocks before control resumed. Sam's ability to stay out of debt at a time others were falling into one trouble after another was to him not a thing to be proud of. By dint of hard work and ingenuity, he transformed *vu compra* into a dependable source of income. However, it was a pittance to what he symbolised. A man might be good in more than one thing but his satisfaction would be total if he is tested in that area of his expertise, otherwise he would continue to grumble even when his modest achievement was already the envy of those around him.

In Italy, he was decaying intellectually until Clara Springer came into his life and provided the tonic to the contents of his grey matter. She was on tour of Naples when they met in 1991. When she returned to London, she began to write him. Even when Sam's family delayed for months or when his friends swayed to tight schedule, Clara was always there with weekly letters that probed his intelligence and challenged his first class education. These verses captured Sam's gratitude for what Clara represented.

> Spring
> Magical liquid mountains emit
> Meander rock cavities searching for exit
> Wailing with rage eventually explodes
> Like urine from virgin holes
> Spring
> Fishes from detractors know no other gap
> Flocks to quench their thirst lap
> Weary shepherds hurry with hands cupped
> Before bottlers who get your beauty tapped
> Spring
> Glad I have found you
> Your fountain I crave to drink from too
> My own spring please grant

To satisfy my ravenous thirst
Your beauty preserved in my cyst
With faithfulness wholesome and gratitude grand

Unfortunately, to drink from her fountain would never be. Sam was a destitute immigrant when she requested to visit during the summer of 1992. He discouraged her. The same period in 1993, she invited him to London. Unknown to her, Sam could not move about freely within the territory of Italy let alone go to London. He could not encourage her to come. The image of Efe loomed like a shadow. Until he was sure of what became of her, there would be no other rival. Clara embodied characteristics that any man could fall head over heels in love with. She was special in her own way. To remain himself, he needed to stay physically severed from her.

Sam lost his Alfa Arna to a patrol police command on the hills bordering Rieti, Macerata and Perugia. The commandant could be only a few years older than Sam. To address him as father was improper. Otherwise, Sam pleaded in the name of God and his son Jesus Christ. When that tactics seemed to inflame rather than appease him, Sam called him *mio amico*, *mio fratello* and even *mio cugino* to no avail. When Sam tried to explain that no license to undertake *vu compra* could be obtained without first obtaining a permit to live in Italy, the officer barked, 'Then go back to your country and don't let me see you again.'

Helpless, Sam grudgingly appended his signature to the paper before him and walked away. Two weeks later, he replaced it with another car. With minimum maintenance cost, he had started saving again. He kept a date with December.

The morning of Tuesday, 30th of November, 1993,

started like any other one. Sam went to the train station piazza where goods for *vu compra* were on sale. He assembled enough goods to last his team for four days and commenced recording what his friends put in their bags. Suddenly, the regional patrol police swooped on the piazza. All his friends fled abandoning hundreds of goods to the care of the risk bearer. He stood beside his goods which were scattered on the ground. The police confiscated almost everything. About ten persons were taken to their office along Via Cavalleto in Prato della Vale, properly identified and slammed with fines ranging from one million to one million and five hundred thousand lire for transacting commercial activities at unauthorised places.

Among those fined was a lady who had a resident permit and was merely passing-by at the time of the arrests. She was in no way part of the commercial activities and was not associated with any confiscated wares. Through an English language speaking officer the lady tried to explain her position to the man who commanded the operation but he replied, 'You should go and say that to the Mayor. He ordered for this operation and only he can change this decision.'

Once again the authorities preferred to impoverish illegal immigrants as a practical and more effective way of warning them of illegal conduct of *vu compra* or occupation of public places.

Sam was still feeling the pains of the seizure when the world moved into the new year.

1994, for him, was different. He did not make any clear resolution. He got into it like a rudderless ship, tossed about by waves, desirous of reaching safely ashore but having no command about when or how. His anxiety and frustrations gradually gave way to anger and finally indifference. He called Grace but one of her former girls told him that she had gone finally to Nigeria. She fell for a man who promised to marry her. The man appeared so genuine that she gave him fifteen thousand dollars to travel to Germany and buy a fine car for their wedding. She informed her family and the date for their traditional wedding was scheduled. While she waited anxiously, news reached her that the man was hobnobbing with women in Palermo. The man did not know that Grace had got wind of his escapade when he rang from Germany and requested another fifteen thousand dollars to be able to buy a brand new Mercedes Benz.

'You son of a bitch! Better bring back my money before I lose my temper on you,' rumbled Grace.

'Why this outburst Grace? Are you changing your mind about the car?'

'Yes. Just bring back my money intact.'

'But I have already paid it to a car dealer who has started fitting the car with burglary proof and remote control mechanisms.'

'You are a liar and a swindler. I am not interested in who is staying with you in Palermo. You are free to do whatever you like so far you return by the next available train and give me my money.'

For minutes, the man remained dumbfounded. Eventually, he recovered to shock Grace the more.

'I did not really intend to go to Palermo. I missed my flight and took the opportunity to visit my auntie's sister. While I was here, I received a telegram from my mother. My father died last week and as the first son, I was supposed to give him a befitting burial so I remitted five thousand dollars to them. I am sorry, Grace, but I will endeavour to make up the difference before I travel to Germany.'

'I am not interested in all these cock and bull stories

and ...'

Grace could not complete what she was saying when there seemed to be a struggle at the other end of the telephone followed by a feminine voice which pummelled her mercilessly.

'Ugly and shameless old woman, you heard that your father-in-law died and instead of anguish and tears, you have the temerity to insult my cousin for ordinary fifteen thousand dollars. Let me tell you, he is not cheap. If you think that you could lure him into marriage with scrappy fifteen thousand dollars, you are crazy. You know he is young enough to be your son. You have tasted him and seen that he is full of vitality. You are wrong to assume you are the only woman who wants his hands in marriage. Right here now, there are two young girls who can do anything to have him. I do not want to be unfair to an old woman so that people will not be unfair to me when I get old. Give me a call, I am Alice, when you have forty thousand dollars to get him back or keep your bloody money and give him up as a bad debt.'

Disgraced and heartbroken by a former motor-park tout who could neither read nor write, she packed her things and left Italy forever. Sam was sympathetic towards her and thought she was smart to have returned to Nigeria. She had the proper profile to fit into the Nigerian society again. He wished he knew his fate with Efe. Perhaps, she might not have gone through the humiliation. She might have gotten from him what remained to crown all her efforts, a man to call her own and to father her children.

'Uncle, when are you coming to visit us?' asked her former girl with a voice laden with suspicion.

'I do not know. I wish Grace was around. I will tell you when next I call. Pass my greetings to others.'

Sam did not go or call again till date. With news of Grace's departure, Sam became suddenly scared. 'Assuming Efe has gone... to marry a stranger, in fact, an untested woman would be difficult,' he thought. The next person would have been Clara. But from the beginning, he had been stunned by the rate of divorce in Europe. The Igbo man in Europe won't go through that type of experience without getting seared. Sam's parents, for example, had lived together for decades. They had had their bad times. They reconciled. They had their good times and it had never been an opportunity to see how inferior or deficient the other partner was. They teamed up and saw Sam and his siblings through childhood. As the search for a better living standard took him beyond the frontiers of his hamlet, he came face to face with the agonies of children whose parents parted ways and concluded there could not have been a better legacy parents could bequeath to their children than the belief in the sanctity and permanency of a happy marriage.

Above all, Nigeria was Sam's greatest love. The leadership formulated policies that deprived him of the opportunity to grow. His resources, just like that of most ordinary people were wasted. Nonetheless, it was the country of his birth. Whatever his achievements in Europe would be meaningless unless he reunited with his roots. His vision has remote chances of being transformed to reality, and even at that, would not alter the European landscape. It is in his native Nigeria that his vision would be meaningfully put to the test.

Getting more intimate with Clara and eventually marrying her would impede the mission to Africa. In his own opinion, it would be difficult for a woman born into comfort and all the security that goes with it to abandon them for a journey to Africa. Unsure of Efe, with Grace gone and scared of walking to the altar with a stranger, Sam started wondering if he had not made a grave mistake to have shunned the overtures of Clara. More so when she claimed to be adventurous and full of curiosity, qualities that would have enabled her blend into African way of life. While Sam was lost in his own quandary, Clara woke him up one Sunday morning and told him she was at Heathrow airport.

'What are you doing there by this time?'

'Lewis is arriving from New York. I am waiting to receive him. I am so happy, Sam.'

'Who is Lewis and what is he to you?'

'Oh, Sam, I did not want to fool myself. I had waited to be very sure before telling you. Lewis met me while I was on vacation in Cuba. He said he loved me and wanted to marry me. I told him we could have fun and return to our respective countries after the holiday. But he followed me to London instead and only agreed to go home after I had promised to give his proposal a serious thought. From New York, he called me almost every night. Sam, I was overwhelmed with the torrent of attention. I have accepted his proposal. He is coming to take me with him to the United States. I have cross-checked the manifest; he is listed. He is on board Sam. Oh, Sam, I am excited. It is now that I realize how badly I had wanted to leave London. It bores me. I cannot wait to see new places, meet new faces and confront new challenges.'

'I am very happy for you Clara and sad for myself.'

'Yes, I guess you will miss my frequent letters and calls... But I assure you I won't forget you. I will always write you.'

'Thank you but even a thousand letters a day and a

hotline between our houses won't be enough to blot the despair at the loss of you. It was only last night I made up my mind to tell you that I would like to marry you.'

'Do you mean it?'

'Yes, I do.'

'Please, Sam... you make me sad now. I thought you were going to tell me years ago. Saaam!'

'Don't be sad, Clara. There is no blame for you. It was my fault. I procrastinated until my proposal was overtaken by events. Bear in mind the love I feel for you and my wishes of good luck and prosperity always. Life is not a bed of roses. Do not presume that it will be sweet always with Lewis. There will be ups and downs. Remember that Sam will be glad to hear that together with Lewis you overcome bad times; that you did not throw in the towel. No matter where the tide carries me, I will be there always if you need my help. May the love of God see you through. I want you to know that these wishes come from Africa, a place where the beauty of nature has not been plundered or tainted by industrial waste; a place where the chord between God and mankind is still very strong.'

'That does not relieve me either. Sam, I miss you. Maybe you would have decided earlier if I had put more pressure on you. I regret I did not. I thank you for all your kindness; for all the joy you brought to me when I was depressed. I share your dreams for your country. I wish there could be more gems like you. No matter the setbacks, do not give up your ideals, they endear you to me and based upon that, you are destined to alleviate the sufferings of your people and alter the years of mismanagement. It would interest you to know that my father-in-law to be is a senior senator. Lewis is a chip off the old block. I think he and I can make it to Washington like his father. A vantage position to lend an embattled idealist a helping hand. Your friendship is forever, Sam.'

Clara got Lewis to speak with Sam from the airport.

'I have read your poem to Clara. It sounds great,' Lewis said.

'We hope to see very soon.'

They had written regularly and would not accept his refusal to attend their wedding in 1995 until he told them that he had no resident permit in Italy and so could not obtain enabling visa to the United States.

Sam's brief affairs which blossomed in 1994 had actually started in 1993 when he was mesmerised by the beauty and reserve of Nora. Her father died when they were still infants, leaving the mother with the onerous task of raising eight children by herself. She was the first child and started dating men at the age of fourteen. Though Nora's mother did not give her any word of encouragement, yet she never cared to know the source of money with which Nora bought dresses for herself and supplemented what her mother could scrape together for food. Her mother did not conceal her gratitude and before long, Nora went for multiple, wealthier and older men. For telling him about herself with frankness he had never witnessed, he fell for her.

Among her clients was an importer of cars. He took her to Germany, France, Japan and Sweden. She would have been satisfied with the mogul's trickle of favours if she had not run into a woman in Lagos.

'He takes you to places most girls enslave themselves to go. You return with crappy shoes and tawdry dresses and a little stipend to keep you perpetually dependent on him. He moved you into a flat at the outskirts of Lagos, vows to strangle you if he catches you with another man.

But every night, he leaves you alone and joins his wife and children. He adores his family and won't ruin it because of you. Yet you dare not mention that you would wish to be like him someday, with a man and children you can call yours without being thrown out of his life poorer than when you met him. Do not be under any illusion about love. He has none for you. He is exploiting you. It is not his fault. It is yours. You watch your youthfulness wasted. By the time your breasts sag and your skin shrinks, he will cast you out for younger girls. I was like you many years ago. I thought it would be sunny always. That is why I am suffering today. Your sugar-daddy pays me generously for washing and setting your hair, I will be guilty if I don't give you this piece of advice. In return for the pleasure he derives from ruining your future, I want you to go for something that will help you go through the long and rough road ahead. A lot of rich bachelors prefer well-educated and homely women. A woman's money is not an attraction to them. So, count them out as targets. You would be left with only the wretched ones who cannot afford three square meals or a flat for you. However, if you make hay while the sun shines, you can continue without any hindrance to your flamboyant life-style. A bit of your wealth extended to your wretched man ties him to your apron string forever. So, it is your responsibility to decide for yourself now.'

Nora thanked her for the advice and left. It took many more months before she acted. The previous time they went to Holland, the man made a tour of the red light districts of Rotterdam. Nora had earlier concluded that it would not matter to her if she formally hawked herself for money to help her family. But she was appalled by the way human beings were displayed inside glass closets. Men moved from one closet to another, appraising legs, waists, breasts and heights while the occupants grinned and wriggled suggestively. If the prospective client eventually decided on which caged ware to buy, he went to the brothel manager and paid. Apart from the tips he might give, the woman depended solely on her share of the payment. More disgusting to Nora however was not really the debasement of womanhood but the risk of being inspected by somebody well-known to her at home. When she heard that prostitution was not organised in Italy, she prayed for an opportunity to go there. Her chance came when they were in transit in Rome en route to Holland. She sneaked out of their hotel and went for good. The mogul woke up to find a note which informed him that she had gone into the Italian 'jungle'.

Ten years had passed since many of her younger brothers and sisters had been seen through school. Those who opted to go into trading had been firmly established after years of apprenticeship. She had bought an apartment for her family and a car for her mother. She had changed the miserable standard of living of her family but regretted the road she took to achieve that aim. Nora further held Sam captive.

She was very prayerful and attended church service every Sunday at the Basilica of Saint Anthony and recited her rosary everyday. Fasting was an unsurpassable means for her to ask for favours from God. She was a good cook, and neat. She neither smoked nor drank alcohol. She liked a good laugh without being noisy. She was a bit reserved. When Sam was not at home alone with her, she devoured gossip magazines. Sam gradually started seeing her as somebody who could be a wife someday. Her resolve to abandon prostitution and commit herself to a better-or-worse marriage had not been tested.

1994 was more fateful than the previous years. The

patrol police at San Severino, a small community between Castel Raimondo and Tolentino in the province of Macerata confiscated his goods. Within the same period, he also lost some to municipal police at Pievepelago, a hilly community ninety-five kilometres from the provincial capital, Modena.

The spate of misfortunes reached its climax when an oncoming vehicle collided head-on with his car in October. His car was damaged beyond repair. He had broken limbs and was hospitalised for months. One of his friends who was slashed by shattered glasses, bled profusely and required emergency surgery.

Before Sam was wheeled to the theatre, he telephoned Nora to inform her of the accident. In her absence, he left a message with her flatmate. It took her two days to get to the hospital. But as soon as she arrived, her presence made a great difference. Nurses and people who volunteered to assist hospital patients gave way. She took over. She fed, cleaned and played with him. She stayed awake to ensure that the ice water bags, pillows and other props were in place. Very little sleep crossed her eyes on the chair as she constantly kept vigil over him. He quickly forgot her initial delay in coming to the hospital. He felt more affection and indebtedness towards her. With his limbs still in casts, he was unimpressed if not shocked when two days later, Nora packed her things to return to her house.

'If you are afraid of losing your job, maybe I can tell your employer. I need you. Without my parents, sisters or brothers in this country, I guess the hospital would not have discharged me if I had not told them that you are my fiancee and would care for me.'

'Perhaps, I forgot to tell you. I do not work with that family anymore. I resigned two weeks ago.'

'Why? Two good weeks. What happened Nora?'

'I could not take their insults anymore. It was too much for me, so, I left.'

'So, you have gone back on the streets!' Sam cried. With one of his crutches he hit her. 'How can I explain this tragedy to Reverend Father Cuomo who got you that job and saw to it that you were issued a work permit. How dare you do this to me and expect me to marry you!' He was almost in tears.

'I can as well tell you that you are wasting my time. After one year, you can not claim that you are still trying me. We come from the same ethnic group and you understand our traditions. If you are serious, instruct your parents to go and see my family. If you are not, well, there are a thousand and one men who are ready to marry me immediately. If you need me to stay around your sick bed and be bruised by your crutches, make a move.'

She stormed out and went home. And for two weeks, despite Sam's telephone calls, she did not come back nor return the calls to ask how he was coping. Sam was devastated. His temperature skyrocketed. The pain from his fractures heightened. To prevent heat from gangrening his injuries, he swallowed more antibiotics. Afraid that he would never wake up anymore, he resisted the urge to swallow tranquillisers too.

One morning, nine months later, he did not know what came over him. From nowhere came courage to accept that the affair was over. To lock in on that development Sam started to write to let her know.

Ever since the debacle, I have thought about you
without ceasing. The only time I have been free from
this torture has been in my miserable sleep. Even
then, dreams of you mar it and waken me, hence I

would be consumed in my thoughts again, to be terminated by another bout of sleep. As I bow my bloody head to write, I cannot hold back the tears which well in my eyes from rolling down my cheeks and staining these pads. Tears of anguish and defeat in a battle in which victory seemed available for me to grab. Tears for all my love and concern for your welfare. I am reeling in pains today like any betrayed lover. Often I wish most past evil and deceitful incidents can be reversed. Not because I derive pleasure from humiliation and pain but because of the opportunity it grants to soothe my agony. However, I know they won't be. You have gone, abandoning me to be consoled by the Almighty God. Nevertheless, those on whose lips falsehood runs like a river or in whose hearts wickedness and treachery dwell like an evergreen, misery and betrayal shall overtake them.

Chapter 6

Embattled without Respite

All the residents of the White House had only one postal address. It belonged to Mama. The letters were put inside one basket free for all the residents of the White House to check through. Because none of Sam's friends – Cento, Richard or Louis knew his real name, no one could retrieve his letters. They often joked about seeing him reading letters without seeing when he received them. Efe did not know Sam changed his name to Billy as soon as he entered Italy. There were some individuals in the Nigerian postal system whose policy was to hijack overseas mails for reasons known to them. So from the beginning, Sam's deluge of letters did not reach her. Only a few did. Her replies were very slow. They took months to arrive Italy. He decided to see if the telephone could help bridge the communication gap. Efe heard about the cost and protested vehemently. 'We need the money, Sam. Write me instead. Three letters posted at an interval of two days, hopefully, whoever steals the letters will be away on any of the days.'

The device had its setbacks. Sometimes, she received two or three letters that contained basically the same theme. At other times, the flow of information was slow because of loss of letters in transit. Nonetheless, the hit-or-miss patchwork kept the two lovers in touch for eight months. It was in pursuit of the same goal of keeping her informed that Sam described the things he was going through without holding back anything. Efe wept. Not because the six months deadline would not be realistic but because survival had been such an uphill task for them. Sam knew it was not the best thing to tell her but he guessed it would be the worst thing to keep away from her.

Efe was sent to a firm of computer technologists in Enugu with some other secretaries for computer training in office administration. Two months later, they returned. Immediately, Efe was deployed to Abuja, the new Federal Capital of Nigeria and was there for six months. Communication collapsed completely. The ministry's telephone through which Sam called her in the past had broken down and had not been repaired for one year. By then, Efe had left. On the other hand, Sam had been sacked from the White House and relieved of his employment in Naples. Then came the last straw that broke the camel's back. Mama had moved with her soft drink business to another town.

Her life in Lagos which took a new turn when Sam departed remained the same on her return from the rocky new federal capital territory. She spent more time with her ailing mother and occasionally returned to their Ire-Akari Housing Estate, to the very room which accommodated Sam's belongings and still smelled of his fragrance and bore evidence of the good times they had together.

Ministerial job lost its boredom and monotony when she was charged with opening electronic files for documents that dated back to decades and which took a chunk of floor space. At first, installing the operating system required constant reference to the installation disc. When writing file and paging became difficult, she was forced to start the installation afresh. Some of the documents to be filled were either incomplete or illegible. The task was difficult and progress slow much more by constant power failure that wiped away from the hard disc yet-to-be saved data. But Efe was undaunted. Sometimes, she worked an hour or two after others had gone. She cherished it. It engaged her fully and made waiting for Sam bearable. The autonomy given to her to transform the system alone coupled with the increase in her salary and prospects for promotion in future were delightful.

Her father who had been awaiting trial in Kirikiri Maximum Security Prison started losing weight. He thought it was a result of his recent loss of appetite and increased his consumption of food. Soon, he experienced excruciating pain in the bones followed by fatigue and problems with urinating. He was taken to the hospital, given some analgesics, multi-vitamins, antibiotics and sedatives. Two weeks later, though he could urinate with relative ease, the pain elsewhere had not declined and his weight loss continued. A doctor recommended a check-up.

His son, a medical doctor, was invited to the university hospital where he was on admission. Father and son met after nearly three years. Prison guards were everywhere. They listened to their conversation and hushed them when it became emotional or when they flouted the rules and used native language.

His son demanded a PSA test. It was done and the score was well over 24. A biopsy confirmed the old man had prostrate cancer and it had degenerated. He was not taken back to the prisons. Within weeks, his prostrate enlarged so much that passing urine became very difficult. His condition was not the type that could be operated and there was not the money to apply the only likely treatment of blocking male hormone function responsible for stimulating the growth of the prostrate with estrogen infusions, to be followed by injection of anti-coagulants to avoid blood clots. His life could not be prolonged.

He was released from jail when all that was left for him was a few painful weeks. He was released to go home and die. The gloomy atmosphere that set in did not lift until his death one month later and years afterwards. His wife, son, daughter and daughter-in-law surrounded his death bed. He struggled to make himself heard. He spoke to his son.

'I, your father, am not a criminal. I am innocent of all the allegations against me. I have served my country with all my heart. I am simply a pawn in a dubious socio-political agenda. Cancer did not kill me. Incarceration did. I die today happy that I have robbed neither my country nor neighbours. I do not stand the judgement of man anymore. I stand before He who knows what my mouth has not uttered. He from whom nothing is concealed. And this is what I charge you to tell the world. The mission is over. Awaiting me is the love of God which nobody can deny me. Take care of your mother and Efe. Live in peace with your wife as I lived with your mother. Teach your children the right morals when they are young so that they will not stray into darkness when they grow. Keep the light shining.'

Efe was already in tears when her father finished with her brother. He beckoned to her. She sat on the bed with his hands on her laps which he tried to raise to console her but they were very feeble. He exhorted her with more effort.

'Tell Sam, my son, that I love him and wish him God's blessings. I am sad he is not with me now. It is not easy for him. Let him not despair. The darkest hour comes before dawn. To you, my dear daughter, do not be swayed by the difficult times ahead.' He paused for a very long time. The pangs of pain were immense. His eyes rolled backward. He recovered to conclude.

'This house will someday be for you and Sam. I have kept another one in Ikeja for your brother and...' A spasm of pain shook his body. The women burst out in tears. He never recovered. He passed away at the age of sixty-eight. His remains were conveyed to Benin for burial. While his son returned after two weeks, the women remained until the end of the one month compulsory traditional period of mourning. Thieves broke into their Ire-Akari home while they were away, and carted away electronic gadgets, jewellery and expensive apparels. Efe returned to work in black mourning dresses which she wore for six months before it was removed and burnt according to their custom during a ceremony that brought her mourning to an end. In her desperation to contact Sam; to share her agonies with him and to let off the steam that was tearing her tender heart, she wrote him a detailed and emotional letter even though her previous attempts did not yield any response.

Her work at the ministry remained at the core of her resilience. There were times when official red-tape or corruption delayed payment of workers' salaries. At such times, workers in the public service stayed away from their duties and engaged themselves in other activities that would fetch immediate cash for their families. Efe was different. Boredom, redundancy, lateness to or early departure from office were not for her. She was so busy that she hardly knew when each day came to an end. She planned her finances prudently so that the effects of delay in payment of salaries were cushioned. She was highly motivated.

There was no gainsaying the fact that Efe enjoyed her job.

Soon she secured a job with a prosperous indigenous firm of architects, planners and builders with head office in Racecourse on the Lagos Island. Though she had not had post qualification cognate experience, yet her knowledge of computing was more than a compensation. Later, she competed vigorously with senior partners in the application of Graphic User Interface to her designs at a time other architects and engineers had not touched a keyboard. But she did not leave the ministry without reasonable notice. It took her three months to give her replacement the much needed induction course.

Efe was the only professional female employee, the other woman worked as a typist, receptionist, messenger and cleaner. She served tea, took dresses to dry cleaners, paid telephone and electricity bills. She addressed all the architects and engineers by their first names. To some, she was too warm and to others, she was too cold for a healthy official relationship. Nobody was complaining. It did not concern Efe either. Her job specifications were clear.

Soon, the other woman started seeing her as a rival. Efe became one of those who should be snubbed and hated. All her colleagues, single and married, started admiring Efe. The junior partners went underground for safety, leaving the rich and powerful senior partners to sort things out themselves. They told her how great she looked, rambled in and out of her office, bought her expensive gifts which she politely but firmly rejected, offered to be transporting her to and from work daily. When these approaches did not prove effective, they suggested that she should visit their homes for dinner with their families. Others exploited every opportunity to narrate with a gauntlet of innuendoes the stories of Nigerian women whose hearts had been broken by their fiances abroad.

The other woman was annoyed that the whole focus was on Efe. But Efe considered the episodes sexual harassment and loathsome. She neither succumbed to them nor allowed herself to be demoralised. Sam's photographs stood constantly on her drawing board. She came to work in long skirt suits or gowns whose sleeves were lengthy. She avoided personal conversations or gestures that could be misconstrued. The job was interesting but she was having a terrible time coping with sexual harassment. One of the harassers told her she possessed the attributes common with the senior partners. He thought the sky was her limit. The only problem was that she did not understand, and did not want to play her cards well. He promised her a superb performance appraisal.

'I do not know how to do anything else for advancement on my job apart from working to the best of my ability. If it is enough to earn me the praise of my superiors, promotion and salary increment, fine. If it does not, that means my performance is either below expectation or is not good. If I merit any benefits, I think this organisation will give it to me as it gave to my male counterparts,' replied Efe.

'There you go wrong again. If you keep waiting until somebody points at you and says you deserve it, you may be stuck to your present position forever. Use what you have to get what you want.'

The torture reached its crescendo when the other lady proceeded on annual leave. Efe helped with typing and tidying the office occasionally. Every morning, she prepared and served tea to everybody. One day, she went into her boss' office to retrieve empty cups. He rose from his chair and advanced towards Efe. He stopped abruptly when his eyes met her fiery looks.

'What is it?' she asked.

'I...I...I... am sorry if I embarrass you but you look sweet and I think somebody like you can make a perfect wife.' He forced a grin but his fingers were quivering with nervousness.

'Listen sir, you are married with children. Your wife has lived with you for three decades. If after so long she does not make an ideal wife, a lady the age of one of your daughters who works in your office, cannot. It is natural for a man to admire good things but it is evil for him to use his official position to compel his female subordinate to do his bidding against her wish. I did not come to this firm in search of a husband or a man to sleep with. I deserve every penny paid to me. I am here as an architect and I want to be treated as such. I wish you can as well tell your men that I do not only feel embarrassed but sexually harassed by their behaviour.'

'I am sorry, Efe. It is okay. I like your courage and still believe that lucky is he whom you have sworn to love and live with. I am surprised that there is yet a Nigerian woman to whom money and power do not sway,' he said and retreated to his seat, wiping away sweat from his face.

Efe kept to herself, neither keeping intimate male nor female friends. Her only confidant was her mother to whom she complained about her experiences working with men.

'Don't they see single women? Can't they leave a married woman alone?' her mother wondered.

Efe was grateful for her concern but was frustrated by her inability to see the overtures as harassment. There was a lady who worked on the Island too and who had ridden on the same bus with her from Western Avenue to Racecourse for so long that they had become acquaintances.

'She belongs to my generation and unlike my mother, she would understand my problems,' Efe thought.

One day, Efe tried to get a bit intimate with her.

'It seems you work at Tafawa Balewa Square?'

'Yes. I work with a travel agency as a ticketing clerk. And you?'

'I am an architect with a group of consultants, planners, builders and engineers.'

'Mmm... that sounds very interesting. I have seen very few female architects and I am sure you are the darling of your male colleagues.'

'I like my job but I feel embarrassed and harassed by the men. Everybody wants to befriend me or take me to bed. I ...'

'My sister, you are lucky. I am not surprised nonetheless. You have a very elegant frame. I doubt if there is any man who would see you and won't look your direction a second time. I wish I were as beautiful as you are. I graduated with honours in Biology three years ago. I know how many men who slept with me, with promise of job offer. None of them delivered. Except my present director, I would still have been roaming the streets and falling for bogus employers. My only headache now is my immediate boss. I am at his beck and call. I won't worry if it is limited to my official hours. But recently, he has always encroached on my weekends. I have a fiance and he is threatening to abandon me. I have explained my plight to my boss but he won't take it. He threatens to fire me any day I turn him down. My friend, I do not want to lose this job or ruin my marriage either. I have decided to go to my director at our headquarters, and see...'

'This is a clear case of sexual harassment.'

'Who cares about sexual harassment in this country?

194

Of course, neither the harasser nor the harassed. It is one of those western imports that would not survive the odds. Personally, I do not mind so far as it earns me commensurate reward. True. My grouse with my boss is that he has the authority to discipline or sack but none to promote or increase salary. I must go and see the director. If I were you, I will cooperate and obtain what I need. What does it cost after all, just a few minutes or at worst a night with the right superior to advance and grow on one's job with the speed of a gazelle. My sister, you are wasting your chances. Believe me.'

Efe was feeling very sad and disappointed when she alighted from the bus and said good-bye to the other lady. She was undaunted in her resolve to stand firm against abuse and exploitation.

One day away from the memorial service of the death of her father, her mother sent for her and her brother with his family.

The following day, a church service was conducted at St. Dominic's Catholic Church Yaba. Her mother's eyes were sunken. She told her grandchildren stories and played with them.

'There is one member of the family who is not here. I wish he was with us today. By the time he returns, a lot of water must have passed under the bridge,' the woman said with a frown.

Efe thought that the most terrible thing that occurred in the absence of Sam was the death of her father. There was no way she would have known that more terrible things were yet to happen.

'Didn't daddy implore you to tell him? That would be your duty mum when he returns. I won't know how to start telling him that the man he loves like his own father has passed away.'

Efe's mother changed the topic. Everybody, especially the children were merry throughout the evening. She went to bed in high spirits.

The first person who alerted the household was one of her grandchildren. The little girl went to Efe and complained. 'Auntie, I have greeted granny. She did not respond,' the girl started sobbing.

'Do not worry,' said Efe. 'She is asleep. If she wakes up she will respond.'

'No, auntie,' the girl persisted. 'She does not love me anymore. I shook her and shouted. She does not love me anymore.'

'All right, let us go and see her. She loves you believe me. Mummy loves all of us.'

She took the girl by the hand and went into her mother's bedroom. Granny had died of heart attack. The family went into mourning again. More than anybody else, Efe missed her mother. The loss left a vacuum which could not be filled. The Surulere residence was locked up. Efe searched for what to hold on to in order to avoid being tossed about by waves. An opportunity came when her brother left for Saudi Arabia where he secured a new job as a medical doctor. Her brother's wife provided the much needed company on Saturdays and Sundays.

Among the clients of the firm where she worked was a very prosperous young man. He was once a business associate of Benson's. Endowed with a better foresight, he invested in banking, real estate, stocks and bonds. He also obtained a license to market petroleum products. He was fond of carrying cartons of currency notes in the boot of his cars. On approaching crowds of people or market places, he ordered his drivers or escorts to bring out the cartons. With the straps removed, he started to scatter the notes far away from his human wall of bodyguards. He relished with pleasure as people trampled on one another to scramble for the currency notes. He was always at any public function that involved donations so far as the organisers were patient with his flamboyance. He had a knack for turning traditional weddings and burial ceremonies into money spraying events.

Outside public glare, his wretched relations could not squeeze even a dime from him and were regarded as a disgrace if they participated in the public scramble for money. The man was literate and dashing too. He could have any woman just with the snap of his gold-studded fingers. His request for the design of a mansion was handled by senior architects and supervised by the most senior partner. Efe was assigned to use the computer to design a befitting landscape. With a new software produced and marketed by an American company, it required a continuous simulation of various layouts and patterns until an optimum mix was achieved. Sometimes, what the designer considered as beautiful might end up in the dustbin of the client. Efe was simply lucky that the client was very impressed by her work. To further demonstrate his feelings, he breached official protocol, walked into her office to thank her. That would not have been very suspicious if he had not gone as far as showing his appreciation by offering Efe the sum of five thousand naira.

'I thank you for your compliment but I do not deserve so much money when the design was a group effort. I am paid to do this job. Even then, I think it is the senior partners who pieced beauty, practicality and cost together that deserve all the respect and the gift, maybe.'

The man was shocked but not discouraged. He said

that he would like her to supervise the construction project.

Again Efe replied, 'I am not a building engineer. But if my employer wants me to oversee the architectural aspect of the project, he will discuss it with me and prepare me because I have not handled such a project alone before.'

'Do you mind if I call you tomorrow?' he pleaded.

'Well, if my boss trusts my competence to discuss with you. I will be glad to welcome you.'

Two days later, the man called to invite her to his office.

'Do you want to see me in the office at Ilupeju Industrial Estate or the other office on Victoria Island? Though I would have preferred to host you in my Allen Avenue palace or fly with you east of the River Niger to my mansion in Owerri from where we shall attend the anniversary celebration of my conferment with the Igwe title by the traditional ruler of Amamiri.'

'Excuse me, is my boss aware you are having a problem with the design?'

'It is nothing to do with my building project. There is a personal matter I want to discuss with you.'

'Can you let me know what it is now? Since recently, I have been very busy at home preparing for the membership examination of the Institute of Town and Regional Planners that I do not even have any time for myself. Perhaps we can save each other some inconveniences.'

'Since I met you Efe, I have had problems sleeping. You are a different woman, much different from what I have been seeing. I want to marry you immediately.'

Efe inhaled heavily, and slowly she picked her words as if a mistake could cost her the whole world.

'Thank you for the proposal. I think no woman would have it from you without counting herself extremely lucky. I would have been glad to give you a trial. Incidentally, I gave out my love to a man nearly ten years ago when we were still on campus. Presently, he is outside this country, toiling to save enough for me and our children. He has preserved himself for me. He writes me everyday and tells me how much he misses me. My parents were aware and approved of him when they were alive. I won't let him down. He is returning soon. I am already gone. I have taken time to make this explanation to you so that my decline will not be seen as playing hard-to-get. Once again, thank you very much but please, forget me.'

The man went through Efe's boss to no avail. He located her aunts who lived at Agege with their families. Securing their consent to persuade Efe was one thing, succeeding with her was another. Like other efforts before that, it was abortive. However, through them, the man learnt that Sam had not written for five years.

'How can a very intelligent woman like you be so dumb? It is fantastic that a man who, perhaps, has died in the hands of mafia drug lords or languishing in jail exerts so much influence on you, slowly and irretrievably wastes the bloom of your youth and beauty. You are under a spell, no doubt and God has sent me to redeem you. I won't...'

'Who told you this bullshit by the way?' Efe interrupted him. 'He went to Italy because he could not rob himself to affluence like others in Nigeria. It was our initiative. It was indeed for me that he could be in jail or killed. I do not have the conscience of sluts to deny him and cannot tolerate a situation whereby a man, no matter his accomplishments in life, says sleazy things about him. Maybe, now you will understand why he is precious to me. He cannot be saying such dirty things to another man's fiancee. He cannot describe an affection that has lasted longer than a decade as fetish. And let me tell you, I will either marry him or spend my life his widow.'

'Supposing he is married?'

'It is none of your business and please do not call me again.' Efe banged the telephone.

He swore to marry Efe by hook or crook.

Efe was going through a period of depression and it reflected on her job. When her work was not shoddy it was tardy. She became touchy too. She lost the psychological equilibrium with which she had managed her relationship with her abusive colleagues and jealous office clerk.

Her boss called her and compelled her to resign or be fired. The senior partners thought she would beg for leniency but she did not. Within minutes, she tendered her resignation and headed to a miserable home and turbulent future. The leasehold of their Ire-Akari Housing Estate residence paid by her father became due for renewal. Her brother's wife and kids had joined him in Saudi Arabia. Without a job, she could not undertake the lease so she moved into her family's Surulere residence. The place she shared with Sam; the place where her parents lived.

Sam had gone very far away beyond her imagination. Her parents had died there. All the good times that she had had in that house had been shrouded by gloom. It was her fortress when Sam left her for Italy and her father was in jail and later died. It had become the only place in the world she could call hers, the only place she would not be told to give up Sam in return for love and kindness.

She stayed indoors. Sam's photographs were everywhere in that house. She read his five-year old letters more than three times daily and kept some in her handbag. One of it was a letter he wrote to her in December 1990.

My beloved Efe,
It seems three weeks of my life have been lost.
It has been three weeks since I read from you last.
I have dropped twelve letters in the post office for you,
hoping that it will yield a solution to this woe.

This night, I return to sleep in my dunghill;
after spending all day thinking about how wonderful you have been.
Up the hill stood bandits ready to kill;
or take you away in my presence still.
Resolved as I have never ever been;
began the bloodiest battle not for silver or gold
but that together with you I must go.
Tripped one off the cliff, the other to his death, I strangled.
To the valley, the last enemy and I fell.
The just must triumph. You, I rose to tell
as I looked at the enemy on the ground mangled.

The fall had severed us far apart;
but your tears from the peak touched my heart.
It is a hair-raising dream I have gone through.
I won't sleep again until I tell you.

Against those wont to destroy, be on your guard.
I am a marching carcass when you are gored.
Unless you hear that I am dead,
bear in mind that I live for you as I said.

Gradually, her savings depleted. She was not interested in looking for a job. Age was not on her side but she believed in the theme of that letter. She avoided any street where men who admired her lived. One weekend, her two aunts came with another woman, Madam Angela. The aunts told her that in the absence of her parents, they were the same though she might be more educated than they were. The young mogul had paid them generously to come and talk to Efe for him.

'He is an Igbo man like Samuel, handsome, very rich and generous. He has everything. Many women in this country will do anything under the sun to be married to somebody like him. Our family will not be poor again if we have a son-in-law like him. I wish your parents are alive. They cannot watch you waste this opportunity for a wretch who has since forgotten you. Please, Efe, we have come to tell you that the days when love was blind are gone.'

'Auntie, Sam is my husband. He has not forgotten me and will be back. He will be back soon and if you see me in his arms, you won't need to be told that it is there that I belong. If I had wanted to leave him, that would have been five years ago when unknown to you, one of the heirs to the most powerful aristocratic families in Nigeria fell head over heels in love with me. Sam is my own share of men. It is not his fault that he was not born with a silver spoon in his mouth. Let us try to be a bit reasonable.'

'We are surprised that despite your education and natural intelligence, you still want us to come out openly with the truth about Samuel. Look at this woman,' one of her aunts pointed at Madam Angela. 'She lives in Italy. She has a small scale business and is very popular there. The last time she returned, we begged her to find out what happened to Sam. Within days, she located his house. Please, my sister can you explain the investigation,' said the woman to Madam Angela.

'Efe, my daughter, I do not like meddling in people's personal affairs but the tears of your aunts touched me the previous time I was in Nigeria for business. I know Sam very well. He used to associate with other Nigerians until four years ago when he started dating one Italian girl who comes from a wealthy family. Years ago, they got married. He has two children now and has even acquired Italian citizenship. You could not have obtained a degree in architecture if you were not good in arithmetic. See if this statistic corresponds with the last time he wrote to you. It was not his fault. You should not have left such a man to travel without any voodoo assurance that he would return to you.'

'Do not expect that of me. This is a christian family. Everything is in the hands of God,' Efe said feebly.

To drive her message home, the woman brought out her residence permit and showed Efe. 'Can you read the local authority that issued it?'

'Naples,' Efe replied.

'Good,' one of the aunts interjected. 'Maybe, you can now believe what we are telling you.'

'My daughter,' Madam Angela continued, 'I live overseas with men like Sam and, I understand them more than somebody who has not crossed the frontiers of Lagos before. He had problems actually like other illegal immigrants. His case was unique because it did not take women long to notice that he is attractive. It is unfortunate that you bear the brunt of this development but I do not think that any reasonable person would blame him.' She looked at Efe's face and saw that her story was yielding the desired impact. She continued, 'Had it been they had not gone to Switzerland on holiday, I would have photographed him with his family. Ah, Sam knows me well and like other Nigerian kids, calls me mummy. I think he was on vacation with his family somewhere in Africa, Kenya, to be precise, at the time your father died. If you still want to wait for him, it is your business. I have done my best.'

The pain and shame was too much for her to bear. Efe broke down and cried. The aunts shot glances of triumph at each other.

Madam Angela consoled her. 'My daughter, I will advise you to listen to your aunts. They are the only people you have in this world now. It is quite disheartening that Samuel abandoned you despite all your family did for him. I think it is the will of God. He has blessed you with a successful man; somebody who will wipe your tears away.'

Amid tears Efe protested, 'I am not interested in him or people like him. I want a man in whose life I will mean a lot because we toiled and made it together and have mutual respect for each other. I have spent all my affections and hopes on Sam. I cannot love any man anymore.'

'Who is talking about love these days? Accept to be his wife, have his children and enjoy all the good things wealth can afford. Is there any other thing about love and marriage?' Asked Madam Angela.

'My own opinion about marriage is different. Tell that man to look for somebody else. I need time to decide If I will marry again or not.'

'He telephoned your office and was informed by your former colleagues that you have resigned. Thoughtfully, he came to our Agege residence and left the sum of twenty thousand naira for you. I think that will go a long way in cushioning the effect of unemployment. He also pleaded that you call any of his houses to tell him what type of car you want him to buy for you from Sweden for your next birthday. Great. Isn't it?' disclosed one of her elated aunts.

'Please, return his money to him. I do not need him. I do not need his money. Without my parents and deserted by Sam, I have no birthday to celebrate. He has money.

He is handsome. But there is something about his character that I will continue to find repellent. Tell him to give his car to someone else. And for God's sake, do not accept anything from him on my behalf. If he must continue to visit your homes, do not come to my late father's house again.'

'But you need money?' retorted the other aunt.

'Yes, but not his. Not even a dime from him.'

'Soon your savings will be exhausted and you will be in a mess. Our friend has promised to help assemble your travel documents and offer you a job in one of her companies in Naples. If you won't marry the oil mogul or look for another job in Nigeria, you cannot have anything against this proposal,' her aunts stated.

'Give me time to reflect on it. Maybe later in the morning I will tell you my mind,' Efe promised as all the women retired to bed.

Madam Angela fulfilled her promise. With only Efe's international passport, she left for Victoria Island, Lagos, where most embassies were located. By the time she came back, there were visiting visas to France and Holland inside Efe's passport. 'Italians are always stubborn,' she told her. 'They could not grant my request for a work visa. However, I managed to secure a transit visa for two days for you. That will enable me to contact my lawyer and regularise you for the job.'

'Thank you, Ma,' Efe said.

'The money it has cost me to get you across is enough for five persons. It does not matter. I have no doubt you will repay me promptly.'

'I will, Ma. I am very grateful.'

'See you again on Friday. I will leave immediately for Ufeke-Mbede to ensure that the other persons I want to help are well equipped for the trip.'

'Are they travelling with us?'

'No. I told you that it is expensive. I will procure their passage through Eastern Europe.'

'Do not forget you have not given me my passport yet.'

'Oh yeah. I know. I will use it to confirm our ticket for Friday's flight. I will bring it with me on Friday.'

Murtala Mohammed International Airport evoked bitter memories. It had been nearly six years since Efe came there to bid farewell to her heartthrob. She had come again to set off from there to Italy to face the fact that Sam jettisoned her for an Italian woman as a relief from the burdens of illegal residence. Her aunts were there. She had made spare keys of her Surulere residence and given them.

'Do not disappoint us, Efe. You know the difficult times confronting all of us here. Please, do not go there to waste your time on a good-for-nothing Sam. We admire your courage to embark on this journey and to rule him out of your life. Our daughters are watching. Inspire them by striving to make money which is badly needed in this country. Set aside your education for now. Respect Madam Angela. She is your boss. Once again, do not let us down. Good luck,' pleaded the eldest of the aunts.

'Thank you, auntie, for everything. I will do my best to accomplish it. God will do the rest.'

Chapter 7

Grateful for Self, Solicitous for Others

One weekend in October 1995, Sam called Idowu, Joe, Obanye, Ethel, Philip, Roland, Eddie, Mag, Ikuku and Chris, past and present members of his work force who had become his personal friends and told them that it was high time he left the stage. He lamented that he came into Italy as a nobody and would leave as one. Since 1990, hopes for resident permit had been dashed one after another. Illegality had left him with no opportunity to manoeuvre himself into the professional cadre of the society. It had robbed him of every form of contact with Efe and loss of money and wares at the hands of law enforcement agents. Moreover, it denied him a wider latitude of choice and subjected him to the wickedness and pomposity of Nora. She was the most attractive Nigerian girl he had seen in Italy. If it were at home, there would have been millions of women like her. Losing her would not have been very bitter.

'Gentlemen, I have struggled to put her behind me. That chapter is closed forever. I leave for Nigeria a few months from now. I thank you guys for your cooperation.'

'No matter the hardships you have encountered, Sam, suffice it to say that your trip to Italy has paid off,' said one of his friends.

'At least, you have made more money than you would have made as manager in Nigeria in fifteen years,' said another.

'You are right. But considering what I hoped to achieve or the abundant opportunities for growth in this country, the money I have made is intangible.'

With them, Sam traversed the hills and plains of Reggio Emilia, Parma and Bologna for six days every week. No police confiscated his goods. His car did not break down. There was no idle time. Sales were encouraging too. His plans looked unstoppable until December.

Suddenly debates in Rome about the issuance of resident permits to illegal immigrants gained momentum and culminated in a law which came into effect on the 18th of November 1995, three weeks before Sam's scheduled departure.

The conditions for obtaining permits were overwhelming. The situation was not helped by the introduction of further requirements by various Foreigners' Offices. Sam and his friends prematurely dropped their *vu compra* bags. He fuelled his car and contacted all the persons who had withheld jobs from them before when they had no permit or who had accused them of shying away from hard work or thought they were lazy.

The excuses proffered were as diverse as the places they hunted for jobs. Some said there were no accommodation for them. Others said there were no vacancies. Many more complained about their lack of skill. Precisely, one thing was common among all of them: a very strong resentment against the taxes imposed on all prospective employers.

News of those who had satisfied the conditions could

be heard faintly at a distance. One month after the law came into effect, no one known to Sam had been regularized. Yet he and his friends could not be discouraged. There was a day their search extended to all the industries in Sassuolo, Formigine, Castellarano and finally Rondella. They started by nine o'clock in the morning. Only the closure of company premises for break forced them to rest until two-thirty in the afternoon when they continued. They were given employment forms to complete and asked to attach written applications. Before the end of the day, each person had completed at least twenty-five employment forms. In some cases, they were referred to administrative offices in Reggio Emilia or Modena. They followed up every clue yet none of them returned to Padua with any offer of employment.

The next day, they stormed Vicenza and began to have more positive response. The trend continued until three weeks later when their efforts began to yield positive results. Ikuku got a job in Padua. Mag in Venice. Iddy in Vicenza and Eddie in Treviso. No matter the frustrations and agonies of queuing for long hours, their demands were accepted. Once again, Sam went to the Gadiba family. The husband and wife set aside their busy schedule and met with the director of Systems Marketing Srl who would have hired Sam four years earlier. Since that period, the company had grown larger and moved from Faenza to Ravenna, a town bordering the Adriatic, well-known for its blue oases with golden beaches, crystal clear waters, safe moorings, important monuments, precious mosaics and sea port. The company's scale of activities had included software engineering, voice processing, telecommunications and a gamut of other computer-related activities.

But Nigeria had lost its appeal. The news of incessant

human rights abuses, flagrant closure of media houses and inconsistent change of monetary and fiscal policy measures left prospective overseas investors with cold feet. The indigenisation decree which came into effect in the seventies rendered a devastating blow to the drive of Systems Marketing Srl to invest in Nigeria. By that decree, overseas investors were required to go into joint ventures with Nigerians. Only Nigerians could have majority shares. Companies in existence before the promulgation of the decree stopped operations because of this formula. Many foreigners pulled their capital out of the economy. Few genuine ones remained. Those who fled the harshness of the decree created a vacuum that was either occupied by speculators and fraudsters or that were not filled anymore. For some reasons, decision makers had pretended that the decree was not an anathema to genuine foreign involvement in Nigerian economy.

By the time the director of Systems Marketing Srl invited Sam for interview in March, the emphasis had shifted to eastern Europe. Though the West competed fervently for investment opportunities, yet they found it safer and more predictable, he affirmed. Fortunately for Sam, a reliable source had disclosed to him that the decree had been abrogated. The interview began with, 'What do you consider your special strength?'

'Learning, the ability to learn quickly and accurately,' responded Sam.

'Your weakness?'

'My nationality,' he answered again.

'So, if it is possible, you will renounce your citizenship of Nigeria for Italian, for example?'

'No.'

'Then can you explain what you mean my young man.'

'Permit me to refer to a TIME INTERNATIONAL report of 28th of April, 1994. A widow and owner of a successful manufacturing firm in Bavaria, received a letter from a Nigerian. The letter stated that her husband bought stock in a dam in Kaduna before his death and the investment paid off richly. Her share was a whopping $23.6 million. In Lagos, the widow was met by a lawyer. "Why are you coming so late?" he asked disarmingly. "The money had been ready for collection since last year." He escorted her to the bank where she filled out a transfer order. There was just one problem. Naturally, fees of $235000 were due up front. She had $140000 transferred from her account at a New York bank and obtained loans to pay the balance. Over the next few months, she made several trips to Lagos and gave the lawyer additional $133000 for unforeseen charges. She never recovered a penny when the whole thing turned out to be a scam. Worse still, an American physician named John White had lost thousands of dollars, attempting to secure a pharmaceutical contract from agents claiming to represent the government. At the urging of a fraud investigator, he returned to Lagos to identify the culprits and reclaim his money. Two days before his scheduled departure, White was found dead in his hotel room.' Sam paused and looked at the director, aware of his gaze.

'Go on, go on,' the director nodded.

'The scam was not limited to only the ignorant and inexperienced. Laurence Martin, A British businessman who had been doing deals in Nigeria since 1988, was taken for $80000 in 1991 after his company sought a contract from somebody claiming to represent the defence ministry.'

'I'm aware of this mess. More of it were reported by Italian news media. As an international investor, I find such reports very interesting.'

'I guessed so. That is the reason I decided to bring them up. We cannot dispose of trash by sweeping them under the carpet. Let us call a spade a spade. Nigeria has earned such a reputation for drug smuggling that fellow citizens travelling abroad, regardless of credentials, must routinely undergo humiliating body searches. Our legitimate businessmen find the fraud industry a profound embarrassment. No matter how much the Central Bank of Nigeria and some image making apparatus try to disavow any official connection with tricksters, the reputation of Nigeria as a paradise for fraud still remains secure.'

'I think so, Mr Sam Ogemdi,' concurred the director.

'I have been a victim of the consequences of negative publicity about my country. Not long ago, at a trade fair in Padua, I was attracted to a set of fruit processing machines. I walked into the pavilion. The manager was handy with information about its price, uses and technical characteristic. The discussion on a joint ownership of a canning plant went smoothly. I had assured him of a very large market, availability of fruits and cheap labour. "Where?" he asked me. I told him. The man bluntly said he would never have anything to do with Nigerians anymore. At best, according to him, I could buy the machines at a discount.'

'It is painful to be visited with the crimes committed by somebody else, isn't it?' said the director.

'It is indeed painful, chief. A lot of my colleagues have had similar experience. Some have even been swindled by men whom they strained to convince of their honesty and integrity. Five years after my stint in Naples, I have come to understand why my former employer suddenly gave up on a laboratory and hospital equipment deal with me.'

'But this cannot continue forever, Sam,' the director

retorted.

'Certainly. Nigeria is the country of my birth. My peers and friends are still there. My parents who made sacrifices to ensure I was provided with every necessity as a child and who saw to it that I imbibed hard work, honesty and moral discipline will die Nigerians. Efe the woman who made the greatest difference to me and who displayed such virtues that nearly six years later, I have not experienced in any other woman is stranded there. If I had the opportunity to leave Nigeria's shores, not all the people I love would be opportune as well. Our children and grandchildren would find it difficult if not impossible to escape from Nigeria.

'For instance, when I left six years ago, there were still some personal effects to sell or mortgage. People parted with their money because there was more to provide food and clothing for their children until the mortgagor returned. Various embassies deliberately ignored or had not detected our fake claims in support of requests for visa. But today, the cost of air transport has escalated to an alarming proportion while the real income of the people has continued to decrease. Beyond all, western economies are comparatively stagnant and crying for fresh stimulants.' Sam paused and searched the director's face for a sign of enthusiasm.

The man urged him to go on with a nod. 'Government is moaning under the yoke of welfare programmes. Per capita income of people crumble as more taxes are squeezed out to finance decades-old social and welfare schemes. Inflation goes down less often in a year than it goes up. Cost of living constitutes genuine anxieties. Immigrants become scapegoats of a system that goes awry. They are the pawns on the chessboard of politicians and disgruntled citizens. The fundamental human right to move from one

213

place to another does not mean anything to them. Legal and bureaucratic barriers are deliberately erected to demoralise existing immigrants and discourage intending ones. A critical assessment of the entire situation leaves me in no doubt that the West is not a happy host anymore. In future, unless the trend changes, it will not be a willing haven for seekers of greener pasture. While we continue to hope that the West's cloudy sky will not drench poor, needy and deprived people of the world with irredeemable suffering, it becomes incumbent on some patriots at home and abroad to start the onerous task of building Nigeria into a psychologically balanced, politically stable and economically strong country.'

'Are you trying to tell me that there are reliable Nigerians?'

'Yes there are. Millions of them. I feel sad that the atrocities of a minority have never been brought so heavily against the majority as in the case of Nigeria. They make news headlines at home and overseas while innocent and genuine businessmen who still believe in the Nigerian dream go into negotiations with foreigners as underdogs. To them, Nigeria is not a badge of honour any longer. They are neither comfortable at home nor welcome abroad. Though I need a job, I won't like to be presumed guilty because of my nationality until I am tried.'

The director smiled. 'And so?' he asked as he jotted on the pads in front of him.

'Nothing stops a booming business in eastern Europe from expanding profitably to Africa. I know that I can develop the Nigerian market, spin it into a gold mine for Systems Marketing Srl. But I am obviously reluctant to present my ideas because I am afraid of being mistaken for another smooth-talking Nigerian. By now, perhaps you

can see why my nationality is my weakness,' Sam concluded.

The director bent down his head and bit his lips. When he raised it again, his eyes conveyed what his heart felt. Sam knew he had scored a point. Definitely, a special chord in his heart had been struck. 'Do you hear from Efe and your parents?'

'I have been able to contact my parents by letters and telephone. These, certainly are not substitutes for physical contact. The most distressing of all is that one year after my arrival in Italy, Efe and I lost contact. Lost too was any clue about her parents – her imprisoned father and sick mother.'

'So you are sure that there are still many genuine Nigerians?' The man asked again.

'Exactly. I have said that before and can make that claim anywhere. Though terrible are the nefarious activities of the conmen and gangsters on our foreign image, more terrible are those who are filled with prejudice against every Nigerian. Without holding brief for my country's woes, suffice it to mention that no nation is free of criminals. The West, Italy, for instance, has not helped the struggle and determination of some of us to make it genuinely so that we shall be guiding stars for those who are in doubt about what road to follow. It is my contention that a clear and commensurate reward for talent, honesty and hard work will reduce the thieves to shame and disgrace.'

'Tell me once more. Is the atmosphere conducive for investment in Nigeria?'

'Yes. In saying this, I am not driven by patriotic zeal or sentiments. Let me quickly clarify myself. I will collect, collate and furnish you with statistics which will be used to decide and perhaps measure performance in future. Once again, it requires substantial level of trust and autonomy which I may find myself ill disposed to ask for.'

'In eastern Europe, we go into business with our technology and capital. There are no provisions that a certain number of indigenes must be employed or that certain positions in our organisational hierarchy be reserved for them. We hire whatever number of persons we find necessary. There are no cases of missing files in government offices, arrest or detention of expatriates or illegal confiscation of personal or corporate assets. These are the things we find enticing and conducive for further investment. Nigeria is different, Mr Ogemdi.'

'Yes, Nigeria is different if you are talking about market size. It is more than the populations of ten former communist countries put together. In addition, it is a member of ECOWAS (Economic Community of West African States) which increases an investor's market and tariff-free zone far beyond Nigeria's physical boundaries. Moreover, the dreaded indigenisation decree has been dismantled. Foreign investors are free to operate business solely and repatriate as much profit as they deem fit. There are strong reports of changes in the conduct of government. However, business decisions cannot be based on hear say. It is my desire to discount rumours as I stand before you today. I need to visit Nigeria, see the changes myself and present my report to you. The crux of the matter is that you will not send me or rely on my report if you are one of those who presume that all Nigerians are liars and criminals. Many young Nigerians today do not know whether it is safer to appear intelligent or dumb in this type of situation. However, I must express myself. Do to me what pleases you.'

'Mr Ogemdi, I will reflect on your proposals. We have had enough. See you sometime next week.'

Sam visited Mr and Mrs Gadiba the following day. They were impressed by his performance. The man had already telephoned to tell them about his session with Sam. The Gadibas had consistently vouched for his character and prodded the company to give him a chance.

'Definitely he is testing you on computer operations next week,' they disclosed to Sam.

'But I have never operated one before!' Sam protested.

'We know. He does not expect you to write programmes or repair hardware. You need to know its applications to business and designs. I think he will be impressed if you can learn very fast, you will spend tomorrow on our personal computer.'

The next interview was all actions and no words. With a thorough preparation, Sam looked good as he touched off the keyboard. Out of nervousness, he made mistakes but his performance was generally superb for a novice.

On the 31st of March, the managing director of Systems Marketing Srl formally presented Sam to the Foreigners' Office for work permit. One week later, millions of lire were paid as tax on his behalf and he started working. Grasping the technical jargons and operating procedures were daunting. With time however, Sam learnt those aspects that were relevant to his job as a data analyst. With the assistance of the same Gadiba family, he moved from Padua to a mini flat in Ravenna. For the first time since he came to Italy, he was living alone. His departure from Padua was not total nonetheless. His job included visits to study corporate clients in Ferrara, Vicenza and Padua by observation, questionnaires and through published reports. It was on such visits that he met his friends. Iddy worked in a carpentry factory. He logged in a minimum of ten hours of work Mondays through Fridays and a minimum of four hours on Saturdays. He found his boss and colleagues very congenial. They moved from one town to another, constructing new roofs, or renovating old ones. With his personal car, he got to such places conveniently and punctually. He was having job satisfaction. Ikuku's employer was in the metal mechanical industry. He had not demanded to know nor been told his hourly pay. The company was located at an area accessible by public transport. To be punctual at work, he left his house as early as five o'clock in the morning every working day. However, he credited his young boss for patience when he was slow to learn or when he made mistakes.

Ben was the only friend whose health bothered Sam. He was employed as a trainee welder. His eyes were red and tearful. He felt pepperish sensations. Sam was scared the young man's sight could be impaired or lost completely. So Sam called the supervisor who blamed the situation on Ben's intransigence. He pleaded with Sam to tell his friend that welding glasses were made for the eyes and not for the forehead. Another telephone call Sam made that same day was to Ikuku's boss who claimed that Ikuku's wages and other conditions of employment had been made known to him. Perhaps he did not understand them because of language barrier. If the terms and conditions the employer disclosed to Sam were anything to go by, they did not vary much from acceptable conditions for his sector.

Roland had a unique case. He fell victim to a ghost employer who promised him a job in his building construction industry if he could pay the tax himself. He gave the swindler the sum of two million five hundred thousand lire. The period stipulated by law had expired when Roland found out that the man had robbed him of his money. There was no construction company or job to offer. Roland secured a genuine job in Treviso. The foreigners' office had to be convinced to recognise the new and genuine contract as a replacement for the fake one. The new employer had to be persuaded to go through the daunting task of paying another tax on Roland's behalf. When these afflictions and obstacles were surmounted, Sam heaved a sigh of relief for himself and his close friends. After many years of waiting in the wilderness, they were a stone's throw to being legal residents in Italy.

When the first date given to him for retrieval of his work permit became due, Sam arrived two and half hours before the opening time of the Foreigners' Office. The staff acted with speed and efficiency. In a couple of hours, nearly sixty persons had been attended to.

'Are you really working as a data analyst?' one lady asked him as he stood in front of her.

'Why are you asking me when I submitted my application with a contract of employment?'

'It is my job to ask," replied the policewoman.

'Madam, I do not know how to defend myself unless you give me access to your computer.'

'Access?' she asked obviously baffled.

'Yes. The secret code. The password. Anything to enable me enter into your system.'

She started smiling.

'Do you have photocopies of your tax receipt and employment card?'

'You should have told me this, madam, instead of pulling my legs,' Sam started laughing.

He gave her all the requested documents. She put them inside his file and took them to a superior officer. Sam was later asked to come again after forty days.

The waiting which started in March when the request

was made ended in July when he was issued with a work permit renewable after four years. Sam had submitted an application to the embassy of Nigeria on Via Orazio, Rome a month earlier for the replacement of his lost passport. The appointment became due too. He went, and after the usual formalities, was issued with a new passport. Finally, Sam returned to the Foreigners' Office for a re-entry permit that would run concurrently with his work permit.

There were very many persons to tell that he was departing Italy for Nigeria, east of the River Niger. There were heartfelt gratitude which should be expressed to certain persons. But they were scattered like starlets in the sky, from Naples to Padua; from Perugia to Reggio Emilia and from Ancona to Bologna. Short of time and desperate to go, he decided to leave a letter with his colleague in the office who would see to it that they were informed accordingly.

Letter to the Romans.

You were neither the man and woman whose blood runs in my veins nor the country whose identity I carry like a shadow and have sworn to carry all the days of my life. You were not the beginning of my tribulations and perhaps not the beneficiaries of my triumph in the material sense. Many years before I set sail, I had heard your name faintly across the Mediterranean. The more I was pulled farther away from the shore of safety into the avalanche of death, the louder your voice resonated in my ears. As the drift into the valley of despair continued, neither the anguish and genuine concern of family and friends nor the personal resolve not to cave in to the scorn and evil machinations of my detractors tamed the tide.

The opportunity you offered to my deprived colleagues and promise of a greener pasture for me was more than a magic wand. It resuscitated my hope and renewed my energy. Neither with shield nor armour, I came with only my determination, drive, sense of hard work and honesty. I came, I saw and I knew I was wrong to have set out to capture so much so soon, armed with only blunt weapons. Before my own eyes, loving parents, adoring siblings and heartbroken fiancee were abandoned, not for six months but six years.

However, as I pack my luggage today to return, all my bitter experiences have been overcome by a feeling of victory. Not because of the money made, let me quickly point out for the avoidance of doubt but because of the obstacles and temptations I have surmounted to be where I am now; the experience I have acquired and the resolve never ever before known to me to contribute to a new Nigeria. In this regard, my mission to Rome, though time consuming as every journey to a promised land is wont to be, is a success. Whatever qualities that saw me to this moment would have been meaningless without certain persons, organisations and institutions. I want our Mama through whom we received letters when we were in the White House to know that she is still part of my life. Only few persons in this world could condone the nuisance we constituted and the inconveniences we caused with such equanimity.

The battle is not yet over but when I begin to take stock of my blessings, indeed Mama, you stand out tall. The letters I received through you were the only link between Efe and me. I appreciated your help more deeply when the White House collapsed. Letters dried up and deadly silence which has not lifted till today pervaded life. Albaflex Snc may not be existing anymore as a legal entity, the promise of indefinite employment was broken not long after it was uttered. How much we give others is important. But the importance assumes another dimension when such charity represents a substantial proportion of our income.

Naples was besieged by unemployment, nothing could be more magnanimous than the job you offered to me. You provided me a stepping stone, from where I moved forward. Jehovah's

Witnesses from Corregio to Communanza, you are a special people. You brought light where none existed and rain to a scorched earth. Due to lack of time and space, I cannot mention your names. Be assured that your acceptance of people, regardless of race, does a lot to our self-esteem. Assisi was one police command whose warehouse must be brim full of goods confiscated from us and whose computer hard disc must be bursting with the names of illegal immigrants stored there.

The same Assisi provided my friends and me the most comfortable home away from Padua. The benevolent spirit of Saint Francis manifested itself through the owners of Fina filling station along State Road 75. You had allowed us into your premises before one of you disclosed to us his years of employment in Southern Africa. The gesture showed you were appreciative of that stint in Africa. When we flocked to you in large numbers, you accepted us. I concluded you were above all, magnanimous. You left nothing undone to ensure our safety. From Terni, Arezzo, Ancona and even Siena, we came every night for the peace we couldn't find elsewhere.

When we were daring into zones known, we left some of our wares in your care to reduce our risks, and returned when darkness fell to meet them intact. Not all of us would be disposed to contact you again but our story is incomplete without giving you a mention. You are wonderful. Caritas and Mappamondo are two organisations immigrants in Ravenna found very invaluable. By coming to the rescue of some people who were very close to me, you touched my life. No words would be enough to salute the doctors, nurses and lawyers who freely availed us of their services. It is with unparalleled sense of humility and respect that I thank the honourable gentlemen and ladies of Palazzo Chigi, Montecitorio, Qurinale, Piazza Madama and other public functionaries in Rome and elsewhere who made my dreams come true.

I have followed the debate which culminated in the granting of the permits of stay. Only people with your kind of determination and wisdom could overcome the bitterness and *hatred in those who argue that immigrants take away their jobs and homes. I am pretty sure of your convictions. However, as some immigrants get involved in crimes or roam the streets without jobs, some may find a cause to blackmail you and fan the embers of xenophobia and some of you may begin to wobble. In this regard, I make my supplications. Immigrants are people full of drive. Many of them are endowed with talents. Many have acquired skills and learning which can be harnessed.*

The United States is a shining example of how intelligent, talented, hard-working, highly motivated and ambitious immigrants can stimulate and sustain prosperity. It must be made clear to all and sundry, no matter how painful it may be, that immigrants have become an inevitable and integral part of Italy. They ought not be the pariah of the society. To impoverish them or restrict their integration will boomerang in the future. It was not by accident that Italy sprang from the devastation of the Second World War to become one of the world's industrial giants. The same sun continues to shine over its territories, the same seas splash at its coasts and the same blood continues to run in the veins of its citizens. Hence in you still lies the power to invent genuine and enduring infrastructure necessary for the total integration of immigrants. If you do that now, many years to come, posterity will continue to salute your courage and foresight.

Finally, I wish to tell fellow immigrants that nothing can be as self-destructive as a feeling that you are pests. Your sweat on odd jobs sustain the pension funds. There is no gift worthier than security after retirement. It is worthy to note that not by government fiat but by your monthly contributions that this security is guaranteed. The present generation, perhaps, has forgotten but history will still bear you out that Italy has been one of the highest exporters of human beings. Even in the most wretched of all countries, Italians are present, gainfully employed and comfortable. Migration is natural. It has been as old as creation itself and will continue regardless of any artificial barriers. Therefore, as it presented a choice in our times of distress, let us contribute meaningfully to sustain its prosperity so that future generations will have a choice too in their times of deprivation.

Chapter 8

Double Shuffle

Their flight arrived Fiumicino six hours after its departure from Murtala Mohammed Airport, Lagos, Nigeria. Efe, with Madam Angela, marched the same soil that Sam passed through six years earlier. It was a Saturday. From there, they boarded a metro which took them to Rome train station in good time for the next available train to Naples.

'African Restaurant is across the street but we do not have any time now. Let us go to the market to replenish those items in my shop that are either finishing or completely exhausted. It is a weekly market and if we miss it, I will have a hell of problems to contend with.' Madam Angela told Efe when they reached Naples central station.

Leonardo Da Vinci Airport, Rome, Naples, African Restaurant, in short, everything so far, had been vividly written about by Sam. She was only experiencing them herself. Every inch of the way, they assured her that sooner or later, she would meet Sam again. It was with a very rare courage that she resisted the urge to ask Madam Angela about him.

'This is Naples' Prisons,' Angela said as the taxi

emerged from the tunnel into the chaotic traffic of Via Poggioreale. 'This is the home for most people their families in Africa think are studying or working here.'

'Why are they in jail?' Efe asked.

'They deal in illegal drugs. One is exceptionally lucky if after a year of active involvement, one has not been caught and thrown into jail. Most men, including that idiot, Sam, are prone to it without work permit or any other means of survival.'

'No, Ma. Sam would not have touched cocaine or heroin even with a ten-metre pole. I trust him," Efe said a little flustered.

'Eh, you trust him, He abandoned you and married another woman. You still trust him. Women like you learn in their graves.'

Efe remained silent as Madam Angela insulted her.

'He is saved from imprisonment like other young men by his marriage. Anyhow, he has been reduced to servitude. He has run from state prison to domestic prison. People who saw him before I returned to Nigeria said he cleaned their house, prepared the children for school, cooked, washed dresses and ran errands while the wife did nothing.'

Efe did not know clearly how she felt about Sam. Whether it was pity for his loss of a woman who had treated him respectfully and had adored him and in her place, another woman who mistreated him and reduced him to servitude simply because that was the only means of remaining afloat. Or anger and disappointment that when the moment of trial came, Sam did not persevere but went down, leaving behind a trail of promises not kept and dreams shattered. While the feelings of pity and anger struggled for supremacy, she continued to be filled with a desire to see him again. She had vowed to herself to stop at nothing until she met him face to face.

Madam Angela walked the length and breath of the entire market, hovered here and stopped there. She sauntered into a grocery, haggled and eventually bought negligible number of items.

'The men who bring the type of wares I sell in my shop are not here today. I wonder why,' she complained. 'However, let me use the opportunity to get some Italian dresses for you.'

With hunger and anger raging inside Efe, more out of relief that the loitering was coming to an end than the promise of a new outfit, she cheered up. "That's very kind of you, Ma.'

They walked past five rows of shops to arrive at where dresses were sold. There were very fine linen, silk and cotton skirts, gowns, trousers and blouses which were elegantly displayed. Madam Angela bent down and rummaged through a basket of clothes. Efe thought that perhaps she wanted to buy some napkins or new rags for her household. She stood and waited. By the time the woman got up, she was clutching a nine-inch-long mini skirt and an undersize blouse with a crew neck. Efe could not conceal her shock when Madam Angela gave them to her and nudged her to test them. Efe entered into the match-box cabin of cloth located deeper inside the shop to test them.

'Come out, my daughter, so that I can see how elegant you look inside them.'

No matter how much Efe tried to pull it down, the skirt receded upwards as she walked. The blouse revealed her entire cleavage. While one of her hands tugged at the skirt, the other hand covered her breasts.

'This is indecent, Ma,' she protested and returned to the cabin to remove them.

'Don't say that, my daughter. Listen, after many years in this country, I know what is in vogue. I know what will make you look smart. This is Europe. Get that right into your head. To make it here, you have to discount decency. So far as you are here, you are a hustler. Hustling demands that those morals you learnt at home be tossed out of the window and you may well play down on that feelings of superiority because of your university education. Take my advice. You will not regret it.'

'I have heard you, big mummy! Ma, don't people eat in Italy? I am hungry.' Madam Angela started to laugh. 'I will treat you to a very delicious meal. Just exercise a little patience. It is remaining your shoes. You need to be fitted out in the right attire.' From there, they went to almost where they started for the shops that sold shoes.

'What is your size?'

'Thirty-nine, Ma.' She went for flat soled genuine leather sandals that blended with her tall stature.

'I think you can allow me to choose for myself this time, Ma,' Efe said as she unfastened a pair of sandals to show Madam Angela.

Once again, she was rebuffed. 'Have I not told you that inside an engineering studio, I will not jostle for supremacy with you. I will be a fool to do so. Italy is my domain. It is one in which you are a total stranger. You won't be a fool if you relinquish to me the privilege to decide your welfare. You do not know how profoundly short ladies here wish they were taller. The taller you are, the more attractive you appear. These materials I gather for you are bound to enhance your beauty, and dazzle guys.'

Efe nodded her head in agreement, her face expressionless. Madam Angela picked a flashy high heeled shoe made of synthetic material and paid for it. Shopping over, the ladies headed home. Madam Angela's three bedroom flat at Vomero, a few kilometres away from Naples, was full of people. Apart from the stench of cigarette, the rooms were clean. Efe could count up to seven girls and four boys. They were apparently happy that Angela had returned. The giant refrigerator inside the parlour was full of bottles of beer. The mini bar had assorted bottles of hard liquor. On top of every table and stool, there were bottles and cups of drinks. There were no vacant chairs for the new entrants. One of the girls vacated her seat for Angela. Two boys shifted their buttocks and created a small space where Efe reluctantly sandwiched herself. The aroma of a very tasty food spread through the parlour and the clatter of china wares could be heard as somebody went into the kitchen.

'Please, Jessica, hurry up so that my daughter can eat. She is famished,' Madam Angela told the girl inside the kitchen.

She turned to Efe. 'Soon, food will be ready. These girls must have been sleeping with their boyfriends otherwise lunch should have been ready by now.' Efe looked at the boys, then at the other girls. They were amused by the woman's remark. It was only her who felt that Madam Angela was vulgar.

'Ma, I do not know if it amounts to breaking the rules of the game if I opt to bath before lunch is ready,' she said. Everybody broke out in laughter.

'Which rules? Please, Doris, go and show her the bathroom and make sure she is provided with whatever she needs, okay?' Madam Angela instructed another girl.

Immediately the girl left, three more men came into the house. Out of the seven, only one had not had carnal knowledge of Angela. Three out of the six were not regulars, the other three, were on her reserve list to be used whenever and wherever it pleased her. She was not the type of woman that sat back and cried while her partners cheated her. She warned them of very grave consequences if they were caught. She was also inherently jealous and craved to be admired and seduced instead of her younger girls. All the men knew and maintained their distance from the girls in her presence.

Efe had hardly settled down to bath when people who were pressed with urine began to knock. Two minutes later, she was interrupted by another person.

'Open the door! I want to urinate,' requested a feminine voice.

Efe considered the person rude. Moreover, she was entitled to some privacy. When she did not respond and only splashes of water could be heard inside, the person grumbled away. Efe had never known so much confusion and obscenity all her life. She remained calm in order to be able to accomplish her mission.

In the bedroom shown her by Doris, she arranged her few possessions in the wardrobe. With disgust, she brought out the mini wears Madam Angela bought for her and flung them into a drawer. Below the drawers, she tried to make out a space for her shoes when she stumbled on three cartons of condoms containing one thousand pieces in each. Beside it was a half litre tube of creamy spermicide. 'Can this lascivious old woman be selling or using these?' She asked herself. Nothing had made sense to her yet. As she pondered over it, Jessica came in and told her that their madame wanted her in the parlour.

'Perhaps, now, we can eat,' Madam Angela announced to her.

'Ma, I am glad you realise how much the fragrance of

this food has wetted my appetite,' Efe said.

'By the way, won't you introduce yourself to these men?'

'Until you tell me, Ma.'

'I did not know you have so much sense of humour,' said Madam Angela as she introduced the men one after another, and formally disclosed her name to them.

The Igbos joked that her name meant dress or time depending on the tone. A Yoruba man said that it implies faithfulness. Two Itsekiri men gave their own version of the name's significance. One of the men from the middle belt had opened his mouth to ramble like others when Efe quipped.

'It is interesting that my name means something to different ethnic groups, but my name has only one meaning and inspiration known only to my kinsmen and my family. I will tell one of you someday. Meanwhile, let us eat.'

They all assembled at the dining table. There weren't spaces for some of the girls. With smaller plates, they collected some food and went away. Efe would have been glad to be gone too but the men quickly created a space for her.

'If you won't feel offended gentlemen, can I go to the parlour where I can be more comfortable?' Efe requested.

'Relax, or do you want them to vacate the table so that you will be comfortable?' Madam Angela admonished her.

Others were amused but Efe was embarrassed.

'There are five others who are arriving soon. They departed Nigeria three days ago.' Madam Angela explained to the men.

'No matter whom you have in transit, big mummy, I do not want to miss this one. Take a look at her long legs...'

one of the men declared. He lifted Efe's hands and shouted. 'Man, see the freshness and radiance of this skin. This is the ultimate. *Mama mia!*'

The ovation was very loud. Some people clapped their hands or banged on the table, others whistled at the choice of his words and the effect it generated. The ladies pursed their lips in envy. Efe thanked him and continued to eat.

'I guess I have not told you guys that she is an architect. She is computer literate too. Anybody who wants her does not need to be told that a good meal costs bucks,' added Madam Angela for good effect.

The guests were part of the dinner too. Late into the night, there was no sign that they were intending to go. Efe felt she has had enough of the dirty jokes and needed some sleep.

'Ma, I am having headache and would like to go to bed,' she pleaded. 'Good night everybody.'

Inside the bedroom, she reflected on the day's events; the ladies who guzzled liquor and discarded cigarette butts every ten minutes; the mature men who ought to be fathers but had no sense of time, the group of girls who left for or returned from work at odd times and those condoms. She was still thinking about it when she fell asleep. Efe heard the clanging of metal gates outside. She looked at her time, it was nine o'clock in the morning. She remained in bed. Soon, Doris, who had shown her places the previous day but was not there at meal time, gently pulled the door knob and came in. Efe turned to see who entered.

'I am sorry I disturbed you, my sister,' Doris pleaded as she perched on the edge of the bed. No one needed to be told that her slender seventeen year old frame was saddled with a burden too heavy for it to bear.

'Doris, where did you go to yesterday? I did not see

you.'

'I went to afternoon work. By the time I came home to eat and prepare for work at another location in the night, you had gone to bed.'

Efe knew that any display of shock would cost her a lot. To have time to comport herself well, she took advantage of the silence that befell the household.

'When did those men leave last night?'

'They are sleeping. You have not seen anything yet. That is how they pest on us. Lazy and shameless people. Men, who are worth it cannot go and dump their women at one corner of the street for other men and later bring them home to tell them how much they are loved and admired. You can imagine the risks we take. Two weeks ago, the charred remains of one of us was found many kilometres away from Naples. It was only her gold necklace that helped her friends to identify her corpse. Otherwise, her parents would endlessly look for their daughter. Exactly six months today, a girl, who came into Italy with me after three months of waiting in Slovenia and whose madam is staying in Turin, was slaughtered by a client. Though the killer was apprehended by the police, the court was told he was a psychopath. The news reaching us from Vicenza since yesterday is that another girl was recovered drowned in a river. This our job is very hazardous. As soon as I finish paying my *igbese*, with anymore amount of money I can scrape together, I will go home.'

'Are all of Madam's girls doing the same job?' Efe asked.

'Does Madam have any other industry apart from prostitution? Did she not tell you in Nigeria what you were coming here to do?'

'No.'

'I am not surprised,' replied Doris.

'Why?'

'Because she did it to me. Madam and my mother come from the same village and grew up together. While my mother decided to get married, Madam was satisfied with two children she had with different men and...'

'Sorry to interrupt you. Where are these children now? They are supposed to be adults.'

'Yes, they are grown ups. The female child is about eighteen years old. Madam feels that the girl won't work very hard in Italy, so she banished her to Rotterdam where in the absence of her mother she will pay her rents or buy her dresses, she would be compelled to hustle very well. Madam's son is in a university in Nigeria. 'As I was saying, dear sister, Madam opted for business. She came home with much money and invested in real estate. Each time she visited our house, she brought a lot of gifts for my brothers, mother and me. On one occasion, I came out to greet her. She looked at me and said I had grown into a ripe woman since the last time she visited. I was still smiling for her compliment when she disclosed to my mother that a few vacancies existed for washing plates and dresses for reverend sisters in Rome and would like to take me along for the job. I did not really want to miss my friends at school. My father vehemently opposed anything that would terminate my education prematurely. My mother explained to me that the family needed money to put meals on the table for all of us and to see my brothers through the university. My father and I were finally bent backwards when Madame hinted that I did not need to spend my entire lifetime on the job. Only six or nine months were enough to make money that would change the poor status of my family. That's how she deceived me from my family into slavery. And I am trapped until I finish paying her.'

'How long have you been in Italy?' Efe asked.

'Eighteen months.'

'Since then, you have not been able to tell your family the truth?'

'I am ashamed to tell them, their letters are full of encomium and gratitude for my financial contributions to the upliftment of the family. They even wrote to congratulate Madam for giving me the opportunity. Above all, my father is highly religious. He is a devout Christian. I am afraid he will either disown me or die of guilt for ever allowing my mother to prevail. This is why I work day and night to liquidate my debts and go home.'

'Are you saying that after eighteen months, you have not been able to raise enough money for the flight ticket Madam provided and maybe, some other incidental costs of obtaining your passage to Italy?'

'Sister Efe, from all indications, you are as ignorant of this industry as I was one and a half years ago. *Igbese* does not have anything to do with the cost of flight ticket, visa or passport. It is an amount that madam arbitrarily charges every girl they bring into this country or they buy from a trafficker and must be paid before a girl can obtain her freedom.'

'About how much is it?'

'It depends on the madames' disposition and greed. Some charge fifty-five million lire. Others charge as much as eighty million lire. Madam Angela wanted seventy million lire from me but when she found out that I was working extremely hard to pay up in less than two years, she added ten million lire on top of it. When I pleaded for leniency, she coldly told me that I could either choose to pay or vacate her house and relinquish my right to the joint she assigned to me for work.'

'You accepted to pay?'

'What else can I do? If I refuse, I have simply toiled for her. Without any joint or accommodation, I am dead. Let us hope that by the time I pay the additional ten million lire completely, she won't invent some other demand to enable her perpetuate my slavery.'

'Does she own the streets and roads where you stand to threaten to expel you?'

'Ha! Yes. She claims the place belongs to her and that she has fortified it. She leases it out to whom she likes for money. Girls who resisted ejection in the past have been beaten and slashed with bottles by hired thugs. No one who wants to return to Nigeria with a smooth face and complete set of teeth dares that devil.'

'Doris, these amounts sound colossal. Does it mean that prostitution is so lucrative that one could pay as much within a very short time?'

'Once again, it depends on luck. When you see the type of monsters most Italian men patronize, you will begin to wonder if beauty is a factor in attracting patronage or something else. Some girls have been paying their madames for years. Some are lucky to catch men who pay for them en bloc. And in return, some of these men insist on unprotected sex or some bizarre sexual acts. Men pay me generously. Maybe out of pity or pleasure. And many of them have become very regular. I must admit that Madam took time to teach us the bait to catch a prospective client and the necessary movements while loving them so that they will come again. There are some girls who develop mental problems or sink into depression because of lack of the prospects of liquidating their *igbese*.

'You go to work alone. Madame does not go with you.

In other words, anyone who finds the burden unbearable or who was tricked into prostitution can run away.'

'It is not possible, sister Efe.'

'Why, Doris?'

'I am afraid of the consequences of the juju which a witch doctor smeared on my body at Ufekeledimba shrine. We were six that day. We stood stark naked before the old chief priest of the shrine. He shaved off our pubic hair and put it in a calabash. After some incantations, he proceeded to make a concoction of our urine, dead toad, excreta of tortoise and so many other gruesome objects. While we lay on our backs with our legs spread wide apart, he rubbed his grubby fingers with the mixture, inserted the fingers into our vagina and scrubbed its walls. Finally, we drank another concoction and were covered with white cloth in a dingy room till the next morning. The witch doctor warned us that anybody who defaulted in honouring her financial obligations to Madam Angela would be met with calamity. So, she did not take you to any shrine?'

'No,' Efe replied.

'You are lucky. How much *igbese* did she put on your head?'

'Nothing.'

Doris was puzzled.

'No *igbese,* no juju and no disclosure of prostitution. Only Madame knows what she intends to do with you.'

'She told my aunts that I will work in her boutique as a salesgirl.'

'Do not mind that devil. Her shop is this house. Those condoms inside the wardrobe and we constitute her wares. Nemesis will overtake her someday. She collects this money from us and spends it on those fools who are young enough to be her sons. She has as much insatiable libido as she is greedy for money. Can you believe that she sleeps with as many as three or four of those men at a time and brags about her prowess!'

'Now, I can understand why you do not look cheerful. You are much different. Jessica and others, especially that skinny woman you call Monopoly, are happy and seem to be coping very well.'

'They ought to be. They knew what they were coming for. Jessica was a fashion designer, with nearly five apprentices and three staff. People who knew her at home said she had a booming enterprise. She sold her machines and sent her workers away. With the proceeds from the sales, she registered with an association that trafficks in women. According to reports, there were already fifty persons on the waiting list. To ensure that her application was expedited, she used her savings and bribed the people responsible for calling up applicants for documentation and subsequent exportation. Monopoly has five children and a husband at home. She was a teacher. Don't you hear her English? Her husband lost his banking job when their bank became distressed. Her income was not enough to maintain the family. Another job for her husband was not in the offing. Somebody convinced him to allow her to come here and hustle. She was well-prepared at home. She does not wait for clients. They park their cars and wait for her. Younger and beautiful girls around her do not attract any client until she is gone.'

'Is Monopoly her real name?'

'No. It is the way she attracts men and leaves others without any that earned her the name. Who bears real names in this country? Perhaps, only those of us who were conscripted into the job.'

'But if one lies about one's name, there is always one's

identity card to betray the person.'

'Prostitutes don't carry identity cards. Not even those who have a regular stay permit. At work, they keep it away. Otherwise, the police can tear or confiscate it. I think I allowed my name to be associated with this job by accident and ignorance. A move from Naples to another town is my only opportunity to correct the mistake.'

Efe concluded she had heard enough and needed to hurry up to achieve her mission to Italy before Madam Angela would explode like a dynamite. Doris criticised the madame enough to earn Efe's confidence.

'Do you know Sam, an Igbo man? He has been in Italy for more than five years.'

'I do not know him. What business have I with black men? In the first place, Madame forbids us from any affair with them until she has been fully paid and we are free. Please, sister, do not think about these idiots for now. They will deceive you, drain the money you would have used to liquidate your debts and compound your problems.'

'I think you are right Doris. I appreciate your pieces of advice. I am years older than you. But it will take me many years to acquire your experience. Please, keep me informed of any interesting developments.'

The day was Sunday. The weather was sunny. Madam Angela's household assembled for lunch after which some relaxed in the parlour, others danced to afro-beat music. Efe retreated to the bed for siesta. The intensity of the sun had subsided a bit and the sky was still bright when they left by three different cars for African Restaurant. To the delight of the man who admired her the previous day, Efe hopped into the passenger seat of his car. But she dumped him as soon as she was convinced there was no information to extract from him. Inside the bar, she was outstanding for many reasons: her physical appearance, demeanour, and freshness to the scene. Men fell on one another to talk to her. She was very amenable to their overtures so far as it was limited to knowing her name and collecting their names and phone numbers in return. Not long, the double table where Madam and her entourage sat was filled with food and drinks offered by Efe's admirers. As if Efe had not done enough, she angled for the attention of men who it seemed would be helpful to her secret plot. She went to their tables, started with a familiar face there and utilised the slightest opportunity to pounce on her prey. It was on one of such occasions that she met a man who came from Venice. She lured him away from the table, teasing and embracing him as they went to stand outside the bar for a discussion.

'When can you visit me?' asked the man, 'or do you want me to visit you?'

'I came yesterday and I have *igbese* that runs into millions of lire to pay. You have seen my madame?'

'Yes,' the man nodded in response.

'I cannot afford to offend her. But of all the guys here, you drive me crazy.'

The man was elated and smiled. 'Thank you.'

Efe continued, 'Since I saw you, I have been racking my brain about how to start a clandestine affair with you. Right now, I have come up with a solid idea. My sister in Nigeria is married to an Igbo man. His name is Samuel Ogemdi. He was residing in the White House. The last time he wrote her was five years ago. And was working with another Igbo man in a company in Casoria. Sam is tall, dark and broad shouldered. I promised my sister that I would trace him. I think if I succeed, he will serve as a facade for the affair I want to start with you.'

'Do you know the name or the address of the company?'

'No. He did not write my sister with the address.'

'Which address did he use?'

'Emm,' Efe scratched her hair as if she had forgotten. 'That of one Mama.'

'The person should be living in the White House, indeed. I was a resident there too. But there was no Igbo man whose name was Sam. Was your sister writing him with that name?'

'Yes.'

'This makes the situation more complicated. Casoria is not far from here. Had it been you know the name of the company, I could trace it and enquire about the whereabouts of your in-law.'

'There isn't anything you can do to locate him? Seeing him though important but more important is visiting you at his place.'

For some seconds, the man pondered.

'The person who fits into this description is Billy. And after the collapse of the White House and subsequent loss of his job, he came to Padua. Your sister did not mention these details to you?'

'No. Did the Billy get married to an Italian?'

'Which Italian?' the man started laughing. 'He has been doing *vu compra* since he came to Padua and keeps to himself. I do not think I have seen him with any woman, black or white.'

'Are you sure he did not at time answer Sam?'

'No, Efe. I was there in the White House when he came sometime in August or September. I cannot recollect vividly and until I left, he was known as Billy. However, when I go back to Venice, I will look for other veterans of the White House. Perhaps, they will help to reconcile the description.'

'What year was it?'

'It should be 1990 or 1991. I am not sure.'

'Until you conduct the investigation, I can still call you and find out who is sharing you with me. I am jealous, let me tell you. But you can always be sure I will be there for you. It is your responsibility to work out the cover for my visits and I will be on my way.'

'I will be in Naples again at the end of August. Meanwhile, I will give you the phone number of my friend because mine has been out of service and might take sometime to fix again. Be rest assured that I will leave no stone unturned to locate this Sam.'

Efe had done her best for the day. It was enough to brighten her depressed soul. Efe wanted immediate results. Madam Angela was filled with joy at a corner of the bar from where she saw Efe flirting with different men. She thought Efe was adapting. On their way back to Vomero, Efe found no need for her first admirer's car. She joined her madame.

'Efe, I have delivered your passport to my lawyer. He telephoned his friend at the Foreigners' Office for information. He was told that your transit visa does not qualify you for a work permit. In any case, he has promised to try another office. He assured me of success eventually but said that it would cost a whopping sum of money. Meanwhile, I would like you to go out tomorrow with Amanda. Go out. Have some fun. I mean some real good time. Certainly, before your papers are processed, you will run into a bigwig who will settle the legal bill for us. Amanda will tell you what to do.'

'Ma, where is Amanda? I think I have denied myself a

lot in this world because of a hopeless fiance. I cannot wait to kick it off.'

Madam Angela smiled. 'I have never doubted what you can do, Efe. If these ugly and brainless monsters can make it, why can't you, my daughter? Show them you did not surpass them in education and physical appearance only. Let them know that in hustling, you are a supremo!' She turned to gaze at Efe. Satisfied that the message had sunk, she fired on. 'Amanda has been away with her Italian guy. She will be back by ten o'clock in the evening tomorrow. Forget about the bloody ingrate you call Sam. Bet me, the pain he inflicted on you is a blessing in disguise. With your own money you have a choice.'

'Ma, thank you. I am very grateful for your concern. It is a good thing you are doing for me.'

Efe's roommates were startled by her shrill cry of pain. The more the girls tried to hold her, the louder she groaned. She kicked away the blankets, clasped her stomach and coiled and recoiled her entire length until she fell on the floor. One of the girls ran to wake up Madam Angela.

'Madam, Efe is reeling in pains on the floor. Please come over immediately,' the girl said breathlessly.

Barefooted and her silk transparent night gown unbuttoned, Madame Angela dashed into the room. She screamed 'My daughter... my daughter... what is the problem?'

'Pain...Pain... stabbing my stomach Ma. Oh my God.'

In minutes, an ambulance arrived and carried her to the hospital. Madam Angela's girls thoughtfully brought a wrapper with which she covered her near-nakedness and a pair of sandals for her feet. With two other girls, she accompanied the ambulance to the hospital.

Efe was wheeled into the emergency unit. Three

doctors and four nurses were on duty. While her companions were told to wait outside the ward, one of the doctors who spoke English language fluently took charge of Efe.

'I experience growing pains in my lower chest and abdomen.'

'Do you have diarrhoea or attacks of vomiting?' asked the doctor.

'No.'

'Are you pregnant?'

'No. I have not had sexual intercourse for nearly six years. Moreover, I had my menstruation last week.'

The doctor sounded apologetic. 'I am simply trying to diagnose the problem to be able to render an effective therapy. Are you a heavy smoker?'

'I do not smoke. Since recently though, I have been among smokers.'

The doctor scribbled on a piece of paper and walked away.

A nurse came and transferred Efe to a stationary bed.

'Are you still feeling the bites?' she asked.

'Yes,' Efe answered.

'Don't worry. You will be all right,' she consoled her. The nurse pulled a pharmacy trolley closer, and with a syringe, sucked liquid from three different bottles and injected Efe.

The doctor went to the door of the ward. 'Madam,' he said to Angela, 'You can go. Your sister is having a complication and will be on admission for close medical observation. I promise you that she will be all right.'

'Are you sure, doctor?' Madam Angela demanded.

'Yes. I do not want to base my prescriptions on guesswork. We shall carry out some tests on her.'

'Thank you, doctor.'

The x-ray pictures taken of Efe's stomach and chest revealed no anomalies. Yet as soon as any person approached her, she moaned louder. Her temperature over the period of observation though slightly high, was stable and still within acceptable range. Nonetheless, she was visibly shivering.

Examinations were also performed to detect any diseases in her entire intestines to her rectum. Nothing interesting was detected. More tests were conducted: urine, blood and stool. There was no trace of bacterial or viral infection. However, the mystery was anchored at nervousness coupled with depression and fatigue. Apart from two weeks in the hospital, the doctor recommended additional two weeks of rest at home to enable her recuperate fully.

'This recommendation must be strictly adhered to otherwise you will be risking a complete breakdown of the nervous system,' the doctor warned. The recommendation was devastating to Madam Angela who was desperate to recoup her investment in Efe.

'She did not break down when she was alone and dejected in Nigeria. She has not even stayed alone with smelling strangers inside the bush at night or confronted by three or four teenage boys high on drugs and hell bent on having sex without condoms, torturing and eventually throwing her out of a moving vehicle like a discarded trash. She has been sleeping since she came. And she is eager to begin to work immediately. That doctor must be joking,' Madam Angela said to herself.

Regardless of Madam Angela's self assurances, she did not need to consult an oracle to be able to know that Efe would be a difficult person to handle. She had got wind of the enquiries Efe made about Sam. But that was not enough to give her any cause that Efe was acting.

After three trials of the telephone number the man in Venice gave her and at different times of the day, Efe concluded the telephone was out of service. But she could not afford to give up. She learnt to sneak into the kitchen when nobody was at home, ate enough food to last her for a long time and declined to eat when there were people around. Her colleagues pitied her. One day, she brought out the dresses Madam Angela bought for her, put them on and headed to the parlour where the woman sat, 'Ma, they fit well, don't they?' Efe asked delightedly.

'You look exquisite in them.'

'Thank you, big mummy. You see my misfortune. This god-damned stomach cannot let me go out and knock those bastards down one by one.'

'You will be all right, my daughter. Perhaps from next week, you will go out in the evenings for a couple of hours until you fully recuperate to be away for longer time.'

'Ma, are you sure it will not trigger off another spate of pains?' interjected Doris.

'She can use her mouth and hands meanwhile and ...'

'Sorry to interrupt you,' said Doris. 'Ma, I envisage that she is going to have problems with clients who need something different.'

Madam Angela scratched her head. 'I think you are right Dor baby. With time I will come up with an idea about how to enable her become productive like others.'

The game was erratic for the still-hunter to predict. To play it safe, Madam Angela decided to sell Efe to another woman in Genoa. Doris overheard the secret deal.

'Do you see why our madame is heartless?' asked Doris when she entered the room.

'What is amiss?' Efe got up from the bed. Doris pushed

the door again to ensure that it was closed.

'Madam realises that each day you lie in bed here, her investment in you is wasted. To cut her risk, she has sold you to Sisi, a mischief-maker, for twenty million lire. I am sure Sisi won't set you free until she has reduced you to a walking corpse. The amount is too much. Ten or fifteen million lire would have been reasonable. Twenty million lire for a girl now that prostitution is experiencing its worst times means that your *igbese* won't be less than sixty million lire.'

'When is Sisi coming for me?' Efe asked.

'On Thursday.'

'She is not under any obligation to tell you or to discuss the terms and conditions of the sale with you. She will only tell you to get ready to travel to Genoa with your new madame. I have witnessed the departure of some people from this house before. It has always been the same.'

Early in the morning on Thursday, Madam Angela did not wait in the parlour for Efe to come and salute her. She came into Efe's bedroom. 'How are you feeling today, my daughter?'

'Ma, I am better. Hopefully, if I stick to the doctor's advice, I will be able to start working soon.'

Madam Angela was happy that Efe was not whimpering any longer. She sat on Efe's bed and started to lecture her on the paraphernalia of prostitution, from how to use condoms to how to position oneself to avoid a direct hit that could render damaging blows to the womb; from martial arts necessary for self-defence to the manipulation of emotions to win a stingy client.

'Supposing a client is not satisfied and declines to pay?' Efe asked.

Madam Angela was irritated. 'I don't blame you. You

wasted all your time learning at school while your mates were acquiring experiences needed to survive in this world today. Look at a big girl, listen, before you settle down for business with anybody, collect your money and conceal it. If you wait until he is satisfied, you will be in a terrible crisis sooner or later or you may not even return to Lagos alive. Your workmates are another people to watch. Many of them will be envious of your progress. Honestly, there is a volley of things to learn. It is not my fault that you have no prior experience. However, I know with time, you will understand everything. I trust you. Use your initiative when a client becomes stubborn to deal with him, when in danger, do anything to remain alive.'

Efe went into the kitchen and prepared a very delicious meal.

'Do you want some, Ma?' she asked Madam Angela who was overwhelmed with joy at the turn of events.

'No, my sweet daughter. I have no appetite for food.'

Efe finished eating and was retiring to the bedroom when Madam Angela suggested to her to remain in the parlour, to chat with others and enjoy some fresh air.

'You know I have a delicate stomach. Please, let me go into the bedroom to give the food time to digest.'

Three hours later, Efe heard a strange voice in the parlour, Madam Sisi had arrived. She covered herself with winter blanket under the blistering summer weather and applied some ointment in her eyes.

Angela was so proud of Efe that she boasted to Sisi, 'Go in and see what a fine girl I am giving to you. I have absolute confidence that within months, she will raise your dough for you.'

'Is she aware I am coming today?'

'No, does it concern her who comes here to bundle

her away?'

Sisi found Efe under the blanket. She pulled it aside.

'Please cover me up,' Efe pleaded. 'All my body is frozen, my head, chest, stomach... everywhere.'

The woman bent down and saw that Efe's eyes were red and watery. Her body shivered like a leaf. She mindlessly threw back the blanket and hurried back to the parlour.

'Is it because of that anaemic cow that you collected my money?' She said furiously.

'What are you saying?' replied Madam Angela in surprise.

'You do not know what I am saying? You heartless witch. Can't you go into that room and see for yourself.'

Madam Angela walked in to find Efe still reeling in pains. 'Efe, what is the problem again?' Efe was still explaining that the food might have upset her stomach when Madam Angela grumbled and left the room.

'Sisi, I think your annoyance is inappropriate. This is not the first time people have had stomach upset because of indigestion or change of environment, I have already taken her to a doctor, in a couple of days the period of rest recommended will be over and she can begin to work. Moreover, she has not had sex for nearly six years. I am very reluctant to sell her. I love her and have a lot of regard for the family from which she comes. I do not have the mind to drill her. I want you to understand this fact,' she explained in a subdued voice.

'Angela, I am not interested in buying your lazy cow, give me back my money. As a friend, I will help you by returning to Genoa with her, I will give her a place for work and ensure that she hustles for your investment. As for me, I will not invest even a penny on her. No way!'

'But I have given ten million lire to my boyfriend two

days ago for a car he requested from me,' Angela explained. 'I sent ten million lire home only yesterday. Right now, I do not know...'

'You do not have the money I sent to you just four days ago?' Sisi erupted like a volcano. Bitter arguments gave way to a violent fight when Madam Angela switched gear and returned fire for fire. The sound of broken bottles, doors and windows could be heard far across the street. The crash of the giant television set in the sitting room sounded like a dynamite and sent chill down the spine of Efe. The women tore each other's skin with nails and any rough object they could lay their hands upon. The neighbours were used to the household's incessant brawl but nothing so bloody and deadly.

Three neighbours telephoned the police simultaneously. They were all taken to the station.

At the police station, the ladies were remanded in custody for further interrogation. They were naked, bloodied and bruised when an officer marched them away into the police cells.

Efe told them her story.

'So, you accepted to come to Italy because you thought it would help you to locate your lost fiance?'

'Yes.'

'If we issue you a work permit to enable you look for a job and honestly fend for yourself, won't you like it?' A more superior officer asked.

'It is very kind of you. But that is far from my motive. I do not need a work permit.'

'Because you do not need it to do prostitution like your sisters' chipped in one policeman.

'Do not think that you can fool the police. You intended to come here for prostitution. So, do not spin this incredible story. Tell us the truth or we will be compelled to escort you to the airport instantly,' shouted another.

'Please believe me, gentlemen. I inherited a building in the heart of Lagos from my late father. I am an architect by profession and very proficient in computer applications. You can telephone my former employer whom I am still sure will attest to my claims. I am not a pauper or greedy as to condescend to be a prostitute. I know why I am here and had planned to execute it discreetly without causing ripples. As you have been involved by divine providence, I look forward to receiving your cooperation,' she pleaded.

The policemen looked at one another. 'What is your fiance's name and date of birth?' Efe gave them even more information than they needed. The police immediately entered into the nation's electronic file of immigrants.

'*Positivo*,' came a voice.

'*Positivo*?' repeated the officer.

'*Si*. Foreigners' Office Ravenna under D.L. 132-1996.'

The police in Ravenna immediately furnished their Naples counterpart with the name, address and telephone number of Systems Marketing Srl, employers of Sam Ogemdi. The police dialled the number and got Sam's boss. He left for Zurich an hour ago. He could not secure any seat in the direct flight from Rome. So, he travelled by Swissair to Nigeria. He will be in Lagos in the next twelve hours in the absence of any hitch.'

'His official records do not indicate that he is married?' requested the police.

'Why are you pestering me this time of the day? Is the young man implicated in any crime?' asked Sam's boss.

'Certainly no. We are doing our normal control and wish you cooperate with us.'

'You make difficult demands on me. I feel reluctant to delve into an issue I consider personal,' he protested.

'There is no need to be worried. Just a little cooperation and that is all,' the police pleaded.

'When I interviewed him for this job three months ago, he lamented the loss of his fiancee due to the problems he encountered in Italy. He was assigned a feasibility study to conduct in Nigeria for me. He could as well hold action till December. But I understood how much he craved to see this lady hence I approved his trip. Since he has been with me, no one has telephoned or written him and I have not heard about any other woman in his life.'

The police obtained a return ticket for Efe, went to the Nigerian Embassy for a travel certificate and prevailed on Alitalia to give her a place in the next available flight to Lagos.

'We are already looking forward to when you will be back again as Mrs. Ogemdi. My country welcomes people like you,' the police said as they bade her farewell.

Chapter 9

Delayed but Not Derailed

Aboard the aircraft, Sam picked up a copy of the 8th of June, 1996 edition of *The Economist* which contained a news item about Nigeria and began to read. The first column was disheartening about the country he left six years ago. 'Why can't we imbibe those concepts that make a country great, why?' He asked nobody in particular as he pounded the handrail of his seat. He sighed. This awakened the next passenger who looked at him in consternation. Sam continued into the second column and met what gave him some relief.

'So the world's most corrupt country is being cleansed. The new head of state recently opened a national anti-crime workshop. No longer is it only armed robbers who must live in fear... he spoke of a monumental misuse of public funds and warned the heads of public companies that they will be held accountable for every kobo entrusted to them. The ports are also a target: a task-force had been sent in to catch bent customs officials.'

'Could it be true?' Sam asked himself. When he raised his head, he noticed that the other passenger was reading the column too. Their eyes met. The passenger smiled.

'Are you a Nigerian?'

'Yes...'

'I am Ronco and you?'

'Sam. Your name sounds Latin. I mean French, Italian, Spanish...'

'Oh, yeah yeah. My parents are Italians. I am Swiss though.' Ronco explained.

'It seems you are visiting Nigeria for the first time?'

'No, I am a drilling engineer. I work and live in Nigeria'

'Really?' Sam exclaimed.

'Yes.'

'With your family?'

'Of course. This is my fifth year in Nigeria. And I have just renewed my contract of employment for another five years.'

'How do you find Nigeria?'

Ronco chuckled. 'Nigerians are very good and friendly. There might be socio-political and economic problems but in all fairness, they are accommodating and tolerant of foreigners. Could you believe that my wife and children are so fond of your country that they refused to travel with me to Zurich? The people, the terrain, landscape and climate are alluring. Be it the sandy coastline of Lagos or the arid desert of Kano, my family can talk about it like the natives. Two years ago, we were at Yankari Games Reserve and saw for ourselves the abundance of species that are considered endangered or non-existent. I think Ikogosi warm water spring is the eighth wonder of our time. When my son came from Milan, he visited the West and the East, and saw nature at its best. He made several reels of films he hoped to enjoy with his friends. All his life, he had known only alpine forests with their stunted trees. Honestly, he could not conceal his fascination with the forest in the South;

savanna in the Middle Belt and extensive area of barren and arid land in the north of Nigeria.'

'I'm impressed,' Sam remarked.

'Truly,' responded Ronco. 'It is not easy to find an array of vegetation like this within the same geographical area. My son's friends were so delighted when they watched the films. Some of them have sworn to visit Nigeria. By then, I think they won't have words to describe the sunny and airy climate which contrasts with what they have known in Europe.'

'I'm glad you say positive things about Nigeria.'

'It's a fact Sam. Other expatriates like me will say the same thing too.'

'It's natural for one to enjoy oneself everywhere.'

'You are right. It seems you have been away for a long time?'

'Yes.'

'Where, Switzerland?'

'No. I live in Italy.'

'Italy! *Mama mia.*'

'For how long?'

'Six years.'

'Six good years! With your family?'

'No. They live here. I lost contact with my fiancee five years ago.'

'You do not miss her?'

'I miss her. I miss everybody...' Sam said as he fought back tears.

'I understand. Our fathers and grandfathers went to Africa, America and Asia and acquired all the wealth we boast of now. These people, instead of welcoming them to our tables, we rather introduce barriers to frustrate them. I consider this morally wrong Sam.'

'Mr Ronco, I think it is more despicable for leaders to mismanage national economies for personal gains and in the process, make destitutes of people whose land is blessed with abundant human and natural resources. I blame our leaders for pushing us into exile and slavery.'

'It might be heartwarming that Nigeria, perhaps, has eventually gotten a leader it deserves in the new head of state.'

'Why do you say that?'

'Well, a look at the face of the average Nigerian will show that their opinion about the administration has shifted from that of suspicion to approval. People who pull down banks and their accomplices or people who receive money for unexecuted or shoddy public works projects are in trouble.'

'You sound like a government image maker.'

Ronco started laughing.

'No, I work with DESCO Oil Company. And you?'

'Systems Marketing Srl.'

'Where?'

'Ravenna.'

'It's supposed to be into electronic systems.'

'That's right'

'You work as what?'

'Data Analyst.'

'Ah,' Ronco nodded his head.

'You understand Italian?'

'Not very proficient. Just enough to perform my job effectively.

'You're comfortable with the computer?'

Sam smiled, 'Yes.'

'Your contract is for how many years?'

'Indefinite.'

'You are lucky. I guess your boss has a lot of confidence in you.' Sam chuckled but said nothing.

'Would you like to visit me before you go back to Italy?'

'Yes. But do not expect it soon. I have been away for six years and envisage playing host to friends and well-wishers for weeks.'

'It is all right; any time until you go back. I would like to introduce you to our personnel director.'

The two talked about Italy, Switzerland and Nigeria. But the latter remained Sam's passion. He was anxious to know if *The Economist's* report was true. He was eager to know if there was any silver lining in the sky of his beloved country.

'The general has instituted concrete changes?'

'Yes. Violent crime is on the decline. Foreign debts are paid and investor-confidence in the economy is regained.'

'Didn't I tell you that you are a government image maker?'

'No, Sam. Let's call a spade a spade. My only grouse with the general is the lack of seriousness to hand over the leadership to a democratically elected president. It is the only guarantee against anarchy. Most American presidents had served in the military. Nigerians can copy from them. A Nigerian soldier can see years of excellent service in the military as the road to the presidency through the electoral process. In fact, nothing stops a retired soldier from vying for political power. How do you see his recent plans to try past political leaders for corruption? Who has ever had that courage in the history of your country?'

'It's an illusion, Ronco. Nigeria has known decades of corruption. Over this period, our national coffers were plundered with impunity. The only difference between a former minister and his lowest subordinate was the amount of stolen money in the hands of each of them. Everybody is culpable, the educated elite, businessmen, religious leaders, traditional rulers, and artisans. By omission or commission, we elevated and enthroned graft to the level it became a norm. By putting a former leader on trial, our national conscience will be on trial too. The secretary who types the court summons, the police who investigate the allegations and the judges are not better than the man on trial. I admit that a trial and conviction of these criminals will be a deterrent to others. But the question is this: are Nigerians capable of and ready for a cleansing of this magnitude? Ronco, the answer is emphatically no.'

'So, you recommend that all those beasts should go unpunished?'

'Let me quickly clarify. For every wickedness by man against another man, there is a punishment. It is bound to come sooner or later. The masses of Nigeria have known years of broken promises and shattered dreams. A trial of this nature should not be a hit-or-miss patchwork, a cover or a witch-hunt. It should be free from sentiments. Unfortunately, the present leadership does not possess the moral right to earn the confidence of the people. The administration is a reflection of the previous administrations and all the misrule they symbolise. If the general is serious about trial of past leaders, he needs to start with himself before his efforts achieve legitimacy and credibility.'

Before Sam and Ronco knew it, their flight had arrived Murtala Mohammed Airport, Lagos. Together, they went through immigration and customs formalities. Nobody asked for or was given any bribe. There were no mumbled and irrelevant questions that marked the era of extortion and bribery. Pieces of luggage were handled promptly and precisely. No reports of losses.

Ronco looked at Sam and grinned. 'Did you see what I told you?' They had moved out of the restricted area and were in the Arrival Hall when Ronco continued. 'The general flushed out corrupt and lazy officers from the ports two months ago and replaced them with very young and career-minded men and women.'

'May it be forever,' Sam replied. Ronco's wife and two children were waiting for him. Two drivers briskly came and greeted him. One took his bag, the other collected his suitcase. He embraced his wife, Rosa, children; Daniel and Jean. He turned to his wife.

'Rosa, meet my friend, Sam.'

'It is a pleasure,' Sam said as he shook her hand.

'Sam, Rosa was born in Milan. She speaks Italian, English and French fluently,' explained Ronco.

'*Brava*,' Sam complimented in Italian as he turned to the woman.

'Ronco rarely speaks Italian. He prefers French and English. Can you believe that our children do not have good knowledge of the language of their parents?' Rosa complained.

'No, I speak Italian,' Daniel chipped in.

'And I speak Italian too,' said Jean.

'It's not my fault that my children and I seldom speak Italian. I work with a multinational; I'm a citizen of Europe's melting pot and presently; I live in an English speaking country. So, if it requires English language to make myself understood, or to earn some income for my family, I cannot force Italian down the throats of people. I will pack it up until I return to Switzerland to see my old parents or go to Italy.'

'You are right,' Sam said. Everybody started laughing.

'Sam, I feel more evidence of the changes that have

taken place since recently abound. If it were before, somebody with your appearance would be courting death by standing here for minutes without a retinue of bodyguards. Doing so meant deadly risk to life and luggage.'

'Ronco, I am indeed overwhelmed by this development. But I read a lot about this wonderful governor of Lagos State. I am surprised you have not talked about him.'

'Oh yeah, the colonel. I think he deserves the credit for much of the situation in Lagos. He is certainly a model and if he steps out of army uniform, he can be a great leader.'

Ronco gave Sam a copy of his business card. One of the drivers strode to the Mercedes Benz 200E ahead of him and his wife, opened and held the doors until they were inside. The other driver took the children to the other car. When they were comfortably seated, he walked round to ensure that the doors were securely jammed. The family waited until Sam settled inside a taxi for Ire-Akari Housing Estate. Ronco noted the car's registration number, colour and brand on a piece of paper before he ordered his drivers to leave.

Inside the taxi, Sam brought out the business card from his breast pocket and he took a quick look at it. To his surprise, he had been invited not by a mere drilling engineer but the director of operations of DESCO Oil Company in Nigeria and the Middle East.

***

Aboard flight 701 from Rome, it was an emotional reunion for Izu and Efe.

'How is your wife?'

'She is fine.'

'Why is she not with you?'

'Oh, she is in London. We are expecting our first baby next month and her doctor recommended that she should be on admission before then to avoid any mishap. After six years of trial, you can imagine how precious this baby is to us.'

'This is true. I'm very happy for you.'

'Probably, you will be more delighted to hear that we are expecting a baby boy. He is going to be Izu junior!'

'Izuuu, you have not stopped looking at women as lesser beings.'

Efe grabbed his ear and squeezed it. Both of them reeled in laughter.

'But it is true. I need a son to bear my name!'

'Female babies are children too,' Efe remarked obviously subdued.

'Now tell me, how is my friend?'

'He's fine.'

'You are living in Italy. Aren't you?'

'Yes, we are.'

'Sam is sending you home? How has life been with you since we met last?'

Reluctantly, Efe explained to Izu the things that had happened since he came to her Surulere residence to thank her and Sam for attending his wedding. From the events that led to Sam's departure to the subsequent loss of contact. From the death of her parents to Madam Angela's ploy which provided her an opportunity to come for the apple of her eyes and the efforts by the police to rescue her from the madame.

'You mean Sam is on his way to Nigeria now?'

Efe looked at her wristwatch. 'He will be there only thirty-five minutes before us.'

'I will be happy to see him again hale and hearty. I visited his people three weeks ago. His parents narrated to me the same tale of hardship in Nigeria and his decision to leave for overseas. They told me about their opposition to his plans to marry you. Sam has been away for six years just to provide for his family. From all indications, they are more appreciative of the kindness and warmth of your parents now than ever before. His mother in particular pleaded that I should look for you and pass her heartfelt apologies.

'Sure?' she exclaimed with excitement in her voice.

'I mean it.'

'How was their health?'

'They were fine. But they have missed their son and it clearly reflected on everything they did or said.'

'It has been very kind of you to have thought about going to see them. I'm grateful. I have no animosity towards them. They were protective of their son. Now, it is my duty to prove that I am different. I will see myself as an ambassador of my people.

'I trust you. I have always considered Sam a very lucky man to have earned your love and respect. Apart from rewarding him for his help when we were undergraduates, I think he possesses the discipline and drive necessary for the success of a young enterprise. I had thought about devoting the whole of my next trip to searching for him. Miraculously, I am sitting right here with you.'

'Your in-law plans to constitute an incorporation?' asked Efe changing the topic of the discussion.

'He has already done that. It is scheduled to go into operation soon at Otto-Awori near Badagry. It is a joint venture with an Italian consortium. The man is old and does not like travelling anymore. His male children have engagements of their own. My wife seems to be his only

262

child who has not been provided for. I guess this is an opportunity to do so. With her in the hospital, and her inherent apathy to the amassment of wealth, it falls upon me to follow the old man and see what I can get out of him for our children.'

'The idea is great. I wish you good luck.'

'Thank you. Please, help me to convince Sam to accept to work for my father-in-law. It will be fun if all of us can live in Badagry together.'

Efe smiled. 'If the proposal will be the best for him and me, Sam will work for your father-in-law. Let us keep our fingers crossed until I meet him. Does that sound good?'

'Yes.'

'Was it for the project you visited Rome or are you in transit?'

'It was for it. I am returning from Bergamo. The documentation has been awesome. Good enough, I have been able to steer the deal to a conclusion.'

Izu disclosed to her that Emete served six years in jail instead of fifteen. He was one of the beneficiaries of prison condition review conducted by a special commission last year. He was released on parole. The state had warned that if he was arrested again and convicted for any crime, it would amount to a violation of the conditions of his parole. Presently, he was floating about, more confused than before. He went further to reveal that Betty had amassed substantial wealth and had retired to a home of her own in Anthony Village with a twenty-three year old jobless boy for a husband. She was running a chic beauty centre and boutique in Yaba.

'Any babies yet?'

'No. Her gynaecologists are working round the clock to repair tissues damaged by years of hauling hard drugs into Europe.'

'What of Grace? Lagos is unbelievably big. Ten years have passed-by since her graduation, yet our ways have never crossed.'

'For a long time, I did not see her too. But I saw her recently with a young and handsome engineer whom she introduced to me as her fiance. Two weeks ago, they came to Victoria Island and invited us to their wedding. It is taking place on the 20th of next month at Lagos Sheraton Hotel. With Sam and you around, it is going to be a big reunion. Yeru would be there too. At the recently concluded Lagos international trade fair, he came as his state governor's liaison officer. It seemed to me that he had struck a joint venture deal with some South Koreans and would like to pursue it on his own. He was very desperate for information about how to locate Sam or you. You know what that means. I am sure if I call to tell him that Sam has come home, he will abandon everything to be at the wedding to enable them meet. Once again, Efe, do not forget what I have requested you to do for me as soon as your man is settled.'

'It has been nearly two years since I saw Benson in front of an airline's office at Tafawa Balewa Square. Have you seen him recently?' Efe asked.

'I think his brother was affected by the recent purge of ministries and government corporations of corrupt officials. He has lost much of his ill-gotten wealth and has been under house arrest. Things are not much better. His drug empire collapsed with the intervention of American anti-narcotic squad into drug law enforcement in Nigeria. He lacks the smartness required to make it in swindling. You do not expect to see a deflated man as regularly as before.'

'He has not been used to austerity. Surely, Benson will

find readjustment very difficult,' Efe remarked.

'You are aware Ugo died in his sleep while studying for a postgraduate degree at ASUTECH?'

'Yes. Sam will be heartbroken when he hears about it. All of you were very good friends on campus.'

'Have you heard the latest about your beloved Owerri?'

'No. What happened to it?'

'There are reports that buildings, cars and property worth millions of naira were burnt.'

'What really happened, Izu?'

'The people of Owerri were incensed by the sight of victims allegedly beheaded for ritual sacrifice. Some newspapers reported that most of the alleged fraudsters and ritual killers belonged to an organisation. In 1994, the state government unwittingly appointed several members of this group into a committee to raise funds for the USA '94 World Cup. They used the opportunity to get very close to government functionaries and its agencies, especially the police. In no time, most of them became laws unto themselves. Some of them used siren-fitted cars illegally. Some arrested and detained innocent people in their houses. People were beaten up on the streets by thugs employed by them. They always engaged in sporadic shooting of their guns. They acquired numerous chieftaincy titles. Their mansions sprang up in different parts of the state. Some streets in Owerri were even renamed after them. During this period too, there were several reports of missing persons. The bodies of some of them were found without their heads or private parts.'

'So, how did this horrendous and chilling operation come to the open?'

'Efe, truly, there are many different accounts in this regard. However, one must bear in mind that whatever goes up must come down. God cannot watch such barbarism and wickedness go on indefinitely. With a new administrator and police commissioner, the days of the ritual killers were numbered. Angry mobs took to the streets and destroyed property of these suspected killers and their agents. Police later swooped on what remained of them, made several arrests and recovered over two hundred pieces of human parts from one refrigerator. From another location, they got two human heads.

'What are the names of these cannibals?'

'They bear names which I cannot remember. However, I can recollect that one of them is holding the Igwe chieftaincy title of Amamiri.'

'Can you remember if he has buildings on Allen Avenue and companies at Ilupeju and Apapa?'

'Exactly. Do you know him?'

'Jesus! I do. He came to our office for the design of his mansion in Owerri. Good God! So, that man is a killer?' Efe was shocked.

'Efe, can you believe it that top government functionaries who are paid with public fund attended the opening ceremony of one of the houses of that Igwe title holder? Which other way can a person receive a tacit, if not an open, government approval for his criminal acts?'

'That's not all Izu. They spend tax payers' money in fuelling and servicing vehicles made for these occasions and waste the much needed time which should have been spent in finding solutions to the people's problems.'

'There's hope that the culprits will be brought to book at least to discourage such acts in the future.'

As soon as the plane touched the tarmac, Izu opened his suitcase. He brought out his cellular phone. With it, he dialled his father-in-law.

'The driver is already waiting outside,' the old man's booming voice sounded. Izu turned to Efe.

'We will leave immediately to meet Sam before he kills himself of anxiety.'

'It's very thoughtful of you. I won't say anything until I see him.' Efe said nervously.

Izu hurried into the newsstand for a copy of a weekly newspaper.

'I want an update of the events that transpired since I left, especially the deliberations of the Anti-corruption Tribunal.'

They entered the waiting car and slammed the doors.

'Mahmud, we are going to Ire-Akari Housing Estate. Leave the International Airport Road at Ajao. Pass through Aswani Market, and turn right towards Isolo. When we reach the estate, Efe will tell you the street and the number we are going to. Drive like a former soldier,' Izu instructed the driver.

'With precision and speed. Isn't it, sir?' the driver asked.

'Correct,' replied Izu. Everybody started laughing.

The car gathered speed. Once again, Izu dialled his father-in-law. 'I just want to tell you I will be a little late. I want to see some of my friends, relax general. I am okay.'

He sat back to browse through the headlines of the newspaper. The silence was broken only by fluttering sound of the pages of the newspaper as he turned them one after another. Suddenly, he roared. 'Efe, listen to this! The Anti-Corruption Tribunal has stumbled on a strong evidence that some government contractors were jailed and their assets impounded so as to serve some secret and yet-to-be determined agenda. Though some of these victims are either dead or have been languishing in jail for years, the tribunal has made recommendations to the Federal Government among other things that their bank accounts, impounded assets be released and those still alive be set free with immediate effect. If the recommendations are approved, it is hoped to create space for corrupt past and present public officers who will be goaded to jail in the ongoing campaign against graft. Does that make any sense to you?'

'Yes, it does. They are referring to my father and a few others. My father knew he was innocent but justice was denied him. Lucky are those who are alive to receive an apology from the almighty Federal Military Government. It is comforting that he is absolved of those allegations though posthumously.'

'At any time, you need my assistance to ensure a proper accounting of your father's confiscated assets, let me know.' Izu assured.

'Thank you very much. Maybe, as soon as Sam settles down.'

***

'I am sorry, driver. It's been a long time. I cannot identify the landmarks easily. Just look for 108, Osondu Street. Sam told the driver as soon as they passed Saint Mary's Catholic Church. 'This building is an edifice. What a great work the rest of the congregation did.'

The construction of the building started six years ago and he contributed financially like most worshippers. Twenty minutes later, he got to his former house. The new occupant came out and told him that he did not know anything about Efe and her brother with his family. He admitted that they had been mentioned casually by the landlord that a medical doctor lived in the other flat and had travelled with his family to Saudi Arabia.

'He did not say anything about the single lady who occupied your flat previously?'

'No,' the man replied and returned to meet his wife and children who were anxiously standing at the balcony.

'Surulere,' Sam told the driver as he re-entered the cab.

He reversed the car and engaged it in gear. Suddenly, an oncoming Peugeot 504 stopped abruptly in front of them. Efe dashed out, ran for the door where Sam sat.

'Sam...Sam...Saaaam!' she shouted with excitement.

The neighbourhood looked on in amazement. Sam hurried out of the passenger seat. In the bid, his leg was trapped by the safety-belt. He tripped and fell. Efe threw herself on him. The two were still rolling on the dusty ground when Izu paid the taxi driver and transferred Sam's pieces of luggage into the boot of his own car.

Sam was the first to recover. He lifted Efe up and both entered into the back seat which Izu vacated for them.

'Where is doc?' Sam asked.

Efe was speechless. She simply raised her head and stared at Sam's face expectantly. For some seconds she could not take her large eyeballs off the necklace she presented to Sam on his twenty-fifth birthday. She leaned her head again on his chest.

'What happened to daddy...? How is mummy?' Sam asked in quick succession.

Izu turned to face the couple as he spoke. 'Sam, after over half a decade, our joy, meeting you again, is total. We know how much you love us and would not have wanted to be away from us for so long. Within this period too, there have been many developments – some positive, some negative, there is still time to tell you everything and to hear from you. Meanwhile, let us celebrate the reunion of two persons who love each other.'

'Thank you, Izu,' Sam said as he held Efe who was weeping.

'As Izu said, this is not the moment to account for the events of the past six years. Holding you in my arms now, my joy is complete. The road to this moment has been full of obstacles. Getting here has indeed been delayed but thank God that it has not been derailed.'

Efe sat up and wriggled out of his grip. She looked at Sam's eyes with a steady gaze.

'Are you sure, Sam?'

'Yes, Efe,' Sam nodded his head.

'Mine forever!'

'Till my last day,' Sam vowed.

Efe hugged him. They kissed passionately.

Fifteen minutes later, the car pulled up at 158, Sabon Gida Street, Surulere. They off-loaded Sam's luggage. Efe searched her handbag for the keys and gave them to Izu. Hand-in-hand, Sam and Efe alighted. The lawn was overgrown by weeds and the verandah taken over by a network of cobwebs. Sam looked beyond and noticed the rusty gates and the ominous silence that pervaded the entire compound.

'Where are mummy and daddy? Where are they?'

Efe turned and held him. Tears started to trickle down her cheeks. Sam did not need to be told that they had died in his absence, he slumped on the dusty pavement and wept.'